An Amulet of Greek Earth

An Amulet

Helen Papanikolas

OF GREEK EARTH

*Generations
of Immigrant
Folk Culture*

Swallow Press

Ohio University Press

Athens

SWALLOW PRESS | OHIO UNIVERSITY PRESS, ATHENS, OHIO 45701

© 2002 by Helen Papanikolas

Printed in China

All rights reserved. Published 2002

10   09   08   07   06   05   04   03   02   5   4   3   2   1

Swallow Press | Ohio University Press books are printed on acid-free paper ⊗ ™

Every reasonable effort has been made to contact those who hold copyright to illustrations used in this work.

Library of Congress Cataloging-in-Publication Data

Papanikolas, Helen, 1917–
    An amulet of Greek earth : generations of immigrant folk culture / Helen
Papanikolas.
        p. cm.
    Includes bibliographical references and index.
    ISBN 0-8040-1037-4 (alk. paper) — ISBN 0-8040-1038-2 (pbk. : alk. paper)
        1. Greek Americans—Social life and customs.   2. Immigrants—United
States—Social life and customs.   3. Greek Americans—Ethnic identity.
4. Greek Americans—Cultural assimilation.   5. Folklore—Greece.   I. Title.

E184.G7 P38 2002
305.88'93073—dc21

                                                                2001036346

THIS BOOK IS DEDICATED TO my children, grandchildren, and great-grandchildren, and to all Americans in whose veins an ancestor's Greek blood flows.

Contents

PART 3: AMERICANIZATION

PREFACE

I was an immigrant child growing up in the 1920s when the American Legion, the Ku Klux Klan, and daily newspapers vilified immigrants from southern Europe, the Middle East, and Asia. I could not have imagined at the time that I would one day consider myself fortunate for having been born to Greek-immigrant parents. I did not know then that they had come from a great oral tradition.

I had listened while my father and his friends sang "songs of the table" after feasting. I fell asleep while they related old stories of their rock-strewn country and new ones of their harried search for work and of adventures in this new land. They spoke with the resonance of master storytellers, and what they related seemed to have happened yesterday, not ten, twenty, fifty, or a hundred years past. I often remember clearly the exact words in different dialects that men and women who came later spoke. I remember, also, fragments, which teachers call "dramatic details." Yes, I was fortunate.

Fifty years ago the director of the Utah State Historical Society asked me to write an essay on the Greeks of Utah. He had read some of my fiction published in the University of Utah literary magazine and thought it would be good to have a more diverse quarterly than one almost wholly devoted to Mormon topics. I accepted, because I would learn details of what I had heard and seen as a child, events that had puzzled and frightened me. My memories of those events were stark, but I did not know the reasons for the hate that was spewed daily on the school ground. I was eager to match my memories with history.

I knew nothing about research, but I immersed myself into the immigrant history of my railroad-mining town in eastern Utah while dramatic details rose from inexhaustible memory.

I had stood with my mother at our living room window and watched eight hundred solemn Greeks following a hearse. They were dressed in black and held small Greek flags. The dead man was a Greek, killed by a deputy sheriff during a coal strike. Two years later, in 1924, standing at a kitchen window I gazed at a cross burning on a mountainside and across the narrow valley at a flaming circle for the word *nought,* the answer to the KKK. To Catholics and all immigrants, the word *nought* meant the Klan would come to nothing. That same year a coal mine exploded, killing 171 miners, fifty of them Greek. Their children came to school wearing black-dyed clothes; the girls' braids were tied with black ribbons. A few years later, during the Depression years of the 1930s, fellow Greeks stopped with our family on their grim journey to California where they hoped to find work.

I interviewed many Greek men and women, writing quickly on yellow pads, the words often almost illegible. A panorama of Greek-immigrant involvement in labor wars and the role of labor agents, the *padrones,* shot up from these interviews. At first the immigrants had resented my bringing this disreputable role to light. Later they would speak eagerly about Leonidas Skliris, the "Czar of the Greeks." These sessions endowed me with a lifelong interest in labor strife. Often the respondents' answers became lengthy and veered off into Greek customs and folklore.

I had concentrated on crises and calamities, then I realized I had to learn more about these people who spoke of long-past injuries to their *filotimo,* their self-respect, objectively. I saw history unfolding. I developed a questionnaire that encompassed their early years from mountain and valley villages, provincial towns, occasionally Athens and Thessaloniki to the longer experience in America. The folk culture that emerged became one of my compelling interests and resulted in essays on the Romiosini culture that the immigrants brought with them.

I chose respondents from among those who had come from various regions in Greece, those who had been involved in labor troubles, and others like my Greek school teacher, two priests, and the women of Greek Town, where I loved to visit. A yeasty scent from bread baking in their outdoor earth ovens wafted over the town; their gardens were wonderfully green in the arid western earth.

Later, in the early 1970s, historians began preparing a book on fourteen immigrant groups to celebrate the nation's bicentennial. I was chosen to be the editor and used a heavy, bulky tape recording machine until small models became available. Most of the sessions were conducted in people's homes where the traditional hospitality tray of honey pastries was brought out at the beginning of the interviews.

The two priests had told me that the immigrant men of the West were far different from those who got off ships and settled in one area. Those in the West, they said, were more progressive, more independent. Those in the West had traveled, usually by freight, throughout the Midwest and West, worked in furniture factories, in slaughterhouses, on railroad gangs, in coal and metal mines, and on roads. One of them had been in South Omaha when a mob burned Greek Town to the ground because a young Greek man had walked down the street with an American woman. Others had been strikers in the Colorado Strike of 1913–14 when their leader, Louis Tikas, had been killed in Ludlow. The women, too, had more independence; a number of them were wives of sheepmen who were away for months at a time during lambing and shearing. Most of these interviews have been deposited in the Greek Archives of the Special Collections, Marriott Library, University of Utah.

After *Peoples of Utah* was published, I taught a course by the same name at the University of Utah. I always assigned the students a project to interview people of immigrant background and to write short biographies about them. I also supervised several students who were doing graduate work in immigrant history.

At the same time (in the 1970s), the women's liberation movement, burgeoning ethnic studies, and the Vietnam War became fertile fields for exploration. I became interested in my generation's and third-generation women's responses to these events. I found daughters of immigrants were almost uniformly bitter about the Greek culture foisted on them in their young years: no dating, many marriages arranged, and the resources of the family funneled to providing college educations for their brothers. These women asked for complete anonymity. Although most of them are now dead, I've kept my promise out of respect to their children and grandchildren.

Since the early 1970s, I have given talks to Greek American groups throughout the country. I have met many historians and writers with whom I have a correspondence of many years' standing. We freely exchange information and documents. Also, after my talks people ask questions and offer their views of Greek America. I often make notes of these conversations and ask permission to use what they have to say. Some of my most valuable information has come from conversations with people who wanted to tell of their experiences as Greek Americans. Much of this oral history has found its way into my work in both history and fiction.

When I began giving talks around the country, I was struck by how little Greek Americans and their children knew about the experience of their parents and grandparents and the culture that they brought with them. Often what they knew was damaged by half-truths. They were as little aware as I had been when I first began looking into the immigrant past. This impelled me to write this book, because the Romiosini culture that the Greeks brought with them was remarkable. If people did not know it, they could not value its uniqueness, could not understand why we Greek Americans are who we are today.

Much of the Romiosini culture sprang from the magnificent folk songs of the *kleftic* period, when the Greeks fought for independence to free themselves from four hundred years of Turkish rule. They are included in all anthologies; only when a slight word change or when a song was little known did I document it. Unless otherwise noted, the translations of the songs and poems are my own.

Along with the names of the immigrants I had interviewed years previously, I state their *topoi,* the places from where they had come. So important is this that the second question asked of strangers after "You're Greek?" was "From what *topos* are you?"

Because I did not want this book to be a regional effort, I have made a persistent attempt to include histories and photographs from around the country. In my search, I was surprised to find that state historical societies have almost no Greek photographs. My attempts to work with some churches have proved fruitless. Whenever I could not find photographs to illustrate aspects of the text, I used my own pictures. Greek Americans throughout the United States have been generous with their family photographs.

I hope this book will inspire other ethnics to bring to light the culture their people brought with them to America. In my work with Balkan, South European, and Asian Americans, I found their ancestors' immigrant experiences memorable, each with a certain beauty among the harsh early difficulties. These histories should be made known to those who followed. Otherwise they will be lost, never to communicate the humanity of these early immigrants who helped build America.

Acknowledgments

Many people have helped me over this half-century. I thank mainly the Greek immigrants long since gone who talked to me about their early years in the new land, about their trials, their hunger, their struggle with hostility. I thank Steve Frangos and John B. Vlahos who have altruistically shared their findings not only with me, but with historians and institutions throughout the country. Steve Sargetakis is especially dear to me; when I first began publishing, he gave me valuable immigrant photographs from his large collection to illustrate my work. The late Deno Pappas was unfailingly ready to help with his ten thousand single Greek records of the early years; the translations were done by a good friend, Andreas Dellis. Kathy Politopoulos, publisher of *Laografia,* brought Greek folklore to the children and grandchildren of immigrants, a noble effort. I could always count on John Chipian to compare my minutiae of the Greek-immigrant experience with his and on Dean Athens to review the drafts on religion.

I thank the following: my granddaughter Cleo Papanikolas, who drew the illustrations for the book; my grandson Luke Smart, who has helped me in many invaluable ways throughout the years I have worked on the manuscript; my son-in-law Allan Smart, for photography; my children Zeese Papanikolas and Thalia Smart, for the many discussions on my work; my cousins Thalia and Katherine Papachristos and Helen Anderson, for their time and effort. Many others have helped by sending photographs and in other significant ways. I thank them all with gratitude. My editor, Gillian Berchowitz, has been a pleasure to work with and to know.

Part One

Ancient Lore and Lost Greatness

CHAPTER I

THE AZURE LAND

In Greece, this stony land of thyme and wild honey, a fever took hold of its somnolent people at the end of the 1800s and the early 1900s. Word spread from the arid valleys and reached the rugged mountains: There was work in fabled America, and in one week a man could make more money than in a year of lifting bales on the wharves or of hoeing a landlord's fields.

This small country of 56,000 square miles was so important in the trade routes of the Mediterranean that its entire history was a litany of invasions. Each tribe, each army left some of their blood to mix with the Greeks on the stony land and some of it in children's veins. The invaders left words that were incorporated into the Greek language, but they themselves were taken in and assimilated. When classical Greece lost to Rome, the Greeks became part of the Byzantine empire and were called "Romaioi." After the Turks conquered Constantinople in 1453 and spread throughout the Balkans, the Greeks descended further into a debilitated four-hundred-year Moslem rule. Some other Balkan peoples and a few Greeks themselves became Moslems either through force or through self-interest, but the Greek banner through the dark centuries was "To be Greek is to be Orthodox."

Magnificent folk songs arose from the people pining for freedom and honoring the bravery and lamenting the fate of the guerrilla *klefts*. The word came from *kleftes* (thieves), because they struck at the Turkish soldiers at night. The folk songs inspired a vital culture called Romiosini, which reached beyond to vestiges of the greatness of Greece and to the epoch when the Greeks were subject to Rome.

When France and the United States rebelled to form republics, the *klefts* increased their struggle. In 1821, Bishop Germanos of Patras raised the Greek flag of revolt, and a great body of songs was added to the earlier ones. Foreigners came to fight with the Greeks. But when the Turks were defeated,

The pass over Mount Parnassus, Delphi to Arachova.
Photograph by R. G. Hoegler, from *Greece in Colour* (New York, 1957).

a foreign prince was put on the throne, the economy worsened, and the life struggle of every family continued to be one of providing dowries for daughters and keeping starvation at bay.

Then, at the turn of the century, labor agents arrived; newspapers printed greatly inflated stories of the ease of making money in America. Every family scrounged, borrowed, and mortgaged its land because there was now hope.

Families sent mostly boys and young men. They walked over mountains, crossed barren valleys, forded rivers, took cäiques to seaports. They clutched *kilimi,* woven goat-hair blankets in which they wrapped their few belongings. Inside the *kilimi,* their mothers had placed sprigs of basil or thyme for remembrance. Sewn to the underclothes was the family's meager pool of money, barely enough for steerage and "show money." At Castle Garden, later in Ellis Island, it would be proof that they would not be burdens on the country. Most important was an amulet around their necks, a small cloth square enclosing a pinch of Greek earth.

The travelers had lived with poverty in mountain and valley villages, yet with an ingrained certainty and pride that they were descendants of the ancient Greeks. These were the poor who swelled the great exodus. They left their *patridha* Greece, which had once been a forested land of great marble structures and famed statues, the most ancient with archaic smiles.

Over the centuries giant trees disappeared, cut down for fuel and for shipbuilding, mainly by conquerors who plundered the land. A variety of blood had spilled on this earth the Greeks held sacred: Visigoths, Vandal pirates, Ostrogoths, Huns, and Avars had stormed through it in the universal search for food, for more land to support their growing populations, or for conquest. The barbarous tribes were not interested in the magnificent arts of Greece, nor were the Slavonic tribes that invaded the land more than once and devastated it. Franks, the French, and Turks followed. The great treasures of the past were carted off by foreigners, of whom Lord Elgin was the most ambitious. Monuments were chipped by travelers and sailors as mementos. "In 1818 the Oxford scholar Peter Laurent failed to prevent an English naval officer from knocking off the only remaining nose among the Caryatids."[1]

Sketch of the moscophorus (calf-carrier) from the Acropolis, 570–560 B.C. Illustration by Cleo Papanikolas.

On the way to the ships, the boys and young men passed ruins of that far past. In Delphi, foreigners had uncovered the oracle of Apollo, in Mycenae the Lion Gate, and in Olympia a shameful rock base that told of an athlete, his statue missing, who had cheated in the games. In the seaport Patras, nothing recalled Antony and Cleopatra's winter stay after sailing down the western coast, nor would the boys and young men know who the famous lovers were.

In Athens, foreigners were still digging around the Acropolis, but the young could not take the time to climb it. Those from Sparta and surrounding villages barely glanced at the mountain where the Venetians had built the ruined, once-great city of Mistra, and those from Crete did not deviate from paths leading to the harbors to see the Palace of Knossos, nor did other islanders look at vestiges of temples, altars, and funeral steles.

In their childhoods, some of the men had collected shards of red vases with ancient Greek mythical figures painted on them, which centuries later would prove the continuity of ancient dances to the present. They picked up antique coins that had been disturbed by wooden plows. Sometimes foreigners gave village children a few *lepta* for the shards and coins. The children could not speak to the strangers; they were *ksenoi:* German, French, British, American, Austrian, Dutch, Scandinavian, Czech, and Italian.

While archaeologists dug unceasingly, other foreigners, travelers, and artists celebrated the light of Greece:

> Greece is remarkable for the sharpness of the light, the transparent brightness of the sky. The atmosphere of Greece being so pure and luminous, the spectator could distinguish great distances and in the distance appeared clearer and therefore acquired an accuracy or delineation which is rare in nineteenth-century depictions.[2]

> [Greece is] a land reduced to its essentials of light and form, of rock and sky and sea. . . . The great painter who could render the light of Greece as Van Gogh renders that of Provence does not seem to have been born yet.[3]

Many years later, Nikos Kazantzakis would write: "In every Greek landscape . . . the light is the protagonist-hero. The mountains, the valleys, the sea play a secondary role. The light is the resplendent sober Dionysos."[4]

Many artists were drawn to depict life in contemporary Greece. Edward Lear used pen, pencil, and watercolor in his images of mainland Greece, Crete, the Ionian Islands, and Albania, from 1848 to 1864. They give an instant look into the life of the Greeks in their historical milieu. In *The Rocks of Souli,* Lear captured the wild rock mountain from which the Greek women threw themselves into a lonely gorge rather than become slaves of the Turks. He had an affinity for the Greek terrain, mostly barren, but at times bounteously green with olive trees.[5]

In this rocky land of brilliant light, money was scarce; barter was the medium of exchange. Each day was a struggle to plant and to harvest enough corn, beans, and squash, the food of the poor, to get the family through winter. During those bitter months, they thought longingly of spring dandelions, sprinkled with a little olive oil and vinegar, a festive delicacy. They would wait for the dandelions in America also, where life was not so precarious.

There were always the poor. In the seventh century B.C., Hesiod tells of the hard struggle with the rocky earth. "Perses, you great fool . . . Work! Work," he admonishes his brother, "and then Hunger will not be your companion."[6]

Twenty-seven centuries later, a Greek folk poet wrote: "Few houses make a poor village—feel sorry for them. They have no priest, no teacher, not even a Gypsy [to provide music]. . . . The field is poor, the fatted lambs are hungry. It is a waste of seed to sow it."[7]

The people they didn't eat meat once a month. And many people they didn't have even that. They had to go to Piraeus for any kind of work. They had to borrow shoes to wear. They didn't have any. In the winter time they had to borrow overcoats. It was a pity. It was a very great poverty.—The Reverend Father George Stephanopoulos, Melhounion, Skilinis, Province Eleas[8]

At intervals, folk songs quelled their poverty.[9] Children walked from house to house singing carols on Christmas, New Year's, Epiphany, and during the forty days preceding the Resurrection: Carnival, Clean Monday, the day of Lazarus, and Palm Sunday. Songs of grape harvesting, of brides and grooms, and of the great guerrilla chieftain *klefts,* who fought the Turks for Greek liberty, swept over villages in the valleys and echoed from mountain to mountain, where hundreds of years ago Greeks had fled from invaders and found rugged havens.

Young and old sang of the mountains and the cold streams they deeply loved. Villagers extolled the water of their *topos,* its special *ousia* (essence), and they would speak of it in their American exile. The great mountains talked to each other:

Elympos [Olympos] and Kissavos,
the two mountains quarrel.
Old man Elympos turns to Kissavos and says, "Don't
scold, Kissavou, Turk-trodden,
I'm old man Elympos, renowned in the world.
I have forty-two summits and sixty-two springs,
Every summit a flag, every stream a guerrilla,
And on the tallest summit an eagle sits
clutching his talons."[10]

A bride sang of her misery:

Mother, you married me off badly when you
gave me to the valleys,
and I cannot bear the valleys, warm water I will not drink. . . .
Here the nightingale doesn't sing, and the cuckoo is silent.
Valleys raise horses and mountains manly men,
and [valley] girls languish, and become like the [color]
of a [gold] florin.[11]

The enslaved Greeks honored birds, seeing them as emblems of freedom. They watched the birds swoop down to peck at scanty grain and soar

A guerrilla kleft *who fought the Turks for Greek freedom during the revolution of 1821–29.* Author's collection.

effortlessly above battlefields. They were messengers telling of the destruction of villages and cities, of death on the battlefield—an eagle flying with a severed head in its talons. Chieftains gave them messages of counsel to headstrong younger men. A song tells of a bird sent to a *kleft* leader with the message: "Black bird, black swallow, tell Katsandonis to sit still. Times aren't like last year when he did whatever he wanted."

Illustration by
Cleo Papanikolas.

Streams, rivers, birds, all were wounded by the invading Turks.
Guerrillas ask a giant plane tree:

What ails you, wretched plane tree, that you stand withered,
Water on your roots and yet withered?
Lads, you've asked me, and I will tell you.
Ali Pasha passed by with eighteen thousand [Turkish soldiers],
None sat in my shade, under my coolness,
But all carved a mark on me, and all shot at me.[12]

Yet, at times, they would forego the *kleftic* songs to sing distichs and couplets,
old or improvised, often complaints against one's fate, but more often of love:

Are there no boats at the seashore, with sails unfurled?
Is there not someone in this neighborhood to love me also?[13]

The Greeks were human after all, and songs testify to yearnings for forbidden love between Christians and Jews, between Moslems and Greeks:

One Saturday night, mercy from God,
One Saturday night, one Sunday early,
I set out to wander in the Jewish neighborhood. . . .
I see a young Jewish girl, washing her hair,
with an ivory comb she combed it.
I ask her, "Jewish girl, will you become Christian
and wash your hair on Saturday, and change [wear her

best clothes] on Sunday?"
Your eyes shine
like the flowers of the valley.[14]

A Jewish girl tells her mother the stars and dawn tell her to "marry a *Romaion* [Greek] man, be baptized, and with a wedding crown [be married by] eighteen priests and one abbot."[15]

While women, boys, and old men tilled the resistant, arid land, the *klefts* lived high in their *kleftouria,* their mountain strongholds. They wore white pleated kilts, copied from the Albanians, or the full black breeches of the islands, with heavy guns and long knives in their cummerbunds. Their thick mustaches, denoting manliness, were twisted sideways. It was said of them: "Warm bread they never ate; the battle was their dowry; the yatighan their talisman, and off they sped like a bullet." In battle they stopped long enough to cut off the heads of their fallen comrades to keep the Turks from taking them as trophies.

Songs of the *kleft* heroes were sung from generation to generation. Yoryios Karaïskakis from Roumeli on the north, born of a nun and a guerrilla fighter, was escorted to his grave by "a thousand priests ahead and two thousand behind"; the deacon, Diakos, was caught by the Turks and roasted alive while he sang "Live on high mountains and crystal streams"; the illiterate General Yiannis Makriyiannis learned to write to give a remarkable account of an early revolt.[16]

Surrounded by Turks, the *klefts* survived through cunning. Karaïskakis said, "Sometimes my prick plays the trumpet and sometimes the *toubelekia.*"[17] The trumpet was a Greek instrument; the *toubelekia* was Turkish. The guerrillas were both heroic and ruthless—they took livestock and grain from the impoverished villagers to sustain themselves. They quarreled among themselves. The Roumeliot *stratigos* (general) Theodoros Grivas had married the widow of Panos Kolokotronis, whose father was the supreme Peloponnesian general Theodoros Kolokotronis. The Turks were advancing, but Grivas would not join Kolokotronis until his new wife's dowry was returned to her: "Every day she keeps after me to get her dowry back," Grivas complained. Negotiations went on: Kolokotronis insisted she had very little, although her mother was the famed Bouboulina, who had taken over her fallen husband's ship in a naval battle. Kolokotronis's aged mother was brought out to weep: "Where did she find those that she asks for? We saw none of them." After spirited argument, dowry pieces were delivered and the war resumed. When the war ended, the two Theodoroses tossed their *tsarouhia* aside and danced the *tsamiko* together, barefoot.[18]

A central government did not exist; *stratigoi* were leaders of their provinces. They acknowledged no man-made laws, but they held *filotimo* (honor) as the highest good; in a poor country a man's only possession was his honor, in which his daughters' chastity was all important. The Greeks also prized *leventia,* the love of life, gaiety, and courage. In folk life the *klefts* were giants with their own codes. Theodoros Kolokotronis often wore an ancient Greek helmet; in a song his men:

> didn't condescend to tread on ground; on horseback
> they go to church; on horseback they worship;
> on horseback they take the holy bread.[19]

In Crete, they sang:

> When will the skies clear, when will it be February
> To take my rifle, my beautiful mistress,
> And go down to the plain of Omalo, to the road of the
> Mousouron clan,
> to make mothers sonless, wives husbandless,
> to make little children motherless,
> crying in the night for water, in the morning for milk,
> and in the early dawn for their sweet mother.[20]

Leni Botsaris of a famed clan fought openly with *klefts.* Several other women joined them, disguised as young men, until their sex was discovered. A folk song tells of a *kleft* who lifted a huge rock during a respite of play. Her shirt parted: "I've made Turkish orphans and Turkish widows. Now that my breast is bared, I'll go off to become a nun."[21]

Praised above all were the women of Zalongo, of the Souli region of Epirus. From their high mountain village they saw their men being slaughtered by the Turks in the valley below. Rather than become the Turks' slaves, they formed a broken circle. Singing, they danced to the edge of a ravine where the first in line jumped with her children. Round after round they danced until all had jumped to their death:

> Live on, poor people,
> live on, sweet life,
> and you, unfortunate country,
> live on forever.
>
> Live on, little streams,
> woods, mountains, and small ravines.

Fish cannot live on land,
nor flowers in sand,
and Souliotisses can't live
without liberty.

Live on little streams,
woods, mountains, and small ravines[22]

Everywhere the sojourners walked there were reminders of the Turks, who had overrun their land and ruled them for four centuries: wooden balconies and latticework where veiled women had looked out at the passing world, mud-domed Turkish baths, and doorways and windows with pointed arches. Much of northern Greece, Crete, and several Aegean islands were still in Turkish hands. The young Greeks living in the "unredeemed lands" of Asia Minor had even more reason to find their way to America before being forced into the Turkish army for seven years.

The travelers, though, trudging toward the seaports, knew almost nothing about the Frankish barons who had invaded their country after the fall of Byzantium or about the Venetians, who had stored their ammunition in the Parthenon, which a Turkish bomb reduced to its present ruin. The Turks smashed great marble shrines and statues to build roads and transported Greece's timber, minerals, and metals to Turkey. Byzantine churches with their brilliant mosaics, a unique contribution to the world, were converted to mosques. The mosaics were plastered over.

The physical damage to the country was horrendous, but a greater devastation occurred. During the centuries in which the Turks ruled Greece, other Balkan countries, the Middle East, and Egypt, time stood still. The Reformation, the Renaissance, and the Age of Enlightenment were changing the world, but Greece and the other captive countries knew nothing of these great forces.[23]

When the Greeks won their freedom, the country had been destroyed; Athens was left a hamlet of five thousand people. The people looked back to Byzantium, not to antiquity, as the great epoch of their history.[24] The travelers, though, knew little about the Byzantine era; they knew only that the Turks were traditional enemies and that some day Greek lands must again be Greek. They brought this obsession with them to America.

All of them had sisters to dower and parents to help, yet often something more sent them hurrying to the great ships. Need was ever present, but the wonder of adventure beckoned the young, as it had the ancients. As Pericles said, "We have forced every sea and land to be the highway of our daring."[25]

CHAPTER 2

THE BYZANTINE EAGLE

The Greeks had their renowned heroes who fought the Turks and they had their Christian saints to pray to, to keep Charos (Death) from snatching a beloved and to perform miracles against nature's onslaught. When the news of the Christian God had been brought to their progenitors, "they must have felt that it was unreasonable of the Christian missionaries to ask them to give up all their old gods merely because a new god had been introduced."[1]

The Greeks kept much of the old religion, but in new forms. The rites of spring became Easter; Zeus was transformed into the Christian God; Helios, the sun, was now Saint Elias; Hermes, the messenger, was Archangel Michael; Poseidon became Saint Nicholas; and Heracles (or Theseus) the warrior was taken over by Saint George. The goddess of love, Aphrodite, though, vanished.

The Byzantine eagle that looks both east and west to the two divisions of the empire. One head denotes the Christian Church, the other the emperor in Constantinople. Illustration by Cleo Papanikolas.

That the Gospel was translated into Greek from the Aramaic of Christ's time has held a special place in Greek religious thought.

And the "calling of the Gentiles" meant that Hellenism became blessed by God . . . there was precisely as little "chance" or "accident" in this "selection" of the Greek language—as there was in God's "selection" of the Jewish people—out of all the people of antiquity—as "His" people. . . . The real failure of Aristotle was not in his "naturalism," but in that he could not see any permanence of the individual. . . . The idea of personality itself was a great Christian contribution to philosophy. And again, there was here a sharp understanding of the tragedy of death also.[2]

Eastern Orthodoxy took a tight hold on the Christian Greeks. The Greeks were not divided by language and religion into Greek Orthodox, Greek Catholic, Roman Catholic, and Moslem, as other Balkan peoples were destined to be. Greek ethnic origin and Greek ancestral language were secondary factors: "the contemporary Greek was born to his religion"; no nation "presented greater homogeneity" among the Europeans than did the Greeks.[3]

In A.D. 330, the Roman Emperor Constantine dedicated the city New Rome, called Constantinople after himself, to the Holy Trinity and the mother of God. The two-headed eagle, for emperor and God, was the symbol of the empire, looking both East and West. Constantinople lay eastward, between the Black Sea and the Sea of Marmara.

The empire was divided between Rome in the West and Constantinople in the East. Differences arose over the centuries. In the West, the liturgy was in Latin; in the East in Greek. The West used unleavened bread in the communion service, the Eucharist, the changing of the wine and bread into the body and blood of Christ, while the East used leavened bread. Controversies began early over statues of the West and icons of the East; celibate clergy in the West and married priests in the East; baptismal sprinkling in the West and immersion in the East. The West adopted the new Gregorian Calendar; the East retained the ancient Julian Calendar, which lags by thirteen days.

The addition by the Latins of the word *filoque* to the Nicene Creed, by which they expressed the belief that the Holy Spirit proceeds from the Father *and* the Son, caused a deep fissure between West and East. The conflict over the authority of the Pope increased, widened, and resulted in the Great Schism of 1054, when the Pope excommunicated the Patriarch and the Patriarch followed with an excommunication of the Pope. The sack of Constantinople in 1204 by the Fourth Crusade and Venetian rule further embittered the Greeks.

The doctrinal differences between the Catholic West and the Orthodox

Christ Pantokrator (Creator of all), twelfth century, Cathedral of Cefalu. Photograph by Andre Grabar, from *Byzantine Painting: Historical and Critical Study* (New York City: Skira, Inc., 1953).

East continued. The Catholic dogma of the Immaculate Conception proclaimed that the Virgin's mother, Saint Anne, conceived Mary "by God's special decree delivered from all stain of original sin." It is not part of Orthodoxy, nor is, of course, the infallibility of the Pope. Scholars portray Catholicism as legalistic and Orthodoxy as mystical.[4] The Orthodox *oikonomia* (dispensation) is "a judgment according to circumstances," the opposite of rigid moralism. Humaneness is the criteron for judgment.

Roman Catholicism has singled out the *pieta,* the suffering and dying Christ as the epitome of its faith. The sacrifice of Christ on the Cross sets the theme and mood for the whole of the

St. George, protector of the people, the patron saint of Greece. Illustration by Cleo Papanikolas.

Roman Catholic faith. The Greek Orthodox church . . . has found the focal point of its faith in the resurrection of the Christ. "He is risen!" is the stirring theme that is the epitome of the Orthodox faith.[5]

Provinces, towns, villages, and hamlets had their special saints—men and women who had saved them from catastrophes or brought good fortune—

Because of the dearth of trees, thyme was used for fuel and as fodder for animals. Illustration by Cleo Papanikolas.

but the patron saint of all Greece was Saint George, protector of the people. At night, it was said, the hoofbeats of his great white horse could be heard as he rode over valleys and mountains.

Neither the people nor the village priests knew the foundations of the Orthodox religion: that God is unknowable. To reach the luminous light which is God, one must pass through a divine darkness.[6] All those who believed belonged to the Royal Priesthood. Heaven and Hell were not geographical places. Greek Orthodoxy had no folk songs about Heaven, which was also unknowable—contemplating it when each day was a struggle to survive was a luxury few could afford. In proverbs, Heaven was evoked without sentimentality: "Not even in heaven can man live alone"; "Thrashings originated in Paradise." The people responded to reality: "What Fate has written in black ink, the sun cannot whiten." They knew, though, that God was everywhere. When it rained, they said, "God is raining." When dawn came, they said, "God is dawning." They believed in both Fate and God's will: "If God wants," they said.

In their poverty, Orthodoxy became a great passion; it gave their spirits strength. The Greeks believed to their death in the *Megale Idhea* (Great Idea), which would return to them the lands in Asia Minor that were lost to the invading Turks in 1453.[7] A lullaby sung since Turkish occupation times says: "And if they tie you to the cross, my child, endure silently."

Monastery among the monoliths of Meteora (the monasteries in the sky). From *Greece 1980.* Courtesy of the National Tourist Organization of Greece.

Boys were taught to become soldiers and to die for this centuries-old loss, to suffer horrible torture and death for the fatherland until The City, as Constantinople was called, became Greek once more and liturgies were again chanted in the great Aghia Sophia (Holy Wisdom) Cathedral, the center of Orthodoxy.

CHAPTER 3

SEED IN NUMBERS

The Greeks had their great heroes of the revolution against the Turks and they had their religion, Orthodoxy. They also had a vital, dramatic folk culture. At engagements, weddings, and baptisms, the Greeks sang and danced away, for the moment, their poverty and bleakness. Mothers and women relatives began preparing dowries from the day baby girls were born. They raised silkworms, whose voracious appetite required enormous amounts of mulberry leaves. The women soaked the cocoons, spun the silk threads, dyed them with berries, nuts, flowers, and herbs, and wove scarves and curtains for their future households. For carpets and bed covers, they spun, dyed, and wove sheep wool and goat hair.

Matchmaking was discussed with lively interest and conjecture in coffeehouses and across rock walls. Often, especially if the bride and groom lived in different villages, they would not have seen each other before the wedding.

Many restrictions existed to prevent marriages: first, second, and, in most regions, third cousins could not marry; nor could a man and woman who had the same godfather because baptism conferred a blood tie; nor could in-laws; nor could two sisters marry two brothers, because the "mixing of blood" was viewed as incest. The nomadic Sarakatsani of northern Greece believed that the union of two people produced a unique blood that should not be repeated.[1]

Widows remained unmarried, no matter how young they were. It was seen as an insult to the dead husband if his wife married again. Greeks adhered to God's instructions to Aaron and his sons, making it applicable for all men: "And he shall take a wife in her virginity. A widow or a divorced woman he shall not take."[2] Because mirrors and photographs gave pleasure, widows draped them in black crepe and dyed curtains and draperies black. For the rest of their lives, they wore mourning clothes. Their children did so

Wedding crowns signify that the bride and groom become queen and king of a new household. Photograph by Allan Smart.

for at least a year after their father's death or for an extended time, depending on their *topos,* their region. Only when young orphans had no means of support was remarriage condoned. The new husband, usually much older, married the widow as a *psyhiko,* an act that was good for his soul.

Other impediments involved step-relationships; these precluded marriage because they too were looked upon as incest. When a greater evil occured, such as the birth of a child outside marriage, then an *oikonomia* (dispensation) was asked of the bishop; but that was extremely rare. Brothers killed their pregnant sisters and their babies to uphold the honor of the family name. Dressed in black, mothers followed caskets to the graves, keening laments for murdered daughters and their infants.

Next, the dowry was of paramount importance.[3] Not only were fathers and brothers responsible for the dowry; help was also expected from uncles, cousins, and sons-in-law. Engagement contracts were lengthy; they represented centuries of land acquisition, small plots at a distance from one another. Land had been divided so often through dowry requirements that the parcels had dwindled in size. The Greeks had no love for the resistant plot of land they hoed; it was utilitarian; its purpose was to sustain them. Their love was for "God's mountains and streams."

The dowry almost always included a house and the necessary table, chairs, bed, and linens; land; and a sum of gold coins. An engagement contract from Lidia, on the island of Nysiros, dated 8 February 1915, listed the following dowry items:

A. The house located in Palous as it is.

B. Her brother Gheorghios gives . . . one half the land located at "Akrotyra" Palous, that is from the side of the street of Palous heading towards the mill, up to and including the black fig tree. [Seven more pieces of land are described.]

And in cash, one hundred (100) 20-franc (gold) pieces and another (50) 20-franc (gold) pieces from our son-in-law residing in Alexandria (Egypt). [Fifty gold pieces would be given at the wedding and one hundred six months after the marriage.]

The bridegroom, Nikolas, accepting all stated above, signs personally, and a penalty of twenty-five (20) franc gold pieces is set, which will be paid by the violator as a compensation.

The wedding is fixed from today until next March included.[4]

A Papigo, Epirus, marriage contract from 1855 is more specific.

Our ever revered Lord Jesus Christ, bless this union here, as You have blessed the holy matrimony in Canaan of Galilee, which is intended and undersigned by me Georgakana. In the absence of my husband, I offer in marriage my beloved daughter named Angeliki to the well founded man Kostantinos son of Apostolos Sanoukis, and affix the following dowry below.

3 fezes, 3 kerchiefs, 3 blanket bedspreads two woolen and one linen, 9 chemises, three long sleeved and two short sleeved, five woven, two flokata (ruffled), three aprons one handwoven, one shawl, a handwoven dress with a belt, three camelhair belts and one hand spun, one coat, woolen in good condition and in fashion, and 160 grams of sterling silver belt, 5 *okes* [approximately 2 lbs. ea.] of bronze, and half the field in Moutzali . . . and 800 *grosia* [Turkish coins] and the usual complete bedding, along with the vineyard all of it in Selo, and half of the orchard in the upper part of the village. These I give along with my blessing, and trust that the everloving plentiful God will grant them health and happiness and call upon the ministry of the holiest Virgin Mother Theotokos and St. George and the great sacrificer St. Prokopios. Amen.[5]

Wedding dresses were passed down from mother to daughter over the centuries. They were heavily embroidered, and often came with large metal belt buckles. Dowry coins the clan had provided were sewed onto the bride's headscarf. The poorest of brides had at best an apron of yarns dyed with many colors: red from the juice of a pomegranate or holly-oak leaves, yellow

from the inside bark of an apple tree, black from a black walnut, brown from the heart of a plane tree.

With the signing of the dowry papers, the wedding preparations could begin. In Central Greece an embroidered silk flag, the *flamboura* (bride's flag) flew over her house, secured there by a boy whose parents were living. He pushed a pomegranate into the staff for fertility.[6]

A week of festivities preceded the weddings, which were held after spring planting and harvesting. Marriages were never solemnized during the great church days of fasting; on Christmas; during Holy Week, which ended with Christ's Resurrection; or on August 15, the Dormition (falling asleep) of the Virgin. Although songs were sung about the flowers and birds of May, marriages were not performed in that month; the name itself connoted magic.

With slight variations the activities followed a pattern. Gunshots echoed across valleys and mountains. The bride visited her future husband's family and gave prescribed gifts: silk handkerchiefs, a gold coin placed on the groom's left shoulder (Karpathos). The Wednesday before the wedding, bread for the nuptial dinner was prepared. The parents threw coins into the dough as it was kneaded while boys whose parents were living sang traditional songs of good tidings. Close relatives of the groom rushed into the house and tried to paste pieces of dough on the foreheads of the bride's male relatives—a vestige of bride-stealing days. The relatives of the bride were prepared with their own dough.

Every preparation—the sifting of the flour for the dough, the bathing of the bride, and the shaving of the groom—was accompanied with songs sung by girls from the bride's village. Young males went from house to house on Thursday, inviting guests and proffering wine or liqueur from a tray decorated with basil and flowers. On Friday, the bride's friends, again singing, arranged her dowry linens, which would be placed on a bedecked mule or horse for the walk to the groom's house. On Saturday, the wedding food was cooked. Later the groom knelt, holding a plate with small glasses of olive oil and wine. His friends and relatives dipped a coin into the wine and then into the olive oil, touched his forehead, and placed the coin on the plate. The girls sang the groom's requests to his mother, father, brothers, sisters, and cousins for their blessings.

Weddings were performed on Sundays, holy and joyful because Christ had arisen on that day. Relatives of the groom walked or rode horses or mules to the bride's house. The bride asked her mother for her blessing, pretended she would not leave unless the groom's father promised her a piece of pasture, a portion of his vineyard, and an apple tree—a "sweet apple tree." She pretended to resist while her friends sang her response: "I will not step out, will not go, I wait for my eagle."[7]

In wedding songs, an eagle represented the groom, a partridge or dove the bride. For the first and only time in her life, the bride was the center of village life. She received enough praise to last a lifetime of servitude to her husband and his family, including his sisters, who had formerly been her childhood friends. She would bring water from the village well or from afar, work inside the house, and toil in the fields. Not only had she seen wives' subservience to husbands all about her, but small ceremonial acts before her wedding made clear that for all the fine songs, her fate was decided.

Every province and island had customs that upheld a husband's authority until death. Women in many areas stood up when their husbands entered the house. In Cyprus, the bride's mother touched the groom's

Sketch of an eagle (the groom) and a dove (the bride) by Cleo Papanikolas.

nape with a censer to ensure prosperity in farming. She then gave him a gift, set on the threshold of the house, of a folded rug or blanket with a stick laid on one corner. The groom stepped on the stick with his right foot, broke it, and walked inside, symbolizing the submission of his future bride.[8]

The girls would sing on, as in this Skyros wedding song:

> Two suns and two moons appeared at your window.
> Your hair is golden and your eyebrows black.
> Come, let me kiss you, my dark-complexioned one
> To put out the flame that is my heart.[9]

Eyebrows are often extolled in old folk songs. They took on great importance when the Turks ruled the Balkans: Turkish women veiled the lower part of their faces, and although Greek women did not, the proximity of Turkish customs affected all subjugated countries.

The bride was called an apple in some songs, and the groom was exhorted to pick it. In Crete, when the groom's family and friends arrived at the bride's door, a note of realism sprang out as they sang:

> Open the door, the iron door.
> So we can see the much-praised bride.

> We can see the bride, you can see our groom.
> And if there is any complaint, say it before us.[10]

This was mere melodrama. The arrangements had been rigidly made. The bride and groom stood before the *iconostasis* (icon screen) at the east end of the church, facing the rising sun, which was also a symbol of the Resurrection. They wore wedding crowns of white cloth flowers, signifying their new role as king and queen of a fledgling household. A white ribbon connected the crowns; the best man interchanged them three times with crossed arms, carefully, to prevent their slipping and bringing bad luck to the couple. The priest's long intoning of God's blessing of Abraham, opening the womb of Sarah, giving Rebecca to Isaac, and joining Rachel to Jacob culminated in the Dance of Isaiah. Three times the priest, with silver Bible raised, led the procession; the best man (*koumbaro*) followed, leading the new husband and wife around the table on which the consecrated wine and candles had been set.

After the mystery (one of the seven sacraments) of marriage, the wedding party arrived at the house of the groom's parents for the nuptial dinner. In the poorest villages, people brought pieces of meat, cheese *pites,* and pastries to help the hosts offer enough food. In many regions, the groom stamped on a pomegranate at the entrance of the house to ensure that his marriage would be fertile. In other areas, someone would break open a pomegranate and strew the seeds around the house, again for fertility.

Singing continued. The *koumbaro* was feted with songs, usually accompanied by Gypsy musicians summoned from their encampments. They played their instruments for the most traditional of Greek folk dances, the *syrtos,* and its many variations. Flutes, violins, *lyras, gaidas* (bagpipes), *clarinos,* and often the *daouli* (drum) rang out while the *koumbaro* led the line dance, first with the bride then with the groom. The *koumbaro* had a special status; he had taken a sacred vow to raise the couple's children if they died or were unable to care for them. This vow was made in church in the presence of God and created a relationship that was stronger than blood. Afterwards the relatives joined in and danced until morning.

The festivities were not over. On Monday the house was put in order, and more cooking was done. On Tuesday the newly married couple visited the groom's family and the bride presented small gifts to his parents, his sisters, and his brothers: a shirt, a pair of stockings, a handkerchief.

Singing accompanied all the ceremonial events of life: the baptism of a child, the building of a house, the journey into *exoria* (exile), as Greeks called leaving their country. The couple then began their married life; they lived and taught their children according to the culture they had been born into. It was colored by sayings, superstitions, and the accidents of fate. A child would hear a multitude of proverbs:

> What the householder knows, the visitor does not.
> Ten, fifteen blows on another's behind, what's that to me?
> The crow is born white, turns gray, then black like its parents.
> The apple falls under the apple tree.
> Eat and drink with your family; do business with strangers.
> The fish begins to rot at the head. [Blame the head of every entity.]
> The lid finds its pot.
> Red hair and blue eyes portend the devil.
> A crow does not lay dove's eggs.
> He even argues with his clothes.
> There is plenty of laughter in a fool's mouth.
> Examine the loom before buying the cloth. [Examine the mother
>   before marrying the daughter.]
> Women have long hair and short wisdom.
> The miser's riches fall into the spendthrift's hands.
> If the female dog doesn't wag her tail, the male dog won't follow.
> He who has plenty of pepper puts it even on greens.
> He who has plenty of pepper puts it on his behind.
> If you're not eating the *pita,* don't worry if it's burned.
> Sweet is the morning sleep, bare the behind on Easter.
> If I complain, I reveal my shame.
> When the devil grows old, he becomes a monk.
> When the fox grows old, she becomes a nun.
> When you hear of plenty of cherries, take a small basket.
> My child's child is twice my child.
> Lies are the salt of truth.
> Eat beans, beans betray.
> Stars fell and pigs ate them.
> They're as close as underpants and ass.
> A man without a woman is like a horse without a bridle.
> A woman without a man is like a ship without a rudder.
> A cough and riches can't be hidden.
> Religion is like a fish. Eat the flesh and leave the bones.

Children heard many oaths: "May you swallow your tongue with salt." They learned that when blood was spilled, retribution had to be exacted, or the soul of the victim could not rest. Vendettas were carried on for generations.

Curses, too, if made in the name of the Deity, had to be carried out. A mother's curse was the worst of all curses.

Superstitions abounded:

Don't whistle at night because demons gather then.

Don't sleep under a walnut tree; bad spirits bring death.

Don't hold your head with two hands; it bodes affliction.

Don't travel on Wednesday and Thursday, nor do heavy work. These are ill-omened days. [From Christ's Passion.]

A howling dog smells death.

Bad luck follows when a rabbit crosses one's path.

Those who've died a violent death are susceptible to *vrykolakes* (vampires). Where they died, fires burn at night and shrieks are heard. No one should pass there at night. If necessary clap your hands loudly and hurry away.

Don't lend flour, salt, or vinegar at night.

Don't hold the door of the house open with both hands. This will bring a closure of the house through death.

Nereids [beautiful but seductive nymphs] come out at night to wash their hair at streams and riverbanks.

The screech of the owl near one's house portends death. To escape, it must be killed.

If the song of the cuckoo is heard in very early spring, it means distress.

Don't sweep at night or the progress of the house is swept away.

A person who travels should kick a jug of water outside the doorway. This will bring good luck and wealth.

A traveler should pay attention to the first person he meets at the outset of his travels. There are good shadows and bad ones. If he meets a good shadow, all will go well and he will become wealthy; but not if he meets a bad shadow.

If you meet a priest as you set out on a travel, return home. If you continue, the trip will bode ill.

Don't marry in May. Only donkeys mate then.

Goats are the animals of the devil; sheep are the animals of God.

The *kaki ora* (bad hour), or, as principal investigators Richard and Eva Blum translate it, the "dangerous hour," caused great anxiety for families. There were four dangerous hours: for infants before baptism; for young people during the engagement period and especially during the wedding;

for the *lechona,* the mother, during the forty days after giving birth; and for the old when they lose their vitality.

[As an unbaptized infant] he is not yet accepted into the human community, and is, in a sense, still part of the uncivilized natural world of powers and spirits. With the lechona it is somewhat the same, she is not only vulnerable to what the supernaturals may do to her, but her own powers, her "pollution" associated with fertility, are a source of danger to others.

[When the forty days are over, she attends church to be "cleansed" by the priest's readings, as Mary was cleansed forty days after the birth of Christ. She can then venture beyond her own house without polluting anyone.]

It is otherwise for the youth in courtship and at the wedding. At this time the dangers are not from the supernatural world nor are they inherent from the primitive power of the persons themselves. Dangers come from other humans, for the most part jealous ones. [The common form strikes the bridegroom impotent; this can often be cured by having the bride and groom sleep overnight in a church].

. . . Illness, misfortune, and death [among the elderly] are to be expected; it need not be explained by the actions of supernaturals or sorcery.[11]

The dangerous hour sent people to priests and magicians for help. Protective charms were made into amulets, usually a small square of cloth in which a bit of a page from a holy book, incense, a sliver of the True Cross or a small cross, a pinch of gunpowder, garlic, rue, and salt were sewn. A blue bead pinned to a child's clothes was protection against the Evil Eye. If the Evil Eye was so potent that it prevailed, *maghisses* (witches) dispelled it, but other women were also consulted, those who had received the secret words passed down through female ancestors.

This folklore permeated with fright was bequeathed to children from infancy. Anecdotes of magical happenings sensitized them with terror and delight. They learned of the great heroes of the Greeks, but they also learned that life was precarious and that attention should be paid to survive. Careless Death was always present.

> This earth we tread,
> We will all burrow in it.
> This earth with its grasses
> Eats brave lads and lasses.

> This earth with its flowers
> Eats up little children.
> This earth will eat me too,
> Who my little mother has but me.
> This earth that will eat me,
> Beat it with your feet![12]

Yet there was the sun, which warmed both the rich and the poor, gave solace, and inspired paeans of praise. Near Messenia, in the Peloponnese, villagers greeted the sun in the morning, crossing themselves three times and saying, "Good morning, Sun. As you warm the world, warm me and my children also." At sunset they again crossed themselves and said, "Good evening, Sun. May you happily rise in the morning. May no obstacle be found in your way."[13]

CHAPTER 4

POVERTY AND COMMUNAL CELEBRATIONS

Childhood was short for children. Their future was decided at birth by the Three Fates. By the age of three, they picked beans and removed bits of rock from lentils. Those who were sent to school—often walking miles to reach it—struggled with an unfamiliar language, the purist *katharevousa*. Even before the Greek Revolution of 1821 against the Turks, a movement had begun to supplant this artificial language derived from ancient Greek with the demotic, the popular form of modern Greek.[1] In provincial towns, parents might send their daughters to school, but village girls grew up illiterate.

In the villages, boys and (when death or illness required it) girls herded their family's sheep, often remaining alone on a mountain for weeks at a time. Boys and men tended sheep, the clean animals of God; they did not graze the "unclean" goats—that was work for girls and women.

Poverty sent Peloponnesian village boys as young as eight to Athens with a wooden kit holding paltry shoe-shining supplies. They slept in doorways until they found others like themselves and shared dismal shelters.

Boys were apprenticed for the usual three years around the age of ten to relatives in larger towns to learn carpentry, tanning, and barbering. They worked without pay and slept in barns. "I worked in a cold cellar," one said, "and slept on a straw mattress in a drafty attic with a broken window that I plugged with a pillow. My pay was food."[2] Konstandinos Argyres wrote:

> As my older brothers have told me, my parents had 10 children. My mother lived but 52 years . . . [she died] when I was five years old. . . . My father died when I was only eight. . . . In town [Lefkada] my father had a friend who specialized in grain . . . he asked my father if he knew of a young boy who could watch his

A future immigrant. From Henry Pratt Fairfield, *Greek Immigration to the United States* (New Haven: Yale University Press, 1911), frontispiece.

store during the siesta. [The father suggests Konstandinos.] "Well," said the man, "he is too small to give him wages, however if you want, I'll give him room and board and also, I have a book he can read from and I also have a daughter who goes to school and she can help him because as you know I am unlettered like you." I lived at the store for almost a year. [A doctor needed a small boy to do the shopping and live with the family] and would pay me five drachmas a month! . . . My chores were to go to the *agora* (market) every morning. There were butchers, fish mongers and fresh produce stalls there. . . . The name of the [next village] where we moved was called Kolori on the island of Ithaki. Here I didn't even have to go shopping. As he had promised my cousin, the doctor proceeded to show me how to grind and prepare various medicines. . . . The relationship continued until the next year 1886 at which time Greece and Turkey started to quarrel over lands Greece felt were hers. Greece mobilized her armed services and my brother Yioryis was called to serve his country. This left my sister Anastasia and my brother Gregorios alone. [It was decided to bring Konstandinos, then nine years old, to mind the sheep. He was in full charge of sixty sheep. Three years later, at the age of thirteen, he was put on an uninhabited island to tend sixty sheep. At the age of fourteen, he made all the cheese and tended one hundred sheep, the family's and a partner's.][3]

The young looked at the sea, which could be seen, it was said, from every mountain in Greece and could be reached in a day's walk. Poets, for whom it was a symbol of men's hopes, fears, and loves, have memorialized the sea: Homer's "wine-dark sea," George Seferis's "calm, embittered sea," Odysseus Elytis's "hard dream of storm and sea," and Yiannis Ritsos's "seagull wings over a morning sea."

The young tillers and shepherds saw ruined marble columns in the valleys and knew nothing about them. They played games with the unearthed Roman, Byzantine, Venetian, Serbian, and Bulgarian coins and shards. They were vestiges of countless invasions, blood-land, despotism, and invaders, but the boys and older villagers knew nothing or little about them.

What had come down to them from their brilliant past were a few stories and anecdotes: Aesop's fable of the fox and the grapes; the great orator Demosthenes putting pebbles inside his cheeks to practice speaking clearly; the Spartan youth who hid a baby fox in his tunic and stood at attention

Basil. Illustration by
Cleo Papanikolas.

before his general while his flesh was being gnawed; the heroic stand against
the Persians at Thermopylae. Yet children often carried the names of the ancients: Sophocles, Themistocles, Solon, and Pericles; and a great many were
baptized Alexander after the great conqueror.

Of the Byzantine era they knew of Empress Helen's search through the
Holy Land for the True Cross, and of her being led by a sweet scent to a
spot where a basil plant grew in the desert. There her retinue dug and found
the cross. Perhaps the villagers had heard of the Byzantine Emperor Basil II
(the "Bulgar-slayer") who blinded fifteen thousand invading Bulgarian soldiers, leaving a one-eyed man to every one hundred to lead them back to
their king. The Byzantines gave the Greeks the name Romaoi, subjects of
Rome, and the word remained for centuries.

All knew the *Englezos* (Englishman) Lord Byron, who came to join the
Greek fight against the Turks. He arrived with trunks of silk and velvet, tobacco, tea, and all that would make him comfortable. He wrote in *Don Juan:*

> The isles of Greece, the isles of Greece!
> Where burning Sappho loved and sung,
> Where grew the arts of war and peace,—
> Where Delos rose and Phoebus sprung!

Eternal summer gilds them yet.
But all except their sun, is set. . . .

The mountains look on Marathon—
And Marathon looks on the sea;
And musing there an hour alone,
I dream'd that Greece might still be free;
For standing on the Persians' grave,
I could not deem myself a slave.

Byron was felled by malaria, the scourge of the low lands, in the swamps of Missolonghi. Trying to cure him, doctors bled him repeatedly until he died. His statue stands in the center of the Garden of Heroes in Missolonghi, surrounded by those of the leading *stratigoi* in the War for Independence.

Other foreigners had flocked to Greece to help them in their revolt. Among them were men with high military experience, but the guerrilla leaders had no use for them. The *klefts* had been harassing the Turks for a hundred years before they formed a united, yet loosely organized, revolutionary force. Like Lord Byron, many foreigners were dedicated to Greek liberty, but their governments had self-serving reasons: Greece was in an important strategic position in the Aegean. The wily General Makriyiannis (1797–1864), who learned to write his memoirs phonetically, wrote:

The Europeans disparaged the unfortunate Greeks. England wanted them to become Englishmen, in keeping with the English justice prevailing, like the barefooted and hungry Maltese; the French wanted them to become Frenchmen; Russia wanted them to become Russians and Austria wanted them to become Austrians. And whichever of the four could, would devour them.[4]

The Romaioi did not know all that was transpiring in their quest for freedom. What they did know they heard during communal celebrations. Every village had one or more renowned storytellers, who told of the great events and battles of the past, for the Greeks had come from an ancient oral tradition that bequeathed its history and song down through the generations. The storytellers repeated again and again the old stories of brutal enslavement: Greek boys taken to Turkey *(pedhomazima)* and taught to forget their people and to hate them, the feared janissaries, and Turkish pashas who tyrannized the Greeks and closed their churches and schools, forcing children to make their way secretly at night to caves. Greeks were possessed by the poem of those years:

The Garden of Heroes in Missolonghi. Lord Byron's monument is in the center, surrounded by heroes of the Greek Revolution. The monument on the left is that of General Theodoros Grivas, the author's great-great-grandfather.

My little, bright moon, shine on me as I walk
to learn letters and the things of God.[5]

Children grew up in huts or narrow two-story stone houses. Animals were kept in an excavation in the dirt below. Most families lived in one room above them. The parents slept on a curtained platform at one end of the room, the rest of the family on hand-loomed rugs or corn-husk mattresses that were rolled up in the daytime and set against walls. A rudimentary table, a few chairs, and a fireplace in which thyme, the only fuel available, burned were the hut's furnishings. Thyme was also the fodder for animals. In the harsh winters animal heat rose up and provided a little warmth.

> The family was seated around a warped wooden table—father, mother, and children—the oldest a girl near his own age. In the center of the table was a pot of beans. A metal spoon was passed from one to the other to dip into the pot.[6]

> *[The village] was the home of only fifteen families and contained a small church, a water well, and one well-worn dirt road which served as the main street. We had no school or teacher and to learn to read, the children had to walk ten miles to the nearest small village. At the end of the third year in grade school, my father gave the teacher two roosters in exchange for a third grade certificate and a release to allow me to go to*

Easter bread. Dough is braided to form a cross; an egg, symbol of rebirth, dyed red for Christ's blood, is placed on the end of each arm and in the center. Photograph by Allan Smart.

work. . . . my father took me to the city, Tripolis, to look for work. My first job was in a small grocery store where I earned 100 drachmas a year and board and room in the same building. I spent fourteen hours a day on duty—Ernest (Anastasios) Mantes, Manteika, Province Arcadia.[7]

For all the ancient poverty, the great events of the year gave life meaning: Christmas; Easter; March 25, the beginning of the Greek revolution against the Turks; and August 15, the Dormition of the Virgin. With the children following them, the patriarchs presided over celebrations; they read the shoulder blade of the Easter lamb and foretold what the coming year would bring; and in times of crisis, they recited how similar matters were handled in the far past.

Nature and crafts, not luxuries, gave a festive air to important days. Pots of basil and flowers festooned houses and churches, and the bread women baked for those days was decorated with coils and designs made with ropes of dough. In Macedonia, the Christmas bread was decorated to represent families' occupations: farmers with a plough and oxen; shepherds with lambs, kids, and a sheepfold.[8] Throughout Greek lands, children coming to sing the *kalenda* (carols) were rewarded with walnuts, roasted chestnuts, and cookies.

A coin was baked inside the New Year's bread, bringing good luck to whoever found it in his or her slice. Easter bread was topped with a cross of dough, and red-dyed eggs—red for Christ's blood—were embedded at the end of each "arm" and in the center (Christ's heart), where the two pieces intersected. On May 1, children went from house to house singing the Song of May, of wildflowers and crystal springs, of partridges and nightingales, and of mourning doves alighting on fountains. They were repaid with a sweet, at rare times with a coin. Flowers festooned houses and churches, and the bread for the day was intricately decorated.

CHAPTER 5

DEATH AND BLACK FLOWERS

The days of toil were broken into by the ceremonies of life, not only by weddings and baptisms but also by death. Women sang the *mirologhia* (words of fate), eerie, high-pitched laments for the dead. Often a singer known for her repertoire of traditional and extemporaneous laments led the *mirologhia*. The *mirologhia* of Mani, the southernmost tip of the Peloponnesus, were extolled for their beauty.[1] Those of Epirus "are among the most moving in the world and may compete with the famous Maniat laments: both sets originate in the ancient laments of the Hellenes."[2] "Lamentation has always been held by the Greeks to be as essential to the repose of the dead as burial."[3] "There is the religious idea that the dead need a twofold rite, both mourning and interment."[4]

Cypress trees in graveyards are watchers of the dead. Illustration by Cleo Papanikolas.

As in ancient keenings, mountains, birds, streams, and animals were called upon to lament. Charos was a dark presence. As he rode to gather the souls of the dead, black flowers sprang up at the roadside. Once he was the boatman Charon, who ferried the dead across the river Styx to the underworld, but he became Death himself, the feared and respected personage in the laments:

> They tricked me, the birds,
> the swallows of Spring.
> They told me I would never die.
> I built my house high, the walls of marble.

I sat at the window to see the valleys far off.
The valleys turned green, the mountains blue.
I see Charos coming to take me.
Black he is, black he wears, black his horse
And black the kerchief round his neck.[5]

Lamentations are found in Homer: the Trojan women keening for Hector, Achilles lamenting the death of Patroklos. Bion's "Lament for Adonis" begins:

Wail, wail, Ah for Adonis!
He is lost to us, lovely Adonis . . .
Cry to the listening world,
He is lost to us, lovely Adonis![6]

A mother laments her child:

You did not deserve it, a bed in the earth is not for you,
You belong in the garden of May,
Between two apple trees, under three bitter orange trees,
Blossoms gently falling, the apples on your lap,
Carnations a red circlet round your neck.[7]

A widow keens for her young husband:

I had an apple tree at my door, a tree in my yard.
A deep red tent covered the house,
And a cypress of pure gold that I leaned on.
I had, too, a silver votive holder hanging in my house.
Now the apple tree has withered, the tree has decayed,
And the deep red tent has blackened.
The golden cypress fell and broke.
The votive light has gone out. The house has no light.[8]

On Good Friday of Holy Week, the Virgin's lament was heard through-out the villages:

Oh, my sweetest Springtime,
How is it You lie in a tomb now?
Where has Your beauty gone?[9]

The soul was an awesome presence:

Nicholas Philagios was six years old when his mother died. He remembered the family standing at the bedside of his sick mother, watching her and expecting her spirit to leave at any moment. Someone saw a white butterfly pass through the room and said, "There goes her spirit."[10]

It was said that at death the soul swiftly passed through all the places where the dead one had been. It was active and demanding and could "wander about to annoy the living."[11] From earliest times death was looked upon as a struggle with Charos, exemplified by the mythical figure Digenis (two-birth) Akrites (borders). Born of a Greek mother and an Arab father, he guarded the borders of the Byzantine Empire in the tenth and eleventh centuries. For three days and three nights he fought Charos on a marble threshing floor.[12]

While the liturgy for the dead was sung over the body, someone remained in the house to keep the soul, unwilling to begin its journey, from entering the house. If the dead person had been a priest, he was buried sitting up, ready to sermonize at the Resurrection.

To make certain the dead had not been invaded by vampires and because of the shortage of arable land, bodies were dug up after three years, cleaned, and either returned to the grave already holding other family members' bones, or stored in a shed or charnel house close to the church. If flesh still clung to the bones, villagers frantically performed rituals to drive away the *vrykolakes* (vampires), who took possession of bodies.[13]

Cypresses stood in graveyards, sentinels, watchers over the dead. The dead were remembered throughout the year. On saints' days and the great religious events of the year, relatives brought flowers and basil to the graves and lighted candles in the recesses above them.

CHAPTER 6

STORIES FOR THE POOR

Women at the well, in their neighborhoods, and men in coffee-houses had much to report: amazing, purported miracles; superstitions like the Evil Eye; retribution for known or unknown sins; speculations over witches, *maghisses,* when milk soured or babies suddenly died; *vrykolakes* attempting to enter the graves of the recent dead; *kalakanzari,* mischievous animal-like apparitions; and nereids, beautiful spectra who could entice and strike a person with illness, even madness.[1] "The best seed ground for superstitions," Gilbert Murray writes, "is a society where the fortunes of men seem to bear no relation to their merits and efforts."[2]

At intervals villagers found respite and zest in events that disrupted the monotonous drudgery of hoeing the rocky earth:

Before I came to America in 1912, a soldier stationed in our village made a girl pregnant. Her parents looked all over the village to kill her. She hid in the stables under the houses with the animals. The soldier had been transferred to another village over the mountains. My brother was so incensed at his dirtying the good name of our village that he walked to this other village, found the soldier sitting in an outdoor kafenion, *pulled his gun out of his holster—he could have been executed for doing this—and marched him back to our village. There he was forced to marry the girl at gunpoint, then he took her to his mother, and our village honor was saved*—Georgia Petropoulos Papanikolas, Piana, Province Arcadia[3]

"I don't know what it is," Zisimos-Bellos told [the priest] Papa-Christos whenever he was caught [cheating or playing practical jokes], "but evil is in me. I can't help it." ... At two o'clock one morning the village was awakened by the ominous ringing of the church bell of Saint George. The villagers rushed out to find what calamity had befallen the village. Pulling the church bell was a white monster. Paralyzed, the villagers listened to the monotonous, apocalyptic knell. Zisimos had dusted a donkey with lime, tied him by the neck to the bell rope on which, a foot or so beyond the animal's reach, he had bound a sheaf of barley.

Zisimos-Bellos fashioned a dummy with *foustanella* and an ancient Greek helmet—as Saint George was represented on icons—propping it in the bishop's throne and hiding to await fast-weakened Papa-Christos's entrance into the dim church. . . . Papa-Christos [ran] out of the church, calling, "Come quickly! Saint George is sitting in the church! Quickly!"[4]

PART TWO

NATIONHOOD AND EXILE

CHAPTER 7

ROMIOSINI, THE BEAUTIFUL WORD

After the long years of fealty to foreign conquerors, the Greeks developed Romiosini, an identity in which vestiges of ancient Greece, lost Byzantium, the Great Idea to regain lands taken by the Turks, Orthodoxy, language, and folk culture melded. As they developed it, they faced the "persistence of the Classical image in the West [which] poses a painful dilemma: how far should they consciously try to live up to it."[1] The writer uses the present tense because the dilemma continues to the present day.

Although northern Greece and many islands still remained under the control of other nations, the 1821 revolt gave birth to a free state. Just as Philhellenes very early came to see the classical ruins of Greece, to praise its past, to write paeans about its remarkable light, to paint scenes of everyday life and past glories and defeats, foreign scholars were drawn to collect songs, proverbs, and customs.

Folklore studies in other countries played an important part in forming a national identity before statehood, but "the Greek scholars were unusual in having folklore studies virtually forced on them by events."[2] J. P. Fallmerayer, an Austrian historian, advanced the notion that the modern Greeks were really Slavs, the result of South Slav invasions and of the intermixing with the native population. Greek scholars rose up in heated denial. Other historians also contradicted his theory: the Slavs were never so large in numbers and they were assimilated by the Greeks.[3] A great impetus to contradict Fallmerayer's assertion was the catalyst that caused Greeks to search their folk songs and customs to document their classical roots. The Greek folklorists were intent on showing that classical Greek civilization was the foundation of European culture and that contemporary Greek culture was directly descended from ancient Greece. They set out to prove Greeks were European, not Asiatic as was commonly believed.

It did not seem necessary to the foreign scholars that they should scour the towns, countryside, and mountains to gather Greek folk culture. Claude Fauriel, a French historian, compiled the first important collection (1824–25) by speaking with Greeks in Venice and in Trieste; and he availed himself of the work of Greek scholars—especially that of Adamantios Koraes, a nationalist scholar and the most important early investigator of folk culture following the 1821 revolution. Later foreigners, like Arnold Passow, a German philologist, did dedicated fieldwork in Greece.

Koraes had little use for the vernacular culture. Yet he wanted to retain certain demotic forms of speech, in contrast to the neo-Atticists, who fought to restore "the classical Greek of Plato and the Attic tragedians to daily use."[4] This also meant deleting the words of conquerors, mainly the Italians, Turks, and Slavs. The language would lose much of its color, demoticists answered. Scholars, poets, and politicians fought over the use of the *katharevousa* (purist) and the demotic of the people for decades.

Like Furiel, who censored his respondents' songs, early Greek folklorists erased vulgar words. Foreign folklorists challenged their methods as being undisciplined. Yet the Greeks documented a great number of songs and customs, and when later scholars began their work, they retraced their predecessors' steps.

Greek scholars succeeded in bringing together the remarkable folk culture of their people and their ideology to show the roots of national Greek identity. A giant among them was Nikolaos G. Politis, who established Greek folklore as a separate discipline. He gave the word *laography,* a study of the people *(laos),* rather than ethnography, a study of the nation *(ethnos)* to Greek folklore studies. Unlike many Greek folklorists, he welcomed the work of foreign scholars and brought order to the study: "Politis inherited a methodological ragbag and made a quilt, but it was a quilt of remarkably harmonious design."[5]

Almost all Greek scholars thought of themselves as Hellenes, descendants of the ancient Greeks. They abhorred the Romaioi, whom they considered debased, uncultured Greeks. Kostis Palamas, Greece's revered poet, defended Romiosini. "[The word] *Hellene* he said, 'is dust thrown into the eyes of foreigners; [. . .] *Romios* [is] reality. The word [he] urges, is anything but shameful. It may not be garlanded with the victor's wild olive from the Olympic games. But it is wreathed with the thorns of martyrdom and redolent with thyme and gunpowder. The name conjures up the glories of Byzantium, but also its fall and all ensuing sorrows."[6]

Folk songs tell of important battles and fearsome leaders. They tell of honor, respect, guile, and the fight for survival. Romiosini was a noble culture and also one of secrecy, shame, and blame-throwing, both in battle and in ordinary life. Secrecy was essential to hide imperfections, diseases, especially tuberculosis, and family flaws, such as lying about a member who had been imprisoned for a crime other than a vendetta, which had to do with honor. All would cause grave difficulties in marriage arrangements. Shame blackened a family's *filotimo* (honor). Blame-throwing was indispensable, for the poor could not take responsibility for their plight. Even inanimate objects were not exempt from blame. "The cup flew out of my hand," people would say. "*Keratas* (cuckold)!" he exclaimed. "The *Keratadhes!* Two plates and a glass have broken themselves. What awkward, left-handed dishes!"[7]

From the time Greece was rediscovered after centuries of neglect, writers used the word *individualists* to describe the Greeks; and they were so to the depths of their being. They did not accept authority—foreign, civil, or ecclesiastical—with bowed head. Unlike other peoples who succumbed to religious edicts, the Greeks, fervent Orthodox, would say openly, "We love our Church; we don't like our priests."

One writer asks, "Is it the fierceness of the struggle to survive that has produced the sharply outlined individualism of the Greeks?"[8] Another writes: "Individualism is prized and is rampant. . . . Like his ancestors, the modern Greek is an intense individualist. Interference with his personal independence, or his freedom to order his life in his own way, is sharply resented. Every Greek has his own ideas about everything and hesitates neither to express them nor act upon them."[9]

The remarkable folklorist Dora d'Istria, a Romanian princess of Albanian origin, said the ethnic purity of the Greeks was "revealed in a unique combination of heroism and . . . individualism."[10] "The modern Greek," Kazantzakis wrote, "loves life and fears death, loves his homeland and is simultaneously a pathological individualist."[11]

Peoples throughout the world have been enslaved for long periods of time; they have lived precariously close to starvation, their fate decided by despotic rulers and bureaucrats. One wonders why the Greeks remained individualists under crushing forces. For them life was agonistic, from the Greek word *agona* (battle); they warred with nature, which interfered with their crops; they fought with authorities and among themselves, although responsibility to the family usually prevented estrangement.

Boys and young men, burdened by responsibilities and already individualists, buoyed by the hope that life could have rewards, took their bundles and cheap suitcases to the waiting ships.

Others had stood as they now did, amazed at the great ships in the bay, smelling the greasy bits of meat grilled on the quay, worrying, yet eager.

Greek sailors were said to have been aboard Columbus's ships in 1492, and to have served under the explorers Cortez, Pizzaro, de Navaez, and Coronado. Several Greek names appear during expeditions to the New World, the Revolutionary War, the War of 1812, the Civil War, and the Mexican War of 1846–47. Laborers, many from Mani, established New Smyrna in Florida in 1767.[12] After the Greek Revolution (1821–27), a group of Greek orphans was brought to the United States and educated.[13] In 1857, a Turkish-born Greek was hired to guide camels across the American Southwest in the army's futile attempt to adapt the animals to carrying supplies. When he died in 1913, "Greek George" spoke only Spanish; he had long since forgotten Greek.[14] Better known were wealthy Greeks in New York City, who prospered during the years 1830–1910.

These early Greek immigrants were highly literate. They were involved in importing, exporting, shipping, and the cotton exchange. They had ties to cotton exporters in New Orleans. Traveling "in fashionable circles in New York City," several were listed in New York's Social Register and had membership in exclusive New York clubs.[15] The latter-day travelers would have been amazed at such financial and social heights.

CHAPTER 8

TOWARD THE UNKNOWN

Standing on the wharves waiting to board the great ships flying the colors of many nations, the sojourners' intangibles of history, faith, and folklore combined to give them the Romiosini culture they would take with them. They carried their few possessions and their names.

Over the centuries, poverty drove young Greeks to sail throughout the world to find economic sanctuary in isolated, lonely places. Many young men went to Egypt and Africa. Political upheavals and conquests added to the never-ending exodus. A great number settled in southern Russia when their holy city, Constantinople, fell to the Turks in 1453. Scholars and other learned men climbed to monasteries, many to the Meteora and Mount Athos.

When Greece became a nation following the Revolution of 1821, the people elected Captain John Capodistrias president. Not long afterwards, he was assassinated by two members of the "powerful Mavromichalis clan, which he had tried to subject to his authority. The country now lapsed into utter anarchy."[1] The Great Powers, France, Britain, and Russia, sent Otho, a seventeen-year-old Bavarian prince, to be king of the Greeks. Three regents accompanied him. Treating the Greeks as primitive people, they further aroused them by disbanding the veterans and replacing them with well-paid Bavarian volunteers. Ten thousand Greek veterans were left without a livelihood.[2] Many became brigands in the very mountains where they had fought the Turks.

Political chaos dogged the hard-fought freedom of the Greeks. Otho was replaced by the Danish prince William George, who became King George I of Greece. Conditions worsened. During the latter part of the nineteenth century, wealthy entrepreneurs acquired *chifliks* (assorted lands), which had once been owned and worked by villagers. The *chifliks* became large estates in the fertile valleys of Thessaly, Macedonia, and the Peloponnese.[3] So little arable land was available for the destitute villagers that emigration was their only recourse.

The economy of Greece had become dependent on the export of the currants. France imported almost all of the crop for wine-making after a disease ruined the entire French crop for a generation. By the end of the 1800s, France began to control the currant blight, and Greece's economy faltered. In 1907, the currant crop failed, and Greek economy collapsed. The poverty of the country became one of acute suffering.

When boys and young men could not sail, they walked, often to Romania. Those from the Kravara, the most desolate region of Roumeli ("Nothing grows here. Look at those mountains. You could not graze a mouse"), walked through Macedonia, Bulgaria, and the length of Russia, begging. "Orthodox!" they would shout, pretending they were lame, or lifting a cross as a sign that they were unable to speak. They were often gone for years.[4]

The Greek government encouraged emigration, knowing that its young men would find work, send back large amounts of money, and after a few years return with a sizeable sum—all of which would help the country financially. Earlier emigrants wrote braggadocio letters, enclosing photographs showing them in their new American finery. Advertisements by former Greek citizens, now labor agents in America, appeared in newspapers on the Greek mainland and in Crete; and steamship agents traveled from towns to steep mountain villages and astounded coffeehouse gatherings with exaggerated stories of easy money in America. Young men yearned to leave this land on which three-fourths of the people lived but which was so stony and arid that only one-fifth of it could be cultivated.

From this land, with its ancient lore and lost greatness, the boys and men prepared to leave with anxiety, fear, and excitement, but always with the certainty of return. Families mortgaged their ancestral land at usurious rates to provide passage for the great number of these nearly illiterate sons. They were to work for their sisters' dowries, lift their parents out of penury, and return. *Ksenitia* was the word for foreign lands.

Almost all were young men, often not yet nineteen, the age at which they would have been taken into the Greek army, with one cigarette a day as their pay. Those in Asia Minor were once excused from service, but after 1910 they were recruited to do menial work for the Turkish army for seven years. Others, who had left young brides behind to the mercy of their families, had additional worries. A song of emigration begins unrealistically, plaintively:

Mother, I must go to foreign lands.
To foreign lands I must go.
Mother, make ready and knead your son *paximadhia.*

Little mother, don't tyrannize my woman.
Let her have partridge for supper and rabbit at noon
and at the turning of the sun, let her spread her blanket to sleep.[5]

They would come back, the young men said, when they had fulfilled their family obligations. For the young men, like all Greeks, were bound to their *topos,* the region where they were born. Boys were among them; their parents had listened to labor agents representing shoeshine proprietors who promised their parents good, supervised living and working conditions:

My mother kissed me, embraced me, and gave me a handkerchief to re-member her by and inside was a five drachma coin and a sprig of basil."—Harry (Haralambos) Kambouris, Thebes, Province Viotias[6]

[His mother] sat at her loom in a cove of holy oak. . . . She worked until dark weaving a *kilimi,* a goat hair cover of white and dark red dyed with pomegranate juice. After completing the weaving, she embroidered the *kilimi* with many colors of thread. It would serve to wrap her son's belongings and to cover him while he slept. . . . [On the day he left], she said, "As many strands as are in this *kilimi* that many blessings I give you."[7]

Mothers sewed amulets, enclosing in them a piece of holy scripture or a sliver of the True Cross, a dried basil leaf or thyme for remembrance, a bit of garlic or blue bead to withstand the Evil Eye, and a pinch of Greek earth. They pinned amulets to their sons' shirts for protection against evil. If they died in *ksenitia,* the pinch of Greek earth would be sprinkled on them before the casket was lowered. Greek land was holy to the Greeks.

Now that I leave for foreign lands,
and we will be parted for months, for years.
let me take something also from you,
dearly beloved, azure land.
Let me carry an amulet with me,
to ward off evil, to ward off grief,
a charm to ward off sadness, death,
a handful of earth, Greek earth![8]

The sojourners tried not to travel during the forty days of fasting for the great holy days: Christmas, Easter, and the Dormition of the Virgin (August

15). The villages quickened with excitement as the young men prepared to leave. Boys upwards of nine years of age and older young men spent the last evening with friends. The boys played stick games, hitting stones, vying to see who could send them the farthest. The men drank *ouzo,* sang the old songs of the great heroes of the revolution against the Turks, and responded to toasts of good wishes: "Go well," "Hurry back," "Send me passage." At dawn the young men dressed in their traveling clothes, sometimes cheap new suits, more often worn handed-down ones. Many put on the black baggy Cretan and Dodecanese *vrakes* and tied fringed kerchiefs around their heads; others pulled on the white pleated kilts of the mainlanders.

With their possessions wrapped in blankets, in cardboard suitcases, or generations-old leather bags, they walked to the church accompanied by the entire village. Before the icons, they crossed themselves, bowed their heads while the priest intoned the "Rite of Blessing Those about to Travel by Water," crossed themselves again, kissed the icons, and waved goodbye. Friends and women—not girls, they could not be so forward—followed down the mountain paths for a distance, the women singing songs of the cold pure water of their clear streams, of their famed mountains, of swooping birds, of pines and firs, of farewell, of hopes there would be no obstacles to their journey into the unknown foreign place, the *ksenitia.*

Months, years later, the women would sing:

It came, it came, bitter Spring, black Summer
It came midwinter, black gloom-filled, that *ksenitia*
that takes all the young, the brave young men.[9]

Each sojourner remembered how it had been.

> *I was named Nikos because of what happened in our village. A Turkish official was killed and the Turkish soldiers were sent to take revenge on us. The whole village started up into the mountains. On the way my mother's time to give birth to me came. She wrapped me in her underskirt, but the villagers wouldn't let her take me with her because I might cry and give them away to the Turks. She went back to the outskirts of the village and put me under the altar of the church of Saint Nicholas. Three days later the villagers returned and my mother found me, alive. So I was named after the saint. I never had shoes until I went into the army to serve my three years. I got a medal and some money for bravery in the Balkan Wars and came to America. I learned to read and write Greek with a grammar book my first bossis gave me.*—Nikos Linardos, Stromi, Province Fthiotis[10]

My father sent me to cousins in Volos who had a carpenter's shop to learn the trade. I worked from dawn until dark, slept in a barn, for three years without pay. Then I worked in Kavala for my mother's cousin, again without pay. I kept asking him to let me visit my father but he wouldn't let me go. I left. I decided I would go to America after seeing my father. While walking to the seaport, I passed through a field of yellow-flowering weeds. By the time I reached Piraeus, my eyes were almost swollen shut and my face was red and puffed. I went to a doctor who took all of my money. I returned home, walking sixty-five miles, all the way without food. Two years later I made the same trip. I passed the field where my eyes had swollen. It was green this time, and I went on to the seaport without any trouble. — Harry Greaves (Theoharis Gheorghios Grivas), Lafkos, Province Volou[11]

My brother was already in America. When I was nine years old, he sent me passage. By some misunderstanding he was not there to meet me. I was sent back. When the boat stopped in Spain, I thought I had arrived back in Greece. I walked all over the wharves, and then started walking down alleys. A dark, hooked-nosed man grabbed me, carried me to an alley, and threw me down a chute. There were other boys like me in the dark room. I kept clawing to reach the chute, bloodied my hands, climbed out, and ran down the alley screaming in Greek, "Help me! Help me!" A man driving by in a carriage had his driver stop, and called to me. He was the Turkish ambassador to Spain and made arrangements to put me again on a ship bound for America. — George Cayias (Gheorghios Kayias), Likourghi, Province Kalavryta[12]

———— *has no shame. He was a jailer in a prison in Roumeli. Most of the prisoners were locked up for vendetta killings. The prisoners' relatives collected money to bribe him. One night he unlocked the cells and he and the prisoners made their way to the seaport of Patras where arrangements had been made for their passage to America. He has no* filotimo *(honor), never worked a day in his life in America. He lived by his wits.* — Helen (Eleni) Skedros Rizos, Ioannina, Province Dodonis[13]

I was born in [Demirtas] a Greek village in northwestern Asia Minor, Turkey, about seven miles from Bursa, the ancient capital of the Ottoman empire, with Turkish villages all around it. . . . To speak Greek and to know how to read and write Greek meant for us no less than the survival of our ethnic identity in a Moslem world. . . . [The sultan] let his pashas govern the provinces much as they pleased, and the pashas, fat,

A number of
immigrants came
through Castle Garden
and Ellis Island dressed
in their regional wear.
On the left is the
foustanella *of the main-
land; on the right is the*
vrakes *of Crete and
several Aegean islands.*
Steve Sargetakis Collec-
tion, courtesy of the
Utah State Historical
Society.

corrupt, and ignorant, trained to lead in war but not to govern, left us much to ourselves . . . such relative tolerance as we enjoyed under Turkish rule was in contrast to the intolerance and exclusiveness of the villagers to others. No Turk, no Armenian, no Jew made his home in Demirtas. . . . The Turks my father and I knew were our friends. . . . When, at the age of fourteen, I left my village to attend a French school in Bursa, since we were too poor to pay for my residence on the school campus, my father entrusted me to the care of a Turkish friend [Osman Bey], who kept an inn in the center of the Turkish section of the city. . . . Here I lived for three years, with Turks all around me, feeling perfectly secure and in good company. . . . Osman Bey's education was very limited. So many a time in the evening [he] would knock on my door: "Omer,"—that was my name in Turkish—"would you come down to the coffeehouse and read us the newspaper?"

[Political events beginning with the 1908 Young Turks rebellion, the 1912–1913 wars between Greece and Turkey, and the instability that would lead to World War I changed life in Demirtas.] It was time for the young men who could to leave the country. . . . I left in 1913.—Homer P. Balabanis, Dimirtas, near Bursa, Asia Minor[14]

While working for passage on ships, some young Greeks saw the myriad customs of various races in exotic places.

Ioannis worked in a grocery store in Volos. Sometimes on weekends he would go home to Lechonia, which was a long walk along the road by the sea. . . . Living by this large bay with its ships and boats coming

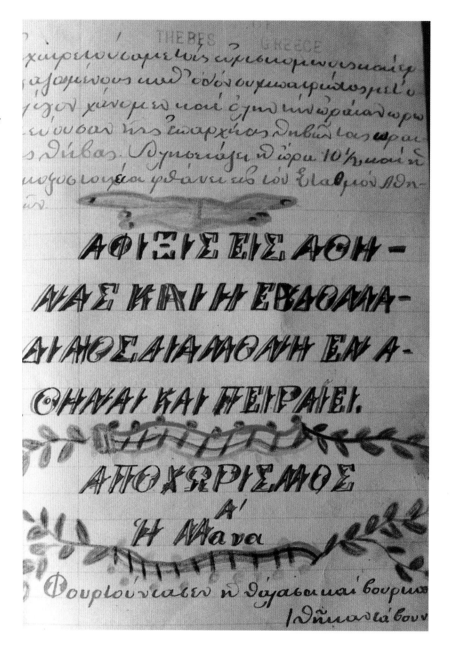

Immigrant memoirs exist, but "Pages from My Life . . . ," by H. K. Kambouris is the only known diary kept by a Greek immigrant of the early 1900s. A page from the diary. Photograph by George Theodore.

and going, Ioannis was filled with a desire to sail the seas and see the world. He bid farewell to his widowed mother and brothers and sister and went to Piraeus, working on the ship to pay for his trip. . . . His uncle [in Piraeus] wanted to send him to school there, but Ioannis wanted to go with the ships and see the world. Consequently, he got a job on a ship at Piraeus and sailed to Salonica, Patras and even-

tually to France. From then on he worked on boats of other nations and went to Italy, England, Russia, and Turkey . . . Rumania, island of Chios, Italy . . . a Norwegian ship to New Orleans . . . an English ship to South America, Cuba and to New York City.—John N. Policandrittis (Ioannis Nikolaos Polykandritis), Kato Lehonia, Thessalia Province[15]

CHAPTER 9

LEAVING THE SHIPS WITH FLEAS

After the young men passed a physical examination in the port of Patras, Piraeus, Kalamata, Zante, or Rethymnon; were vaccinated for small pox; and had their clothing and baggage fumigated, they entered the steerage, the Hades of ships. Left behind were those who could not suppress a tubercular cough or who were yellowed with malaria. Most travelers boarding ships would not remember the names of the steamship lines—Astro-American, Fabre, Greek Transoceanic, Hamburg-American, Messageries Maritimes, and Prince—but they would never forget the iron pipes, the unceasing noise, and the eighteen to twenty-one days of packed bodies. They had only salt water for bathing, and the tiers of bunks had no mattresses over the springs. There was no place to put their belongings; they had to hold them, even while trying to eat repellent food out of tin plates. Within a few days of sailing, the smells of vomit, urine, feces, and unwashed bodies stifled them in the hold. In some ships animals were also kept in the hold and butchered to supply food. On steerage decks, so great was the number of people that they had to stand.[1]

In 1915, 177 passengers had a harrowing experience aboard the SS *Thessaloniki*. The ship held Greeks from every part of Greece and the islands, three Albanians, and a cargo of marble. On December 1, as it sailed out of the Straits of Gibraltar, bad weather forced the ship's engines to turn slowly. A hurricane hit the ship on 21 December. "Mountainous cascades of water smashed lifeboats and skylights, breaking glass on the bridge, swamping the captain's cabin, and flooding the engine room . . . the marble cargo shifted, causing the ship to list over on her starboard side."

An Italian steamer answered the Greek ship's SOS and stood by while the *Thessaloniki* crew pumped water from the engine room. Steerage passengers led by a Greek Orthodox priest begged the captain to let them trans-

Pavli Miloghianni, center, of Hania, Crete, emigrated from the battlefield directly to the United States after the Turks defeated the Greeks in 1897. Courtesy of Catherine Coucourakis Chanak.

fer to the Italian ship. He refused, and the *Thessaloniki* went on. Again a hurricane struck the ship. Passengers and crew pleaded with the captain to send an SOS to American ships. Again he refused. The crew and the captain quarreled violently, the captain threatening to use his revolver. When he left the room, the radio operator sent the SOS. On 30 December, the United States Coast Guard dispatched the cutter *Seneca* to the *Thessaloniki*, now drifting 250 miles eastward. The Greek ship SS *Patris* had heard the SOS and also came to the rescue.[2]

On various ships, immigrants without proper embarkation papers were prepared to swim ashore, crossing themselves and praying that they would not be caught:

> [My grandfather's] courtship of a local Greek widow had brought him into conflict with a Turk who wanted the same woman for a concubine. . . . In a knife fight during which grandfather mortally wounded his adversary . . . grandfather knew better than to place his life at the discretion of an Ottoman court. He borrowed a horse and fled to Smyrna. [After several stops on the way] he was on a ship with cargo destined for New York. As soon as the ship anchored, he swam ashore.[3]

> *After three weeks in the guts of the ship, we got off at Caslegari (Castle Garden) with fleas.*—Louis Lingos (Elias Lingoxegakis), Kefalas, Crete[4]

> I'm not sure why [my grandfather] chose to leave the old world for the new one; I'm sure times were rough [in Constantinople] and he had to earn money to marry off his sisters. . . . He booked passage on a steamer (third class, of course) and came across in 1911. His plan was to hook up with a friend who'd come to America a year or two before; he had his name and address pinned to his lapel. . . . In New York harbor a gust of wind blew that piece of paper into the harbor. Next came the processing by immigration officials. After waiting in an enormous line, the officials asked him his nationality—to which my grandfather responded "Romios." "Romios? What the hell is that?" "Romios!" This apparently went on for a minute or two until someone else in the line said to tell him you're a Greek. "Vre [you]!"[5]

Other examinations awaited at Castle Garden, or Caslegari, the immigrants would call it, and later at Ellis Island. Would some imperfection be found? Would they have enough "show" money to prove they were not paupers? They were asked their nationality so they could be directed to a Greek-speaking official.

Then it was onto a ferryboat bound for New York. Tags tied to their lapels had their destinations and the names of brothers, cousins, fellow villagers, or labor agents written on them. They soon found what *ksenitia* was like:

> *Ksenitia,* being orphaned, bitterness, and love.
> These four were weighed and the heaviest was *ksenitia*
> There in *ksenitia* the stranger should wear black
> so that his clothes will match his wounded heart.[6]

It was good that the immigrants came with the *romaic* values of their Romiosini culture, otherwise they would not have survived in the New World: not knowing the language, searching for work, and learning to accommodate to the hostilities and prejudices that they, as well as other Balkan and Mediterranean immigrants, faced.

Suddenly the boys and young men coming through Castle Garden and Ellis Island were cut off from the color and beauty of their dynamic folk culture. They had known terrible poverty in the land of their birth; now they knew a poverty that was devoid of the mountains, streams, birds, and song; of weddings, baptisms, and, yes, funeral rites of their *topos,* their place.

Everything was strange to the immigrants: trains—there was only one short line in Greece, which most immigrants had never seen; streetcars; American women, often holding their children's hands, stopping on the street to speak to men—only street women would be so immoral in their *topos;* Americans spreading butter on bread and ruining its taste; and even the peculiar banana that the new arrivals tried to eat without peeling. The banana was so exotic that they composed a song in praise of it.

> The banana is a sweet fruit,
> which flourishes in a warm land,
> and brings us the land's wealth.
> As a fruit it is preferred.
> You find it wherever you may roam.
> At the fruit market in bunches,
> From carts you get them at retail,
> From the market the middleman gets them wholesale.
> To eat, to eat a good banana,
> You must, you must pay well,
> And if you want it to be sweet as manna,
> Never calculate, pay well.[7]

The Greeks were among the last European immigrants to enter the United States. Unlike northern Europeans, who usually came in family groups with the intention of staying, they were single men. They met hostility everywhere, as the Irish had when they escaped the potato famine and arrived in the country in the mid-1840s. The Irish were despised, looked upon as backward, uneducated, and boorish. They were turned away from workplaces by NINA signs: "No Irish Need Apply." By the time the Greeks began to arrive, the Irish had progressed to roles as foremen on labor gangs and owners of small stores, and had forced their way into politics.

Between the years 1871 and 1930, 421,091 Greeks arrived in the United

The Byron, a Greek restaurant in the Bowery, New York City, 1904. Photographed by Jacob R. Riis. By permission of the Museum of the City of New York.

States. If they had relatives or village friends already in the country, they went to them. Often they found their kin and friends gone, looking for work themselves. Then they traveled from one town to another, one city to another, mostly on freight trains. Other immigrants arrived in a mill or factory town and remained there for the rest of their lives. Those who went on in search of work had to traverse the width of the United States more than once. For food, they melted lard in a can over hot bricks and dipped bread into it.

> *[My fifteen-year-old] father Christos and his cousin landed in New York City and then went to Chicago, Illinois, and then on to Omaha, Nebraska and then to New Mexico. They made a tour of South America, working for their passage at odd jobs. [He] worked in the diamond mines with his second cousin Tony Sedaris. While he was there, he came into possession of rather a large diamond. In later years this diamond was sold during the depression time in Utah to help enable his family to survive.*—William F. Vigos, son of Christos Gheorghios Vigos, Nemea, Corinthos Province[8]

Labor agents, the *padrones,* found the sojourners—for that is how they were viewed and how they saw themselves—work in New England cotton mills, in screw factories, in the fur business, as pushcart peddlers, or in cigarette factories at $.75 to $1.75 for a ten-hour day, often with Irish foremen over them. Farther west, they might find work in furniture factories in Grand Rapids, Michigan; in slaughterhouses in Kansas City, Missouri, and Omaha, Nebraska; on fishing boats off the Pacific coast; and as dishwashers and kitchen helpers everywhere. In southern ports, many sailors jumped free and filled the holds of ships with cotton bales for Greek brokers, washed dishes in restaurants, and dug sewers. Unwittingly they often paid *padrones* for jobs and found on arrival that they were being used as strikebreakers in factories, mines, and mills. Running from flying rocks and sticks, they arrived bloodied at coffeehouses.

The greatest number of Greeks, 42,086, reached the United States in 1907. It was also the worst of times for immigrants.

> In New York they walked the cobbled streets in a freezing winter, the year of the Panic of 1907 when even Americans could not find work. Neither Yoryis, Zack, Pericles, nor Spyros had an overcoat. They folded newspapers over their chests and backs to protect their lungs and wore their homespun stockings, one on top of the other, their two pair of pants, their caps pulled as far over their ears as they could go, and walked. At the back doors of restaurants and stores they knocked, made signs with their hands, jumped out of the way of pails of dirty water and garbage, learned what the words *dirty foreigners* and *dirty Greeks* meant. They met other *patriotes,* also walking, searching, and like them eating dried beans to stop the gnaw of hunger. "Romios are you?" they asked, stopping each other on the streets.
>
> In the evenings they went to the Roumeliot Coffeehouse. Priests, labor agents, and other *patriotes* wrote their names in little black notebooks and on the backs of envelopes. At night they slept at the ice cream tables, their heads resting on their bent arms, their belongings under the chairs. Yoryis still tied on his mother's red and white *kilimi.* [They] rented a small stable for six dollars a month and slept in the stalls, making small fires to warm their frost-bitten hands and feet. . . . One morning as Yoryis pulled on his frozen shoes, they broke into pieces. He and Zack then took turns going out to look for work wearing Zack's shoes. They were too small for Yoryis.[9]

Employers had little interest in the Greeks, except as an unending supply of workers. In the early years in mining camps, smelters, and mills, they made no effort to provide housing for them and for other "new" immigrants, those who had begun coming at the turn of the century. The northern

Europeans were the "old" immigrants, considered more intelligent and tractable. Yet management learned that the Greeks were diligent, reliable, and willing to work twelve hours and more a day, even though laws had been passed against this practice. Also, the Greeks, controlled by labor agents, were not at first involved in workers rights movements. Labor bosses were unaware that under the immigrants' obsequiousness, false and calculated, lay the trait of individualism that would spring out at the proper opportunity.

> Jack London, the world famous working class author . . . often had negative portraits of Greeks in his short stories and novels. In 1913 he exploded in rage when his views were challenged by Spiro Orfen, an erstwhile Greek friend, who claimed a connection between modern and ancient Greeks. London retorted that the true Greeks had perished leaving behind "a mongrel race." At the end of one letter to Orfen, who had been a carpenter in Seattle, London snarled, "You have behaved toward me as any alleged modern Greek peddler has behaved toward the superior races."[10]

In *Tales of the Fish Patrol,* though, London celebrates Greek courage and individualism: "Big Alec had never been captured by the fish patrol. It was his boast that no man could take him alive, and it was his history that of the many men who had tried to take him dead none had succeeded. It was also history that at least two patrolmen who had tried to take him dead had died."[11]

In "Demetrios Contos," the central character defies the law that prohibited catching salmon on Sunday and the fish patrol that had to enforce it:

> The whole bow of the boat must have been crushed in, for in a few seconds the boat was half full. Then a couple of seas filled in, and it sank straight down, dragged to the bottom by the heavy ballast. So quickly did it all happen that I was entangled in the sail and drawn under. When I fought my way to the surface, suffocating, my lungs almost bursting, I could see nothing of the oars. They must have been swept away by the chaotic currents. I could see Demetrios Contos looking back from his boat, and heard the vindictive and mocking tones of his voice as he shouted exultantly. He held steadily on his course, leaving me to perish. [In the end, Contos decides to save the young man.][12]

CHAPTER 10

SHOESHINE BOYS

Most vulnerable were the shoeshine boys. To circumvent immigration laws, labor agents instructed the boys to say they were the agents' sons. Parents sent boys of eight to twelve to work in shoeshine parlors, not knowing they would be paid little and exploited by *padrones,* who would take their tips from them. *Padrones* read the letters the boys sent their parents so that their complaints were never put on paper. Besides, the boys knew that their fathers had signed documents which deducted the cost of their passage to America from their earnings.

I was eleven years old, and it was in the year 1910. . . . At Charleston [West Virginia] I got off and my uncle got me and kept me for a couple of days, and then told me he was going to Wyoming to find a new job and get a better life. So he arranged for me to work for a shoeshine man, a Greek, for $125 a year, plus board and room. I was hurt and scared that my uncle would do that to me, and he wouldn't take me with him, and I still didn't know any English. . . . There were other boys like me, but I was the youngest. This owner of the place used to get on each train when it stopped in Charleston and go through the cars yelling in Greek if any Greek boys wanted work and sometimes he got some. They kept us in a big house where the man lived and didn't use us too well. And didn't want us to learn English. Also, after my uncle left and the owner saw I didn't have any relatives or friends to take care of me, he cut my pay and I was in a kind of slavery to him.—Nick Mandanakis, Levidhi, Province Tripoleos[1]

Crowded into rooms of little comfort, shoeshine boys awoke as early as 4:30 in the morning to begin work at 6:00 or 6:30. Their breakfast was often

Indianapolis shoeshine boys, photographed in 1911 by the eminent activist for the poor, Lewis W. Hine. Author's collection.

black coffee and bread; for many this had to sustain them until late at night, when they ate their one meal of the day. The *padrones* paid for the food and economized on it.

The boys then walked a great distance to their shoeshine stands; the *padrones* would not give them carfare. They worked seven days a week.

> The only times they are seen at church are during Holy Week and on Easter Sunday morning, at which time they appear at services between 10 o'clock in the evening and 4 o'clock in the morning because the ceremonies in the Greek church are held late at night or in early morning hours and therefore their attendance does not interfere with the business of their employers.[2]

> The shops opened between 6 and 6:30, which meant the boys had to awake by 5:00 to 5:30. Those living some distance from their place of work rose as early as 4:30 a.m. They labored until 9 and 10 o'clock, and later on Saturdays and Sundays.

After the doors closed, the boys generally mopped the floor, cleaned the marble stand and fixtures, and gathered up the shoe shining rags to take home, wash, dry, and have in readiness for the following day. Part of the meal was prepared in the morning and taken to the shop for noon rations, with the rest left at the house for supper. . . . In many instances when many thought in terms of saving all they could and returning to Greece at the earliest opportunity, the meal consisted of bread and olives or cheese.[3]

In 1910, the Greek Consul-General of Greece, a Chicago physician, wrote a letter to the Immigrant Inspector of Chicago decrying the dehumanizing conditions the boys worked under, which disposed them to tuberculosis and other pulmonary diseases. Seven Greek physicians wrote to the United States Immigration Commission of their observations:

The causes [of chronic gastritis, hepatitis, and tuberculosis] we attribute to the close confinement of these boys, the long hours at work, their unsanitary and unhygienic living conditions, inadequate nourishment, stooping position, and the inhaling of dust, from shoes, that is full of microbes and mixed with polish chemicals which irritate and injure the pulmonary organs. . . . [We] believe that the United States government would do better to deport them rather than allow them to land if they are destined to this employment under existing conditions.[4]

CHAPTER II

THE COFFEEHOUSE

Of the three early institutions—coffeehouses, Greek-language newspapers, and churches—the coffeehouses came first. After their long hours in factories, hotel kitchens, restaurants, mines, mills, and smelters, the immigrants washed themselves, replaced their work clothes with their better set, kept for special occasions, and hurried to a coffeehouse. It was important to the Greeks to dress as well as they could, as a sign of respectability.

Shoeshine boys could not call the coffeehouse their home as did older immigrants. They were imprisoned in their servitude to the *padrones*. Even if they had had the leisure, though, they would not have been welcomed there. As in Greece, coffeehouses were for men, for their relaxation. Grown sons and fathers in *patridha* did not frequent the same coffeehouses. Fathers could not enjoy themselves freely with their sons present. Adult sons, also, would never smoke in the presence of their fathers, mothers, grandparents, godparents, or priests; such informality was deemed insulting. In America, the coffeehouse was the men's home, their sanctuary, and their only social life. The men left their savings with the *kafejis* (coffeehouse owner) when they went away in search of work, and they had their mail sent in his care. The *kafejis* took his responsibilities seriously.

Newspapers were read aloud to those who could not read—the illiteracy rate was 28 percent. Avid listeners sat, amazed at events, fearful for their village families, or angry at the election results in *patridha,* the homeland. Coffeehouse owners cut out parts of the newspapers and tacked them to the walls. In the smoky, confined atmosphere, the talk of the printed news enlivened the men; the tedium of their work gave way to zest. Many immigrants went to the coffeehouses mainly to hear the latest news.

The coffeehouse was a true melting pot. Laborers, shopkeepers, labor

In their American finery, Constantine Rodopoulos (Rodis) and his future brother-in-law, Peter Panagiotacopoulos (Peterson), in a Bridgeport, Connecticut, coffeehouse. Courtesy of Themistocles Rodis.

agents, interpreters, Greek government officials, priests, traveling newspaper reporters, gamblers, and procurers met there. In the barren room of crude tables and chairs, basil plants in tall, rusty olive oil cans lined the window sills. Nailed to the wall were calendars of pretty women, pictures of grizzled revolutionary patriots, and of King George (if the *kafejis* was a royalist) or Eleftherios Venizelos (if he was a liberal). Greek and American flags were crossed above the men's pictures.

The men sipped Turkish coffee; smoked the *hookah,* the many-tubed narghile; passed around letters from home; played cards; talked; and listened to representatives of a Greek government organization, the Panhellenic Union, exhort the new immigrants to save their money and return to Greece, fervently reminding the men that they were Greeks and would always be Greeks. Greece needed their money.

The *komboloi,* the string of beads that men fingered in coffeehouses in Greece, began to disappear. Instead the men consulted small, gilt-edged Greek-English dictionaries to learn a few necessary words. They struggled with the English alphabet, in which only eight capital letters, A, E, I, K, M, N, O, and T, corresponded with the Greek. The letters B, Z, H, P, Y, and X had different sounds. In Greek the letter B is pronounced V. There was no

one letter for the English B sound; it was produced by the Greek M and π. Also, the Greek alphabet has no W, and the word *West* was pronounced as "Ghouest." Many immigrants spoke with Greek-English-dictionary pronunciation for the rest of their lives.

Conversation, a great love of the Greeks, expanded from small to larger and larger circles, as the men recounted trivial or horrific incidents on their jobs. They invented nicknames *(paratsoukles)* for certain people: Hrisostomos (Gold-mouth), for a labor agent who had his teeth covered with gold to show his wealth; Diamantis, another *padrone,* for the diamond embedded in a front tooth; Grivas, an interpreter, whose one arm recalled a member of a revolutionary family who had lost his arm in a duel; Mormonas, who had dealings with Mormons. Many were no longer called by their surnames but by the place from which they had come. One, Maniatis, a feared giant, had left the wild mountains of Mani. The Greeks never lost the habit of bestowing affectionate or sardonic nicknames. In the 1930s Depression a jobless immigrant applied for relief. When asked how many children he had, he answered, "Tri-bee-bee." From then on, he was no longer called by his given name Yosifides, but by Tri-bee-bee.[1]

While in Greece students marched and scholars debated poets over the use of the *katharevousa,* the Greek immigrants were adding a few more words to those they found in their dictionaries and giving English words a Greek touch: *eleveta* (elevator), *lasintza* (license), *marketa* (market), *bitsi* (beach), *stanza* (stand, as in fruit stand), *tiketo* (ticket), *farma* (farm), *floori* (floor), *hoteli* (hotel), *karo* (car), *blokos* (block), *Brooklidhes* (Brooklyners), *spitali* (hospital), *visita* (visit), *stampa* (stamp), *treno* (train), *salivouri* (sidewalk), *kori* (quarter), and *politsmanos* (policeman).[2]

Around the coffeehouse tables, the men extolled their sisters' and cousins' virtues for matchmaking purposes. A successful arrangement would save their sending dowry money for the women: in the United States men did not expect dowries. They discussed the peculiarity of American customs and events, world happenings, the life they would lead when they returned to Greece, and, predominately, Greek politics. Without their knowing it, their Americanization had begun. There in the coffeehouse they learned about American laws and rules, asked Greek government officials for advice, and later would get help in passing citizenship tests. There, too, interpreters charged the men a small sum for filling out postal orders to send money to their families. Among them were men who charged exorbitant fees for small services; they were known as "Five-Buck Petes" or "Five-Buck Johns," whatever their given names were.

In the coffeehouses, men also had duties to perform that burdened and grieved them: "And here one night an anxious group of big workmen sat breathing hard over a letter to be sent to a mother in Greece, to say that her son had lost his leg in a tunnel explosion, that by passing the hat for the past few evenings they had collected enough for his passage, and that he would be home soon."[3] The compatriots, straining to write a letter to the man's mother, knew what awaited a legless or armless man in the fatherland. He would not be able to work the arid land or tend sheep on the mountainside; he would spend his days sitting in a chair in his stone house or in a coffeehouse.

Showmen came from Greece with jaded singers, dancing and rattling tambourines, and puppet shows, the Karagiozi, in which the slyly stupid Greek peasant always got the better of the supposedly crafty Turks and officious Greek bureaucrats. Although viewed as entertainment, the Karagiozi performances barely masked seditious sentiments.[4]

Soon phonograph records became available, and every *kafejis* bought a cheap hand-cranked player from the Atlas Company in New York. As early as 1911, Greek recordings were being made in the United States. Men and women singers recorded the old *kleftic* epics, love songs of their provinces, and nostalgic laments for *patridha*, their far-off country. The phonographs played on, even when the records became scratchy and the words were barely recognizable.

The Karagiozis puppet, with his crude, comedic assaults on authority, was a great favorite throughout Greek-immigrant America. Illustration by Cleo Papanikolas.

In cities, though, between 1907 and the beginning of World War I, some laborers were able to buy tickets to sit in the balcony of vaudeville houses and watch the two Combis brothers, the "Grecian Gladiators." In ancient Greek war dress, wearing helmets and carrying spears, they gave tableau performances of "At the Walls of Troy" and "Chariot Races in the Coliseum," using live white horses. In the Hippodrome the immigrants' raucous cheers nearly had them thrown out of the theater.[5] American audiences could not conceive that the Greek laborers in their midst, doing the menial work allotted to all new immigrants, had any connection with those gymnastic marvels, the Gladiators.

In the first three decades of the 1900s, immigrants could see the old, familiar *kleftic* plays at little cost. Amateurs among them took the parts that had been staples since the Revolution of 1821: *Golfo* and *Esme* were popular, combining heroism and love. Esme was a Turkish girl loved by a *kleft*. In the first decade of the 1900s, professional actors from Greece brought plays to America.[6]

In the Midwest and the West, laborers had little entertainment beyond playing the dice game *barbouti* and card games like *fessa*. The lone coffeehouse in prairie towns and mining camps meant an outpost of rescue from homesickness, illness, and even death. The *kafejis* kept a pot of beans or lentils simmering in the back room for hungry sojourners who were traveling on the freight cars, looking for work. The men ate in the warmth and broke off stems of basil, a sign of friendship, which they sniffed and placed behind their ears or in their lapels. Some *kafejidhes* owned phonographs, a lucky amenity for the travelers. If there was neither a phonograph nor a musician among them, the men sang, deeply solemn, the epic *traghoudhia tou trapeziou* (songs of the table).

At rare intervals, wandering showmen arrived with Karagiozi puppets and dancing and singing women. Their visits were fleeting to the men who worked long hours, were paid less than American workers, and were often victims of industrial accidents.

The Grecian Gladiators used live horses in their vaudeville skits. Courtesy of Steve Frangos.

CHAPTER 12

THE GREEK
AMERICAN PRESS

After coffeehouses, Greek newspapers were the next immigrant in-
stitution to appear. "One of the principal factors which led to the
early establishment of newspapers in the Greek communities of
the United States was the Greek immigrants' passion for nationalism and
politics. The desire to be informed about political events in the old country
and to keep abreast of Greece's wars with Turkey in liberating portions of
'unredeemed Greece' made them insatiable devourers of news."[1]

The first Greek-American publication, *Atlantis,* began in 1894 in New
York City. It was a weekly at first, then a biweekly, and later came out every
two days. By the peak "of Greek immigration, several Greek-language
newspapers, including a daily, were already in distribution. The most important challenger to the *Atlantis* was the *Ethnikos Keryx* (National herald)
which began publication in 1915."[2]

The newspapers regularly printed stories and poems written by *patriotes,* a few with incipient talent, most with literary pretensions coupled with
sentimentality. They wrote about *ksenitia,* that old displacement they feared
and dreaded.

Other publications appeared later. *Kampana* (The bell), a "Greek American Humorous review," included tales of miscreants and women as
temptresses; observations on American life; dialogues by two comic antago-
nists, Pericles and Fasoulis (Bean); and pertinent cartoons about Greek and
American politics. Like *Ethnikos Keryx, Kampana* was a liberal publication,
wholeheartedly supporting Eleftherios Venizelos, an anti-royalist leader in
Greece.

Few immigrants would have known Demetra Vaka, of whom Alexander Karanikas says, "For the Greek-American community [she] remains after three decades the First Lady of Letters." She was born into a cultured

Anatolian Greek family, but the death of her father altered the family's finances. She had wanted to become a doctor; without money for medical studies, only marriage or teaching were open to her (and to all women at that time). Turkish political unrest forced her to leave Turkey. She arrived in the United States at eighteen and learned English—she already knew seven other languages. In 1907, she began publishing in English. With her husband, Kenneth Brown, she wrote *The First Secretary,* a novel about a young American and his adventures in Greece. Altogether she wrote fifteen books, most of them interpreting the culture of Asia Minor for the West.[3] Yiorgos Kalogeras, of Aristotle University in Thessaloniki, wrote that Vaka "doesn't hesitate to emphasize her ambition to acquire the political and the civilizing strength as a *woman.*"[4]

The few educated Greeks sat in coffeehouses for lack of a better place to meet. Because their businesses or newspapers needed the support of uneducated Greeks, they assumed a superficial camaraderie that often evolved into lifelong friendships between members of the two groups. Later they would find more congenial places to meet.

CHAPTER 13

PRIESTS AND APOSTATES

The immigrants immediately built churches.[1] Orthodoxy had been brought to the New World by the Russians, and their priests officiated at services for the Greeks until they could build their own churches. The leading members of each community established the churches, to assure that if they died in *ksenitia,* they would be given a Greek Orthodox burial. The men were not regular churchgoers; priests usually intoned Sunday liturgies in empty naves. The young men attended church on their name days and on the great feast days of the year, particularly Holy Week, which culminated in the Resurrection.

Often the immigrants bought abandoned buildings of other denominations, purified them, brought icons from Greece and Mount Athos, and attempted to repeat the accouterments of their homeland churches. The first churches were without pews; later, when women arrived, one or two benches were available for mothers to sit and decorously nurse their infants, a handkerchief covering their breasts. Men sat at the important right side of the church, women and children on the left. In many churches women and children were relegated to the balcony, a reflection of Jewish custom in the early church.

The first church, a white wooden structure, was built in New Orleans in 1864. Others were erected in New York City (1892); Chicago (1893); Boston (1903); San Francisco, Milwaukee, Newark, Philadelphia, Birmingham, and Lowell, Massachusetts (1904); Salt Lake City (1905); Pueblo, Colorado, (1906); Galveston, St. Louis, Omaha, Los Angeles, Kansas City, Portland, Los Angeles, and McGill, Nevada (1907).

No specific order existed for bringing priests to minister to the new immigrants. Each fledgling Greek community formed a *kinotitos* (community council) that managed parish affairs and chose a priest and a Greek school-

Father Markos Petrakis of Crete came to the Utah coal fields in 1916 with his wife and four children and subsequently served in other communities farther east.

teacher, who were paid by the community. Rival factions competed for control. Although the churches' loyalty was to the Patriarchate in Constantinople (Istanbul) and the autonomous Church of Greece, they functioned under local authority; laymen, not priests, dominated the affairs of the churches.[1]

When communities requested the services of a priest from the Ecumenical Patriarchate, they were served by educated clerics. More often the *kinotitos* wrote letters to a village priest one of them had known and invited him to come to America. The priests came gladly, in black robes and tall priest hats, the *kalimafkia.* Feuds over priests and church affairs were especially

Church committee in Denver, Colorado, photographed in the basement of George Allison's Candy Store. He is seated at the front, right. The Greek church was erected in 1908. Courtesy of Andrew Paspalis.

tempestuous between Arcadians and Spartans, and in the West between Cretans and Roumeliotes.

Imposters, though, with doubtful credentials also made themselves known in coffeehouses and were accepted by communities in desperate need of priests. How they had lived before coming to America could not be known. An abbot had paid a pittance for sexual encounters to the impoverished young mother of three children. When they were discovered, the mother was stoned and chased out of the village. There on the outskirts she starved to death. The abbot slipped through the guards with the monastery's treasure, arrived in New York, and was widely acclaimed by unknowing parishioners.[2] Enough exposés were documented to warrant the publication of a small black book.[3]

Early priests left a wealth of anecdotes.

> *My dad told me this story about one of their first priests. The church wasn't much to look at and the priest kept complaining and begging for a new one. No one paid any attention to him. One Sunday he told the members that he had this dream the night before. In the dream the Virgin appeared and told him that on a certain site an icon was buried and there they should build a new church in her name. The parishioners took shovels and went to the place and dug and sure enough there was the icon! Everyone was beside themselves with joy and started talking about getting*

started right away. Then one of the men examined the icon and looked at the back. The words Sunkist Oranges *was [sic] imprinted on the wood.*—James Cononelos[4]

An immigrant who had arrived in San Francisco in 1884 describes the tentative beginnings of the church there. This occurred after a fisherman had been murdered by another Greek. The community of about five hundred Greeks paid a Russian priest ten dollars and his fare to conduct the liturgy for the dead. They then buried him in the Serbian cemetery.

> There was nobody who asked that we might have a church except myself. I was the least among the others in wealth but the one born to do good deeds. . . . Then, I said, when we have things ready, we should give a big dinner and invite some of the big heads, to make a good impression and bring good luck. [The consul, the mayor Julius Kahn, and Professor Putzker "Who loves anything Greek and speaks the Greek language well" were invited.]
>
> The night of the dinner, I put on my diamonds and received the strangers at the door and showed them to their seats. Then, my countrymen seeing me in this splendor of dress, told me that I should be the president of the affair if I wanted success.
>
> "My Greek brethren" [Julius Kahn said], "it seems that I see before me tonight all the Greek geniuses, Pericles, Plato, and many other Greek names that all of you know that I have no time to bring before you. As I look upon you tonight, it seems that I am in the company of the Athenian philosophers . . . I want to tell you that you will succeed and are lucky to have such a leader as Alex Kosta."
>
> Then Martin, the Greek consul, spoke and said that, as long as they had me as a leader, there was no doubt about their succeeding . . . The Professor Putzker spoke. . . . He said he felt as if he were in Athens, amid the wealth of civilization and its great men and that, if he had a wish, it was that he might die in Athens. . . .
>
> Then it was my turn to speak, and God gave me courage, and my whole body burned with the fire of courage, from head to foot. . . . [I] said, "Greeks, fellow men, friends, and brothers, and Christians. We have only one language, one religion, one flag. Let us try and decide to build a church, because it is a bad thing not to have a church. I am sure that we shall succeed and I myself first of all put $100.00 down." Then I sat down. Then you should have seen all the Greeks who were present throwing their hats up in the air and saying, "Zito, Hellas! (Long live Greece!)."[5]

In 1907, the Philadelphia Greek Orthodox Church recommended an African American, Raphael (Robert) Morgan, to the Ecumenical Patriarch for ordination and that the congregation accept him as an assistant priest. Following his ordination, Morgan returned to Philadelphia, and after a few years he went to Jerusalem "never again to return."[6]

In the author's western mining town, the well-liked priest "did not have his papers." He was a chanter, made a priest on the spot during the Balkan Wars of 1912–13, which enabled him to pass through Turkish lines with army plans hidden in his robes. When he left the western town in 1921, colicky, irritable babies were taken to the new priest, who "had his papers," for a rereading of the baptismal service because the former priest-cantor might have left out a word or two. Priests in America continued the role they played in Greece. "The subordinate clergy [in Greece] on the other hand was of mixed quality. . . . Sometimes he was a pious and dedicated man who gave much of his time and sympathy to his parishioners, but more often his role as a spiritual adviser was strictly a secondary one. Generally speaking, he came from the same social stratum as his parishioners and his education was extremely limited—only his clerical garb distinguished him from any other villager."[7]

In America, to the derision and laughter of passersby, priests wore their long black robes, large pectoral crosses, and tall *kalimafkia*. In Chicago, a group of angry Greeks complained to the mayor, who said, "Our American people are peaceable and would never have annoyed your bishop if he had complied with the habits and customs of our country and had attired himself accordingly."[8] As more priests arrived, some voluntarily conformed with church council edicts that they dress like American clergy; others were recalcitrant, but, as church boards had full authority to fire and hire, they capitulated. Archbishops and bishops continued to wear their robes and *kalimafkia*.

Immigrants clutched the "to be Greek is to be Orthodox" dictum with a possessive zeal in the new country. Many priests had come from Greek lands still under Turkish rule, and their passionate pleas to redeem the lost territories kept their parishes in turmoil. Greeks who had fallen away from Orthodoxy were shunned and became outcasts; emigration appealed to them.

When I was still going to school [in Petrochori], I by chance got a BIBLE from a new teacher that came to the village for the starters. I never read the BIBLE in the church. The psalters and the Priest sing everything in that Byzantine chant and you can't understand anything—So, Mike, when I started to read the BIBLE *a new conception of things started to pile up before me, so that when I came to* VERSE 4 *that states "*YOU MUST NOT MAKE YOURSELF A CARVED IMAGE—*" and looked at the Plethora of images [icons] I was flabbergasted.*"—Thomas Gregory (Athanasios K. Gregoropoulos), Province Aitolia[9] [Athanasios K. Gregoropoulos became a Jehovah's Witness and converted all his family except his mother, whose anger at him instigated his stealing money due his father from tobacco merchants and beginning an odyssey that eventually led to the United States.]

The International Bible Student Association and the Mormon Church (the Latter-day Saints) attracted a few immigrants. Nikolaos Efthimios Kotsomichos, born in 1888 in Plessa, Province Doridos, came to America in 1908. From childhood he had wondered about God and his attributes. After working in Milwaukee, Wisconsin, he traveled to San Francisco, where he worked in a restaurant. There he joined the United States Army, served three years in the Philippines, and attended the YMCA and the Disciples of Christ Bible classes. The infant baptisms of the Greek Orthodox church impelled him to be baptized again and to accept the minister's suggestion that he study for the ministry in a Cumberland Heights, Tennessee, seminary, but once there he questioned the doctrine. He then became an Episcopalian in St. Paul, Minnesota. Again he traveled to several cities working in restaurants and as a railroad section hand. He re-enlisted in the army and while in the service, he changed his name to Philagios (Love-of-saints). In 1924 two women missionaries of the Church of Latter-day Saints converted him and he became a Mormon.[10]

Elias Nikolaos Petroulas, born in Moni Tsigou, Province Lakonis, in 1889, was an atheist when he arrived in New York in 1912: "[In high school] we had the parable of the sheep and the goats. That night I had a dream. I saw Heaven opening and Christ coming down with his holy angels to Judge the world. We were gathered together and to my surprise I found myself at his right hand with the sheep . . . my father, mother, brothers and sisters all on the left. I felt I did not want to go to heaven, I would rather be with my people . . . a God who can separate families . . . some to heaven and others to hell . . . is not worthy of worship."

While he was working in Philipsburg, New Jersey, Petroulas became acquainted with young Greeks called The Believers. He asked the Greek inspector about his change of faith. "I didn't change my faith," he replied, "I

The monk Jason Malvis established a self-sufficient religious community in Daphne, Alabama, in 1907. Courtesy of Steve Frangos.

just don't want to believe what the Priest or somebody else tells me. I study the Bible to know for myself what to believe."

This led to Petroulas's becoming a member of the International Students Association and writing articles and translating their magazine, the *Watchtower,* into Greek. After an argument with the president of the society, he

The old Malvis planta-tion. Courtesy of Steve Frangos.

joined the Universal Reconciliationists, and then the Mormon church, whose doctrines of pre-existence, veil of forgetfulness, and eternal progression appealed to him. He translated the Book of Mormon into Greek.[11]

Unusual in the saga of early Greek Orthodoxy in the United States is the story of the monk Jason (Markopoulos) Malvis.[12] He was born in the village Donmena, Province Kalavryta, and arrived in the United States in 1906. Unlike most Greek immigrants, he was interested in agriculture. To attain land, he and a friend worked in a Chicago restaurant for one year for twenty-five dollars a month. During his kitchen stint, he found that others were also interested in agriculture. With his friend, he traveled throughout the United States, searching for a site to build a community of brotherhood. Near the town of Daphne, Alabama, near Mobile, the rays of a brilliant sunset came through a grove of pine trees. He saw this as a heavenly sign and wrote three friends to join him and his companion in buying 120 acres at five dollars an acre, to be paid in several installments. Others, both older and younger, men and women, came to the plantation. Under the highest standards of honesty, it became self-sufficient through farming, raising livestock, and planting orchards. By 1924, the plantation had grown to ten thousand acres.

The plantation became a commercial enterprise with the manufacture of turpentine and the canning of vegetables grown by local farmers. Before World War I the brightly colored Malvis Plantation labels were seen all through the South and beyond, to Chicago, Boston, and New York. More ventures were added: an ice plant, sawmill, dairy, bakery, the landmark Metropolitan Restaurant, nursery, garage, electrical plant, motel, and other real estate enterprises.

The plantation church, The Presentation of the Theotokos (Christbearer), was begun in 1949 and dedicated in 1964. Listed among the treasures of Alabama, it is magnificent, with its three domes, marble imported from Greece carved into ten pillars, and the thirty-foot-high iconostasis. The church bells installed in the two front domes ring out clearly and can be heard six miles away.

Jason Malvis returned to Greece in 1932 and died in Amaroussion, Attika, in 1947. His enterprises continued under Greek-immigrant management that gave help to the destitute and to orphans in Greece.

The Malvis Plantation was a lone symbol of Christian love. Elsewhere chaos ruled. The lack of central authority over church affairs in the United States was aggravated by political events in Greece between supporters of King Constantine and the liberal leader Eleftherios Venizelos, later prime minister. The establishment of a Greek Orthodox archdiocese aligned the liberal followers of Venizelos with Meletios Metaxakis, Metropolitan of Athens, and Bishop Alexander against the Royalist Bishop Germanos Troianos. By the 1920s, many churches were closed for long periods of time, and some offered liturgies intermittently.

The Presentation of the Theotokos (Christ-Bearer), a church begun in 1949 and completed in 1964, is a state treasure. Courtesy of Steve Frangos.

CHAPTER 14

THE MIDWEST AND WEST

The role of the Midwest and especially the West in giving the immigrants a foothold in America has been unrecognized. They were lucrative fields for Greek labor agents, who were able to fill a request by telephone or telegram for ten to a thousand men. Agriculture was giving way to rapid industrialization. The opening of metal and bituminous coal mines, the clearing of sagebrush, the laying of branch railroad lines, and the replacing of narrow gauge with standard gauge rails required many thousands of men.

Earlier, as the country's industrialization began escalating, a few adventurous Greeks left established Greek Towns in New York and Chicago, made pacts with mine and railroad management, trading the promise of cheap labor for privilege, and became the leading labor suppliers of the Midwest and West. From northern and southern Europe, from the Middle East, and from Asia, men came, among them the Greeks. In competing with other immigrant groups to fill this need, the Greeks became the largest labor force in mines and on railroad gangs. Census-taking was haphazard, and the men moved constantly. A recent Master's thesis estimates at least twenty thousand Greeks were working in the Intermountain West.[1]

As in the archipelago of the Aegean islands, mining camps, mills, and smelters dotted the vast prairies and sagebrush deserts. The Greeks rode freight trains over this terrain, hoping at the next stop to find a labor agent and work. They kept a lookout for railroad detectives, who would arrest them for vagrancy, and for officials who would charge them a head tax, a means of keeping immigrants from remaining in an area. Often in a small town they found the maligned coffeehouse, the only home of the peripatetic Greeks. They would remember all their lives the men they had worked with, men who had helped them, men with whom they "had eaten bread and salt."

The Greek government became alarmed at the number of men killed and those who returned with limbs missing. It sent investigators to the United States to ascertain the reports of labor abuses against its emigrés. Deaths were often the result of carelessness on the part of American managers, who neglected to provide even rudimentary training for immigrants, or of ignorance by the workers themselves.

Miners had been warned not to touch exposed electrical wires, but knowing nothing about electricity, a Greek worker brought a pair of gloves from his boarding house, attempted to move a wire, and was electrocuted. The following is from a 1909 report on an explosion in a Utah Gilsonite mine. Gilsonite is a hydrocarbon used in paint, insulation, and paving mixtures.

> The bodies of two Greek miners, who lost their lives in an explosion at the Black Dragon mine . . . were recovered . . . after having been entombed just fourteen months. . . . The cause of the explosion, in our opinion, was. . . . The two men were sitting against the south wall resting. Gervas, who was known to be an inveterate smoker, rolled a cigarette, struck a match to light it; the dust in suspension (and gilsonite dust in suspension will ignite more quickly than black powder) immediately ignited with a flash, both men throwing up their left arm to ward off the flame. Both men appear to have been quickly overcome by carbon monoxide gas, as they had not fallen over but were both leaning back on the south wall of the vein. The flame from the dust set fire to the gilsonite and the melted gilsonite soon poured into the drift, filling it up completely and encasing the victims in the liquid asphalt.
>
> The following notices are kept posted in conspicuous places. . . . "Employees are strictly forbidden to carry matches, or have fires of any description, in, at or near the mine or any workings contiguous thereto."[2]

It took management a while to realize that signs in English were meaningless to the immigrants. They then began posting rules in several languages.

The most important Greek investigator of the workers' dangerous and

degrading lot was the legendary Maria Economidhou, a journalist for her husband's Athenian newspaper *NIKI*. Beginning in 1912, she traveled throughout the United States, Cuba, and Canada. During her travels she attended an evening of entertainment for laborers. She described *Kyria* (Madame) Sophia, who was accompanied by violin and *laouto*, as singing with a voice like a wolf's and dancing with the grace of an elephant. When Economidhou complained with disgust, a laborer said, "If we didn't have even this diversion from time to time, we would become animals completely." The men danced until morning with this "famous Pavlova of the mines."[3]

Almost all Greeks in the Midwest and West used their savings to open stores and restaurants in large cities elsewhere. Though their time in menial work was short, they were of the utmost importance in the industrialization and unionization of the Midwest and West. In return, the immigrants secured their foothold in the new country.

Cretan coal miners in Utah, 1911, had their picture taken with bottles and guns as signs of affluence for the benefit of relatives back home; sprigs of basil are a symbol of friendship. Steve Sargetakis Collection, used by permission, Utah State Historical Society, all rights reserved.

CHAPTER 15

STRANGERS AMONG STRANGERS

By 1920, Greeks were flourishing in the larger cities, as importers of olive oil and other Greek foods; grocery, restaurant, and candy-store owners; cigarette merchants; and autocrats ruling strings of shoeshine stands. The Greeks were achieving what they had a passion for, "being their own boss." Their entrepreneurial spirit was noted early. In Jackson, Mississippi, "a man refused to hire [Anthon Tattis] because of the reputation Greeks had for going out on their own. . . . He said, 'Tattis, you are a Greek. You won't work here six months. As soon as you get enough money you are going to start a business of your own.' "[1]

Greeks became involved so quickly in the restaurant and candy-store businesses that the words *restaurant* and *candy store* were immediately linked to them. "When two Greeks meet, they open a restaurant; when three Greeks meet, they form a political party" was a much-heard expression during those years. A mistaken idea prevailed that they had a special aptitude for cooking. The young Greeks had never done any cooking in their native country. Women there had complete responsibility for food preparation, except for roasting lamb on spits. Greek men and women remained inside the traditional circles prescribed by custom. In America the boys and men began as dishwashers, later became cooks' helpers, then cooks themselves. With their savings they rented small stores with warped wooden floors. Above the doors they hung signs: Acropolis Cafe, Sparta Restaurant, Smyrna Candy Store. The men worked as many as eighteen hours a day, but they were proud of being proprietors, no longer laborers.

Candy stores had a special aura. In many Midwestern, Western, and Southern towns, the candy-store proprietor was often the only Greek inhabitant. Candy stores were meeting places where young people congregated: they sat on the stools or in barren booths, punched out little rolled

Gus Theodore sold shoelaces and pencils on city streets. Later, with the help of his brothers Nick and George, he established a chain of launderies in California. The young man with the cart is Nick Theodore. Courtesy of Georgia Theodore Kyriazis.

paper numbers in hopes of winning a box of chocolates wrapped with gauzy ribbons and bows, and ordered soft drinks or ice cream sundaes. Children gazed at the window displays of penny candy, agonizing over what to buy with their one or two pennies. Hand-cranked phonographs tinkled popular tunes of the day.

For a few immigrants the rise was easy. Euripides Constantinou Kehayas was born in Kotyora, Pontus, Asia Minor; the name had been changed by the conquering Turks to Ordu, the place where Alexander the Great reached the sea on his retreat from Asia. At an early age Kehayas supplied the sultan's court with tobacco. When the Young Turks took power in 1908, all who had dealings with the sultan fled. Kehayas came to New York, where he soon established the Standard Commercial Tobacco Company. It subsequently controlled the Axton-Fischer Company, manufacturers of Spuds and Twenty Grand cigarettes, and the Mignon brand, sold exclusively to private clubs. He went on to own a steamship company and, for a time, the Greek newspaper the *National Herald*. And he expanded his tobacco holdings to include many different kinds of merchandise, which he sold throughout the world.[2]

Thousands of other Greeks were still searching for work, riding freight cars, following every rumor of work. Fellow Greeks, *patriotes,* and coffeehouses saved them. In strange cities, small towns, and hamlets, they asked policemen, "Greek Town?" and were directed to a few stores and houses in

Ted's Sweet Shop, Chicago, Illinois. Courtesy of Steve Frangos.

fledgling neighborhoods that would grow as women arrived. Greek Towns were almost always near the railyards. There the Greeks hoped to find work on the railroads and in their subsidiaries, the coal and metal mines. They were fortunate if a labor agent met an incoming train and with the canny recognition of one countryman to another hailed them. They learned to be fearful of railroad detectives, knew days of hunger, and some spent time in jail for vagrancy when they looked for jobs. They survived by searching for a coffeehouse.

They banded together—those with work helped the jobless—yet assaults on each other over real or supposed insults to their *filotimo* erupted regularly and were duly noted in American newspapers. The men rented houses in poor neighborhoods and pooled their money. In these houses, called *bekiarika* (bachelor houses), they took turns cooking and doing housework, an appalling situation to them. They had been coddled by mothers and sisters, but in America they had to learn to cook, wash and mend their own clothing, and recall the folk cures of their people.

The sardonic humor of the Greek people came to their rescue. In a Chicopee, Massachusetts, *bekiariko* during the economic crisis of 1907, Greeks had been working in a cotton mill for $3.30 a week. Several of them decided to rent a house and pool expenses. They had one table, ten chairs, a stove, two pots, a frying pan, a few dishes, knives, forks, and spoons, an *English Method* [grammar] book, a dreambook, and a picture of the hero Pavlos Melas, who had been killed in the 1897 insurrection against the Turks in Greek Macedonia.

The men had the misfortune of choosing Kyriakos as their boss because he had been in America a year and knew about forty words of English. He also made the great sum of eight dollars a week at the mill. He was good-hearted, an excellent companion, and honest. He also turned out to be a tyrant. His permanent menu allowed no deviation. *Loukanika* (sausages) were his staple.

Mondays: rice with sausages
Tuesdays: potatoes with sausages
Wednesdays: eggs with sausages
Thursdays: lentils with sausages
Fridays: cabbages with sausages
Saturdays: beans in cottonseed oil
Sundays: meat, soup, beer

After two weeks of sausages, the men began to complain. No matter how they tried to sabotage the food when they took turns cooking, Kyriakos would not budge. The men complained that in their dreams, the furniture, the dishes, they themselves were turning into sausages. Kyriakos remained aloof. The men then held a funeral in the backyard and buried a sausage, to the accompaniment of church hymns, the *troparia*. Kyriakos was not amused. Eventually the men separated and did not see one another for many years. Then, one of them chanced upon Kyriakos, now a prosperous restaurant owner. Jubilantly Kyriakos invited him to his home, promising an excellent dinner, the first course of which was rice with sausages.[3]

Generations-old vendettas added to the instability of life in America. The vendetta became ingrained in Greek life during the Turkish occupation: Ottoman officials paid little attention to dispensing justice, and clans took charge of avenging their families' honor—often the rape or seduction of a daughter or sister. Besides needing to mete out justice, the Greeks believed, as did the ancients, that a murdered person required retribution to give his soul rest.[4] Contemporary vendettas in primitive areas of Greece were often undertaken with sorrow and a sense of duty.[5] The immigrants soon learned that American officials were far less lenient than the Greek courts in sentencing murderers for crimes of passion, and they became adept at suing each other instead.

In the early days of the twentieth century, American newspapers attest to the great number of young Greeks, as well as other immigrants, who were arrested for disturbing the peace. Many such incidents stemmed from old-

country politics, labor-agent abuses, marriage arrangements gone awry, and loans. Fists, knives, and guns settled differences, but also brought the authorities. Other charges of disturbing the peace resulted from the men's celebrating their first wages after months of living precariously.

> When the paymaster arrived with their wages, the labor agent was on hand to take the ten-dollar commission from [each of them]. . . . Carrying bottles of American beer, sacks of potatoes, and a lamb that cost them a dollar fifty, [they] walked to the nearby bachelor house of four rooms with bare wooden floors, several cots, a table, and assorted chairs. . . . In the backyard the lamb roasted on a spit. Inside the men prepared the potatoes, sliced a cabbage coarsely and doused it with olive oil and vinegar. Throughout the night they ate, drank, sang and were interrupted at four o' clock in the morning by officers who marched them to the police station where they were fined five dollars each for disturbing the peace . . . they were left with only a few coins in their pockets.[6]

Beyond their Greek Towns, though, the Greeks had little to do with Americans and knew almost nothing about them, just as Americans, unless they were college-educated, had no concept of who the Greeks were. It was commonly thought that they were not white and not Christian. Maria Economidhou, the intrepid journalist for her husband's Athens newspaper *NIKI,* wrote of an American woman in Galveston, Texas, who told her, "Dr. Samson was going to Greece as a missionary." The author asked why. "To Christianize Greece was the naive answer."[7]

Often Greek attempts to show respect for American ways puzzled or further provoked Americans: "In 1908, there were close to 5,000 men in Greek Town in Salt Lake City, Utah. To show their goodwill they entered a float in a civic parade. Utah was founded by the Mormons, and almost all the inhabitants were Mormons. One of their principles was, and is, the Word of Wisdom that forbids the consumption of tea, coffee, and alcoholic drinks. And so our Greeks prepared a float resembling an ancient chariot with several young men dressed in ancient Greek tunics. The float was dedicated to Dionysos, the god of wine."[8]

CHAPTER 16

RIDING THE RAILS

The labor agent Leonidas G. Skliris of Vresthenon, Sparta, became a *padrone* of immense power. Greek labor agents in the West and Midwest either worked directly under him or had a reciprocal relationship with him. Americans called him the "Czar of the Greeks." Commissions from steamship companies for fares and from immigrants for finding them work were lucrative for the *padrones* during America's burst of industrialization. The Czar advertised in Greek newspapers in America, Greece, and Crete. His main office was located in Salt Lake City, Utah, with branch offices in New York, St. Paul, Chicago, Kansas City, Denver, San Francisco, and Sacramento. In coffeehouses, Skliris's agents waited for the young immigrants and sent them to railroad gangs, coal and metal mines, smelters, and mills. Skliris supplied strikebreakers as well, and the Greeks often found themselves in danger of their lives over strikebreaking, which was altogether an alien concept to them. Workers also were forced to trade at the *padrones'* stores or lose their jobs. Labor agents did nothing to alleviate the poor working conditions and discrimination their fellow Greeks endured. An appalling number of men were killed in mines and mills, and on railroads. Management often gave a few hundred dollars to the *padrone* to send to the dead men's families, but the families seldom received it.[1]

As documented in the Dillingham Report of 1911:

> For "white men" without families the [mining] company maintains a dormitory for which the charge is $1 per month. The service rendered includes the supply of bedding and towels. For the Greeks and the Japanese [the lowest-paid workers] the company furnishes bunk houses with running water for the price charged "white men" at the dormitory, but covers neither bedding nor laundry. . . . The

Greeks and Japanese are segregated from other employees. . . . The segregation is partly the result of the difference in the standard of comfort demanded by "American" laborers . . . and partly by the habit—more or less imposed by the prejudices of "American" laborers—these laborers have of living by themselves.[2]

Both management and Americans in general thought of immigrants as being content with a low standard of living. Wherever labor gangs were large,

Wisconsin railroad gang, 1913. The water boy, George Papachristos (second row from top, right) later married the author's aunt. Courtesy of Thalia and Katherine Papachristos.

workers lived either in "foreigners' camps" or "white men's camps." The difference in amenities was most noticeable on railroad gangs. American quarters included a separate railroad car for cooking, another for eating, and a third for sleeping in bunk beds. For immigrants, a single car was used for cooking and eating, with wooden platforms at either end for sleeping. This practice continued after immigrants took over the major industry of laying rails and keeping them in repair.[3]

Almost immediately, the Greek practice of sending money to their families led to difficulties. Southern Europeans sent more money than northern Europeans, and Greeks led all immigrants in remittances to their native country.[4] For years this practice brought censure to the Greeks. "The foreign element . . . spends no money other than for the barest necessities of life. They hoard their earnings, spending barely 10 percent with the business men of the community . . . and send most of their savings out of the country. The native born workingman, on the other hand, spends his money for good living, good clothes and for the comforts of life."[5]

Tragedies and misery quickly began.

[On our railroad gang in Kansas City, Missouri] a tragedy occurred to one of the workers and he lost his life while they were moving rails from one section of the line to another. A [railroad] car fell and crushed him. . . . The man was from Kamaria in the province of Corinth and his name was Demetrios Karmargetis. His father and brother were on the same job.[6]

[Three hundred fifty miles from Seattle] we found but two houses of the company and nothing else. Only endless forests and 8 feet of snow. . . . The snow and cold were excruciating and we found the workers had removed the stove and taken it to the foreman's house. The laborers and foreman were Italians. . . . The house was nothing but a place to put pigs. . . . In the morning we went to work hungry because there wasn't a place to buy anything. . . . My uncle went to a town 8 miles away and bought [food] for us to eat and returned in the evening. There was no place to cook in the house and we put a tub outside and there we cooked. Our only food was coffee in the morning, sardines at noon, and beans in the evening. . . . That Easter 5 [Greek] men celebrated with 2 pounds pork with a few eggs that I had dyed with ink instead of dye.[7]

The men were amazed that Holy Week meant nothing to Americans, who went to work as if the days were ordinary ones. Although a few Greek churches had been built, they were in cities far from railroad gangs on prairies and mining camps. In their country, church-going was women's domain, except that everyone celebrated Holy Week, which culminated in the year's great days connected with Christ, His mother, His Transfiguration and ministry, and led to the supreme event of the year, Christ's journey to Calvary and His crucifixion. Beginning with His birth, the year progressed, following the Evangelists' recounting the events, each one bringing him ever closer to his Passion. Forty days before Easter, fasting began; marriages and baptisms were not performed, and parishioners tempered their greetings on leaving church. When Holy Week arrived, churches were darkened, a pall hung in them. In America, though, the men swung sledges and picks, pushed shovels, knowing that in their villages and towns the week-long commemoration of Christ's journey to Golgotha was being lived again. Haralambos Kambouris writes in his diary, "It is Great Saturday and we are working."[8]

The men had to keep searching for work. Their sisters were getting older; they needed dowries immediately, and parents were waiting to have the usurious mortgages on their land lifted.

I got a job at the Armour's packing house in Omaha for 2 or 3 hours a day at 23 cents an hour. Out of this sum five of us had to live. Fortunately, I thought, a labor agent offered me a job on a railroad 800 miles away; paying him $8 a piece for commission, which we borrowed, and on the freight train we reached our destination but there was NO JOB, neither were we allowed to return unless we paid the transportation charges back to Omaha.

Page from H. K. Kambouris, "Pages from My Life . . . ," relating the injury of a friend and the death of a young Greek when a railroad car fell on him outside Kansas City, Missouri. The dead man's father and brother witnessed the accident. Photograph by George Theodore.

We worked at some farm for 50 cents a day for 19 days and paid our way back to Omaha. From Omaha I went to Castle Gate, Utah, where I was offered a job at the coke ovens, provided I paid $20 commission for the boss and his gang. When I reported to work, as agreed, the agent told me that someone else had bid the job with $10 more and since I had no more money I lost the job plus the $20 commission. . . . I got me a job at the recently started coal mine at Kenilworth. The first month check was 32.50. I got fired from there because not having any money to spare, I refused to contribute towards buying a diamond ring for the superintendent's wife. (We had to please and pay everyone to hold our job.)[9]

James Galanis was in South Omaha when a Greek immigrant took a young American woman to a movie and afterwards to a candy store for ice cream. Reports varied about the woman; she was described as of "questionable virtue" by one source and a "fine girl" by other reports. A policeman accosted the Greek on the street for being seen with a "white" girl. A fight began and ended with the Greek shooting and killing the policeman. The next day a frenzied mob burned down the Greek section of the town.

All the Greek businesses, bar none, were on fire. If [a] Greek was found on the street he was beaten up, and during all these atrocities and barbarian behavior the POLICE standing a short distance watching this destruction of property and immediate danger of human beings (to the police apparently the poor immigrant Greeks were not considered as such and I mean what I say because I was there!)

Three days after this turmoil, anxiety, and fear, a Greek young man was found killed under a small bridge. The hate and determination of south Omaha people was such that unless the MAYOR and police of North Omaha had not come to our aid with automobiles (they were few those days) and street cars to transfer us to North Omaha it would have been possible that a massacre of the worst type COULD have taken place. . . . A vice consul of Italy declared that the attacked Greeks were under the protection of Italy, which was a powerful nation then.[10]

An affidavit declaring the woman a virgin was signed by five hundred South Omaha citizens.[11]

Hostility toward the Greeks was endemic throughout the United States. "Greek agitators" were often blamed for armed conflicts that resulted in killings. An agitator was anyone who insisted on wages equal to that of English-speaking workers. In Rushville, Illinois, Greek section hands, barricaded in their box car living quarters, killed a sheriff and two deputies.

A mob of 1,000 gathered about the city prison at Beardstown [where thirty Greek laborers were being held] at noon, but their threatened violence was frustrated by cooperation of Chief of Police Patterson and a freight crew of the Chicago, Burlington and Quincy railroad. Armed automobiles bearing the Greeks ran along side the running freight train and transferred their prisoners, while the mob raced towards them from the other end of the yards. An unidentified Greek was shot and killed early in the day by a posse which was seeking to arrest four or five men wanted in connection with the killing of the officers.[12]

An account of nativism in the copper mining town of Ely, Nevada, reveals the various forces at work.[13] Americans were determined to rid themselves of the newcomers. For five years, railroad workers had lived in box cars; miners, twelve to sixteen in a tent. In 1909, Nevada Consolidated built "cramped [houses that] lacked running water until the 1950s."[14] In 1907, the board of governors of a building trades alliance asked local businessmen to employ "white labor, meaning thereby an American citizen." On 9 July 1909, the *Ely Record* reported that the International Smelting Company "has prevented, so far, the employment of Oriental or South of Europe workmen. . . . It seems good to see intelligent blonde faces only in such a large enterprise." The county newspapers accused the Greeks of being an inferior people, barbarians, not at all like their ancient Greek ancestors. Further, the few Greeks involved in bootlegging and prostitution blackened the name of the laborers who worked long hours for less pay than Americans received.

In this atmosphere Greek "agitators" were blamed for causing unrest among their fellow *patriotes*. Racism and fear of competition for jobs set the background for a shooting that involved the entire county. When Constable Sam Davis questioned Antonis Vasilopoulos about lumber he believed was stolen, shots were fired. Davis was wounded and Vasilopoulos fled. A posse set out to lynch Vasilopoulos and mistakenly shot and killed another Greek, Dimitris Kalampokas. When Davis did not die as had been expected, rumors rekindled the thwarted lynching plans for Vasilopoulos and predicted a "general uprising of the Greek residents." Many Greeks were told to pack their belongings. "Loaded into two box cars, herded together by armed guards, nearly a hundred Greeks passed last night in Ely waiting to be transported to another point, most probably to Cobre. This will be done, it is stated, this morning. All of the men were found to be unemployed, and as a result of the high feeling caused by the shooting of Deputy Constable Sam Davis were rounded up."[15]

Since the railroad refused to transport the men, who said they did not have the money for their fares, the men were let go. They were more fortunate than other immigrants in the West, who during labor wars were put into box cars, taken into deserts, and abandoned. The Salt Lake Greek-language newspaper, *O Ergatis* (The worker), and the Greek consul general in Washington, D.C., took an active role in the proceedings. The consul general appealed to Elihu Root, the secretary of state, who ordered a complete investigation of the shootings. Vasilopoulos was found guilty of wounding Davis, but the sentence was overturned. Kalampokas's killer was freed a few weeks later.

Greeks began leaving McGill and Ely; sufficient numbers remained until the 1912 copper strike, when many more left the mining town, along with other Balkan immigrants returning to fight in the Balkan Wars: "nativists who had been looking forward to their departure, started having second thoughts as they considered the significance of the loss of large numbers of foreign laborers."[16]

"America swallows the young," families left behind in Greece said. Boys and young men died in mines, mills, smelters, on railroad gangs, and by bullets and knives. They were often buried without anyone knowing whence they had come. Until churches were built, so that men would not "go to their graves unsung," priests had to be summoned from hundreds of miles away. No women were present to prepare the body for burial, to keen the *mirologhia,* the words of fate, to cook the fish dinner after the liturgy, and to prepare the forty-day memorial wheat. The men did their best, and when wedding crowns were unavailable, they often fashioned wreaths of fresh flowers about the dead person's head. These funerals were called *thanatoghamoi* (death weddings). In antiquity, death was believed to have been followed by marriage with the gods.[17] In Orthodox Christianity the tradition evolved into the unmarried dead being buried as brides and grooms: they had been denied marriage, one of the seven mysteries (sacraments) while living, but they would have it in death. The boys and young men were staying longer in America. A mother's lament begins:

> Small bird, there where you fly to America,
> Tell me, where does my son lie down to sleep?
> When he is sick, who tends him?

The men were afraid of company doctors, who hurriedly amputated limbs the Greeks believed might have been saved. On an Oregon extra gang, the young men used an effective American medicine. A teaspoonful of the bitter liquid cured an assortment of illnesses. A skull and bones was printed on the label, and underneath were the English words the men could not

A parade of Greek immigrants, members of the Vizas Lodge, in McGill, Nevada, 1917. From *The Hellenic Colonies in the Western United States of America* (San Francisco: Prometheus Publishing Company, 1918–19). John B. Vlahos Collection.

Μία Παρέλασις τῶν Μελῶν τοῦ ἐν Μὰκ Γκὶλλ Παμμεγαρικοῦ Συλλόγου ὁ « Βύζας »

read: "For external use. For horses 20–30 drops on affected parts. For humans 2–3 drops."[18] The men tried to remember folk cures.

> He had hardly been on the railroad gang a week when one freezing morning his fingers loosened about the pick, and the sharp point went through his shoe and nicked the side of his foot. . . . He went into his tent where he tore off a piece of a shirt bottom and stanched the blood. The pain grew worse in the passing days. Limping, he remembered a fellow villager whose leg had been cut off a year ago and stories he had heard in coffeehouses about company doctors amputating legs and arms and sending the mutilated men back to the old country with a hundred dollars or two.
>
> He wrote to his village asking his parents what to do. A yellow, putrid pus oozed from the blackening flesh, and red streaks spread up his leg. . . . One of the men recalled that he had once gone to a *praktikos*, a folk healer, for an infection on his arm and the folk healer had instructed his mother to make poultices of boiled onions and use them until the infection drained. Others remembered folk remedies, but nothing grew on the prairie, only red grass. Each night the cook gave him a pan of hot water to soak the wound.
>
> Two months later he received a letter from his parents telling him to take a tuft of clean sheep's wool, dip it into the film floating on a

crock of feta cheese, place it on the cut, wrap it, and change the dressing every day. "Sheep, a crock of feta in this wilderness," he said sardonically to the letter. By then his foot had healed leaving a thick scar.[19]

> We were working in the copper mill in McGill [Nevada] when one of our compatriots hurt his insides. We asked the foreman to help him. He refused and the labor agent paid no attention to us. We left our jobs. I had enough money to take a railroad coach, but most of the others started walking to Salt Lake City, over three hundred miles away. On the way they dropped their belongings and arrived in Salt Lake three weeks later.—Louis Lingos[20]

Every factory and labor gang required an interpreter, an *ermineas*. He usually had a year or two more schooling than the laborers and had acquired enough English words to transmit orders from the foreman. On railroad gangs in the Midwest and the West, the interpreter was indispensable: the workers were on prairies and deserts, far from towns. Interpreters rode handcars driven over the rails by pushing and pulling a horizontal bar, or they rented a horse and buggy and arrived on payday to take orders from the men.

Spiros Papachristos, an interpreter, was born in the mountain village Klepa, in Nafpaktias Province, in January 1888. He left the village on 27 April 1907, embarking from Piraeus on the thirtieth of the month; and arrived in New York on 10 May. A small red leather notebook details his sojourn in America. In the following three years he kept a record of the money he sent to his family in Klepa: $630.00, a good sum at a time when railroad workers were making a dollar a day. He made out money orders to the workers' families; took letters, which he sometimes had to write, to post offices; made lists of each man's needs: truss, Cuticura, Doan's Little Liver pills, adhesive plaster, rose water, spirits nitre, Black Wash (which had a label warning that it must be shaken well), gloves, stockings, watches, underwear, and guns. He loaned and also borrowed money.

Papachristos wrote down each worker's requests and costs in the notebook. When he was paid, he crossed out the debt. He recorded a stark fact: "In the year 1909 they cut off my brother Kostas's foot."

In the five years between 1907 and 1912, he traveled a circuit of towns and cities, interpreting for labor gangs in New York City; Pawtucket, Rhode Island; Pueblo, Colorado; Pocatello, Idaho; Barr, Colorado; Spokane, Washington; Heyburn, Idaho; Shoshone, Idaho; Salt Lake City, Utah; Council, Evergreen, and Meadows, Idaho; Kemmerer, Wyoming; Payette and Montpelier, Idaho; Nyssa, Oregon; Chicago; Baltimore, Maryland; Lorenzo, Idaho; Ogden, Utah; Rigby, Idaho; Cedar Rapids, Iowa; Galena, Illinois; Fort

Page from Spiros Papachristos's small red leather account book. Listed is the $630 he sent his family over five years, a great sum when one considers that he was often out of work and that when he was working he was usually paid 75¢ an hour. Courtesy of Thalia and Katherine Papachristos.

Wayne, Indiana; McGill, Nevada; Glen Haven, Wisconsin; and Mitchell and Burlington, Indiana.

He died in Chicago, in 1911, at the age of twenty-seven. A Greek doctor wrote that the cause of death was endocarditis, brought on, his family believed, by the harsh Wisconsin winters.[21]

CHAPTER 17
THE MIDWIFE MAGHEROU

A number of Greek folk healers came to America, but none reached the fame of an Intermountain West midwife. Georgia Lathouris was born in 1867 in the Peloponnesian village of Ahladhokambos (Pear valley).[1] She had been called the *mami* (midwife) since her fourteenth year, when she delivered a woman caught with labor pains while grazing goats on a mountain. The village was poor, and the girl was paid in wheat and flour.

Georgia's family could not provide her with a dowry, but it was her fate, as Greeks would say, that a tall Croatian, Nikos Mageras, came to build a bridge over a river near the *mami*'s village. Foreigners were being brought in to reconstruct the roads and bridges that the Turks had allowed to deteriorate because the Greeks had lost the skills their forefathers had known.[2] Women and girls made up the work crew. The *mami* was among the workers who brought large rocks to the site and hammered them into small pieces.

Soon after work began, Nikos asked the *mami*'s parents for permission to marry her and they agreed. In 1902, Nikos left the *mami* and four children behind to take a job in America offered by a labor agent. A few years later the family was reunited in a copper mill town fifteen miles west of Salt Lake City. Magherou (the genitive form of her husband's name) was one of the first Greek women in the West and became the matriarch of the Greek women who came later. Mine, mill, smelter, and railroad workers throughout the Intermountain West came to her for folk cures.

The *mami* used a wide variety of village cures. For pneumonia and bronchitis she simmered red wine with powdered cloves and tea with whiskey. She placed mustard plasters on the patient's chest and back and on the soles of his or her feet. Powdered Spanish fly *(vizikanti)* produced blisters;

The kind of work done by the midwife Magherou at the age of fourteen when the foreman of the work crew asked her parents for permission to marry her. From *National Geographic Magazine,* July 1928. MAYNARD OWEN WILLIAMS/NGS Image Collection.

when they broke, the "poison" was released. If these measures were unsuccessful, she applied *vendouzis*—water glasses heated with a tuft of burning cotton and then placed lip down on the patient's back. The heat and pressure inside the glass drew up the flesh. If the patient was very ill, Magherou cut a cross on the raised flesh and released the "bad" blood.

To cure jaundice, she made a small cut with a razor blade in the string of flesh connecting the inside of the upper lip with the tissue above the teeth. For abdominal pain, attributed to a spleen that had grown and "traveled," Magherou nicked the skin of the abdomen, drawing black blood and forcing the spleen to "go backwards." For boils, she used flaxseed poultices; for corns, raw tomatoes applied overnight. An injured toenail was immersed in warm wax, then tied with a cloth until it came out.

A favorite remedy for the midwife was bleeding; she used it for almost every ailment, especially infections. In America there was no need to search in ponds for leeches; drugstores sold them. To stop bleeding she used soap or the scrapings from the inside of a leather belt and firm bandages. For chronic backaches she had a small child walk up and down the patient's back. She set bones and saved two men from imminent amputation by company doctors.

Regularly pregnant herself, Magherou delivered Greek, Italian, Yugoslav

The legendary midwife of the Intermountain West, Georgia Latharos Mageras, "Magherou," who used a variety of folk cures for sick and injured Greeks. She is shown with two of her daughters and several grandchildren. Courtesy of Wilma Mageras Klekas.

(then called Austrian), and Mormon women. Young mothers brought their children to her when someone's envy had given them the Evil Eye; when their skin yellowed with jaundice; when they had *soufra* (rickets), for which the *mami* burned a bay leaf with a blessed candle, leaving only the stem. On three moonless nights, she touched each joint with the stem. Her fame spread, and people came from throughout the mountain states with their sick babies and children.

The *mami* prepared prodigious amounts of food, not only for her large family but also for sojourners and patients. She made enough *belde* (tomato paste) to last from one harvest to the next and filled big crocks with *hilop-ites*, minute pasta squares. She began preparing the dough by cracking thirty dozen eggs. She continued working until her late seventies and died in 1950 at the age of eighty-three.

CHAPTER 18

MEN WANTING TO SEE THE SKY

Life in the monotony and noise of factories, in the blackness of mines, on lonely railroad gangs became unbearable for many laborers. Greeks had been advancing from dishwashers to cooks in restaurants and from pushcart peddlers to owners of grocery shops, but other men saw opportunities in difficult or unfavorable conditions.

The Mouyias brothers of Klepa, Province Nafpktias, had worked on railroad gangs throughout the Midwest. When winter came, shutting down work on railroads gangs for two months, they returned to Chicago's Greek Town on Halsted Street. Chicago's railyards were among the busiest in the nation. Over a maze of intersecting straight and curved rails, passenger and freight trains chugged, steam hissing through their great black wheels. The cacophony rose to the blackened canopy. Workers brought their lunch pails and ate wherever they found an empty space.

The brothers approached the railyards' manager about supplying lunches for the workers. The manager agreed, and a small, windowless building, more like a shack than a lunchroom, was equipped with a counter, a row of stools, and a water fountain at one end. Each morning the brothers stopped at a Greek bakery, where they picked up a large beef roast and a ham they had brought there the night before to be cooked. They had a coffeemaker but no stove. The menu consisted of sandwiches with condiments and coffee. The brothers prospered, and a few years later they were able to bring brides from their village. The two couples lived together in a spacious bungalow in a middle-class neighborhood. They considered themselves fortunate, except that they were childless.[1]

John Karrant also left industrial work. "My father, John Karrant [Karrantopoulos], came to America in 1904 where he worked in Moline, Illinois

The baptism of a daughter at the Petropoulos farm in Manteca, California, 1919. The Petropoulos patriarch and matriarch were born in Piana, Arcadia, Peloponnesus. Courtesy of Patricia Manuse.

and Davenport, Iowa as a foreman in a roundhouse for the Rock Island railroad. In 1907 he moved to Fort Smith, Arkansas where he bought a farm and his specialty was growing tomatoes from seeds brought from Argos, Greece. He also made ice cream."[2]

When the Ute Indian reservation was opened to white homesteaders in 1905, twenty-five of the forty Greeks whom Skliris had brought in to break a Utah coal strike in 1902 bought 180 acres each under the Homestead laws. They farmed and raised sheep, returning to the very work they had left *patridha* to avoid.

All through the West, many Greeks left mines and mills as soon as they found a Basque or American stockman who would hire them with the agreement that after a few years their pay would be a small flock of sheep or herd of cattle. They then became prosperous stockmen themselves. John Papoulas of Mavrolithari, Lamia Province, Roumeli, owned five thousand sheep in Colorado by the early 1920s.

Dimitrios Tsiflakos and his brother, the earliest of sheepmen, increased their small band of sheep to five thousand, established the Yolo Sheep Cheese Company in northwest California, and grew tobacco on acreage adjoining their sheepfold.[3]

Demetrios Papadomanolakis (Jim Pappas) was born in Crete in 1893.

When his ship docked in the New York harbor all he had was a 20 dollar gold piece. . . . He soon found himself working in the coal mines around Raton [New Mexico] with his countrymen. . . . One day he was pushing a loaded coal car when it jumped the track. He unloaded the car, replaced the car on the track, reloaded it and started to push again. Once again it jumped the track and with deep despair he threw his tools into the car, walked out of the mine, threw a chunk of coal over his shoulder [an old superstition that assured his never having to return] and headed to Raton. . . . He purchased 544 goats from a ranch in Mora, New Mexico and he and a helper walked the goats 150 miles across country to the TO Ranch where he started a goat-cheese business.[4]

The old taboo of only women caring for goats was immediately discarded in the United States. Feta and (soft) *myzithra* cheeses were a staple of Greek diets. With no women about, the men gave up the superstition, but they did not make the sign of the cross before milking the goats as they did with sheep.

The number of Greeks returning to farming was small.[5] The 1920 census lists farmers by nationality in order of their numbers, but the Greeks were too few to be included. Those who fled from industrial work were negligible compared with the steady numbers coming through Ellis Island.

CHAPTER 19

MARIA ECONOMIDHOU, JOURNALIST

Maria Economidhou, the Greek journalist, was sent by her husband's newspaper, *NIKI,* to give an eyewitness account of the degrading living and working conditions of the men. The deaths of the young, she writes, "nourished the Minotaur of immigrant life."[1] The boys and men lived in shacks they had built themselves out of blasting-powder boxes or in tents with streams of water and sewage running parallel to each other. She lectured the manager of the largest open pit copper mine in the world who told her, "if we did build them accommodations, they would prefer staying where they are."[2] She rebuked the Greek government-sponsored Panhellenic Unions for exhorting the Greek immigrants to remember the fatherland and to return to it with their savings, while overlooking their illiteracy and appalling living conditions. She castigated feuding, illiterate priests as well.

Maria Economidou traveled three miles into the blackness of a Utah coal mine and called to a cluster of shadowy figures swinging picks, "Have life, young Cretans, the god of Crete be with you." The men froze, thinking an eerie voice was warning them of a cave-in. A six-foot young man cried at hearing the voice of a Greek woman.[3]

Maria Economidhou criticized mothers and sisters. An overworked, depressed young Greek showed Maria Economidou a letter from his mother: "Your poor orphaned sisters cross themselves and say prayers to God every night to keep you well and to succeed in your work because they expect help from you."[4] "Oh, sisters," the journalist wrote, "If you knew how dearly you pay for the dowry that your brother earns in America. If you knew the hardships he is subjected to, you would prefer to remain unmarried."[5]

She angrily describes three Greek officials who had come to Texas to buy horses for the Greek government. They had been in the area a month,

Maria Economidhou, Greek journalist who investigated the abysmal working and living conditions of Greek laborers throughout the United States from 1912–1915. From her book *E Ellines Tis Amerikis Opos Tous Ei-dha* (The Greeks in America as I saw them) (New York: D. C. Divry, 1916).

had met only horse breeders, and yet denounced everything American. The army officer had the effrontery to slap the face of a trolley conductor when he did not stop where he wanted. Yet Economidhou remembered Greek government officials at the steel factories of South Bethlehem, Pennsylvania,

Maria Economidhou with railroad section workers in the West. From her book *E Ellines Tis Amerikis Opos Tous Eidha* (The Greeks in America as I saw them) (New York: D. C. Divry, 1916).

who were "gentlemen . . . and this comforted me for the national shame that I felt."[6]

In Wilmington, North Carolina, she was amazed at an advertisement placed by the Presbyterian churches: "Go to church because it will help you with your employer. . . . Go to church you'll be rewarded in this world . . . in your business . . . in your profession."[7] Because she had been bred in mystical Orthodoxy, this practical, cynical advice repelled her.

In Little Rock, Arkansas, she was shocked at the treatment of blacks. At the Muskogee, Oklahoma, post office, she read army recruitment posters that promised three square meals a day, shoes to replace worn-out ones, teeth repaired, and wages continuing during one's illness. On reading this, she recalled a young Greek she had met on her travels who did not return to Greece to serve in the Balkan Wars of 1912–13. "I cannot close my eyes, because I did not go. . . . When I recall the oath I took when I enlisted as a soldier, my blood rises to my head."[8] "With us Greeks," she wrote to a local paper, "to serve our country is our religion."[9]

Throughout the United States, reservists answered Greece's call to return to fight the Turks in 1912 and the Bulgarians, who entered the war later. This puzzled Americans. At the time, Greece recognized no other citizenship but its own.

That night [in Kansas City, Missouri] along with 500 Greeks waving American and Greek flags, the men marched behind a band to the railroad station to cheer a contingent of Greeks from San Fran-

cisco on their way back to fight the Turks. The boys came to the train windows holding small Greek flags. "Long live the king of Greece! Long live the Greek army and navy!" and from the Greeks of Kansas City came another shout "Long live!"[10]

Throughout the United States, Greek reservists paraded down city streets with banners extolling their native country, the "land of liberty." Newspapers printed accounts of the Greeks, both reservists and volunteers, boarding ships for the war. Casualties were high among the inadequately trained volunteers.

King Constantine would say later that most of the forty-five thousand who came to Greece returned to the United States, many with village brides. With the end of the war, immigration resumed and now an increasing number of girls and young women began coming to the United States. The exact number cannot be given because immigrant women were not counted separately from the men until the Census of 1920. They were picture brides, their marriages arranged by male relatives already in the United States or in response to the young immigrants' writing to their parents asking for suitable brides. These brides were younger than the girls who had watched the young men leave towns and villages for America eight and ten years earlier. The girls left behind then had yearned for letters to the young men's parents asking for them, but they did not come. The girls were now young women in their late twenties, an age considered too old for marriage. Parents chose instead younger women who had been children when sons left for America.

A dread happening further cut off young women's hopes of being summoned to America as picture brides. Unaccountably, after a few years in America, a number of Greek men married American women. Editors, priests, and Greek government officials decried this unforeseen development. Editors cautioned the immigrants that American women were only interested in their wages. Maria Economidhou devoted a chapter of her book to "mixed marriages." Ninety-nine percent of these, she wrote, end badly. Women had a higher status in the United States than they did in Greece, and American women were almost always better educated than were Greek village women or immigrant men. Even though the American women the men came to know were waitresses, helpers in boardinghouses, and store clerks, they had the advantage of having been born American. Maria Economidhou says, "It is dangerous to attempt to place her in the position that Greek tradition reserves for women."

> The Greek woman has been taught that the girl and wife must do whatever the father says. . . . When the man steps into the house, the atmosphere is transformed into a barracks when an officer enters. . . . The Greek woman has heard from her mother that she must not have an opinion different from her husband's, that when her husband is worried, she should not talk to him, when he is angry she should be silent, and when he sometimes raises his hand, she should take it. . . . However, American women haven't been taught these ideas about married life. She considers herself the equal of a man.[11]

Maria Economidhou's observations were true. Marrying an American woman was risky for most immigrant men:

> *Then I decide to get married. But I started to be bald headed. I ask one good [American] girl to marry me, but she doesn't want me. Then I order a toupee and start to wear it and I look like a young and rich man. Then I go to dances and meet the [American] one I want. Then I ask her if she wants me and if we will get married, and she say, "Yes, I love you dear." Then after one month I am ready to get married.*
>
> *We send out invitations to our friends and they come to church about 500 people. Then the best man starts to change the wreaths on our heads, and my wreath catches on my toupee, it dropping down. The bride turns and looks at me, sees a bald headed man and starts to cry and insults me with all kinds of names. She calls taxi and goes away.*

Some of the people are laughing and some are saying "poor George, what is the matter?" "Too bad for you." Then I jump on a chair and say: "Ladies and gentlemen, the bride is going away because I am baldheaded but I will try to find another. [He never did.] You people come to my home to finish the lamb and wine and we will have a good time." . . . Do not camouflage. Be honest.—George (Gheorghios) Kyrianakos, Kastania, Vion Province[12]

The men were marrying ethnic women as well. They met them in the cotton mills and in Polish and Italian neighborhoods, where the men lived in boardinghouses and bachelor houses until Greek Towns became well established. Older immigrants counseled the younger men against marrying women who were not Greek:

Manolios in his simplicity was the incarnation of a good soul and of the proverbial Cretan hospitality. He gave us advice and watched over us with paternal affection and his love increased when he believed we would not marry the Polish girls. Most of the household chores [in their *bekiariko* (bachelor house)] that belonged to us, he did himself so that we wouldn't tire. If one of us caught a cold, he would leave his door open and if he coughed, he would go in at night to see if the cough had broken out and see if the sick person wanted something hot he could boil. . . . He left for Colorado to become a miner. We accompanied him as far as the station in Springfield. "Greek women, Greek women, no *ksenis,*" was his final message. . . . Whenever we meet . . . and his name comes up, we say, "A good hour to you, poor Manolios, if alive and God forgive you if you're dead."[13]

Laborers usually heeded such advice. They often contributed to passage for one among them to marry in Greece and to return with young women for them, the waiting bachelors. Immigration officials became suspicious of these lone men surrounded by women. Newspapers and magazines published reports of girls being sold to immigrants. Women detectives were stationed on ships and trains to watch for revelatory signs. Invariably, the bachelors complained that their friend had chosen "the best one for himself" and had charged too much for expenses. Yet so thankful were they for Greek wives that their complaints were momentary.

CHAPTER 20

PICTURE BRIDES

Young Greek women arrived, each sent by her family with a picture in hand to recognize the man she was to marry. A few women were fortunate to have a mother or father accompany them until the wedding took place, after which the parent returned to Greece. Several brides often traveled together, but most came alone and afraid. Future grooms wrote that the women should not bring their hand-woven dowry linens with them: "In America they have better, machine made." Families sometimes did not heed the advice and hump-backed trunks accompanied the brides. They were filled with woven and crocheted linens and bed-spreads the women and their mothers had worked on for years: raising silk-worms, soaking and spinning the thread; shearing sheep, carding, spinning, and dyeing the wool with nuts, berries, and herbs.

> *I didn't know what to expect when I was sent to America to marry him. I wasn't sure they had wedding crowns here so I brought my own. They were made of red silk roses.*[1]

> *I met him on Thursday. We were engaged that day, and on Sunday, we were married. The next day at the train station, he asked me to sit down and wait for him while he got tickets for Ann Arbor [Michigan]. When he left me alone, I was worried that I wouldn't recognize him when he'd come back to get me.*[2]

Not all women wanted to come. A song of those years begs:

> Don't send me, Mother, to *Ameriki*.
> I'll wither there and die.

Several women wanted to become nuns, but their parents refused permission. One ran away to a nunnery; her father followed and forced her to board ship and then travel to a Wyoming mining town, there to marry a man she did not know. The father of another woman who yearned to enter a nunnery took a stiletto out of his cummerbund and told his daughter she would marry the man chosen for her in New York or he would twist the knife inside her.

Other women wanted desperately to leave their villages: without dowries they would be unpaid servants to the entire family until they died. To escape, they conspired to achieve illegal entry, pretending to be married to immigrants already in America. A Cretan woman accomplished this by going to Hania with her brothers. There the brothers found a stranger on the street who agreed to a fake marriage in return for a small sum of money. The wedding certificate was presented to the French embassy, and she was given the necessary papers to leave for the United States, where she hoped to find a husband. Once, in America, her *horiani* (fellow villagers) arranged a marriage for her.[3]

By far, though, immigrant women pined for their villages and their people. More than homesickness fed the longings of women who had no male relatives in the country. In Greece, fathers, brothers, and uncles protected women against abusive husbands; in America they had to depend on their husbands' *filotimo* (self-respect), which was often lacking. The author recalls a story she heard as a child. An immigrant had left his wife and infant son in his village. After nine years, he sent them money to come to America. They crossed the ocean, the prairies, and the high mountain country. The train made a stop on a deserted sagebrush flat bounded by distant mountains. A man approached the wife, speaking the unfamiliar Roumeliot dialect.

He was an interpreter for a railroad gang fifteen miles away, where her husband was working. Her husband had not wanted to lose a day's wages to meet her. Frightened to be alone with a stranger, a violation of her culture's rigid code, she and her son rode in the wagon to meet the husband she had not seen for almost ten years.

If husbands had family members in the United States, the brides could not consider themselves *nykokyres* (ladies of the house). As in Greece, they would be under the authority of their husbands' families.

My mother had lived with her aunt in Tripolis most of her life, worked as a seamstress and kilim *(rug) weaver and from time to time made articles for her dowry. . . . She did not know my father because he had come to America at age 12 but the families knew each other. Her dowry items were packed and she was bringing with her a little money which she wanted to keep for herself for some emergency which might arise in the future. [She was traveling with her husband's father.]*

. . . Soon after the ship left the dock at Piraeus, grandfather asked Mama if she had any money. Mama was startled that he would ask about something so personal but answered that she did. He asked for her money which she reluctantly but obediently gave to him, but years later Mama told us she managed to hide a little money because she didn't know when she might need it and didn't want to be penniless.

When the ship docked in Italy, Mama anticipated being taken on a tour of the immediate area but grandfather decreed that Mama should remain on board while he disembarked with the other passengers. . . .

When they arrived in America, grandfather took Mama to his daughter's home in New York City where they prepared for the wedding. Mama was not consulted about any of the arrangements. . . . What should have been a beautiful time in her life was tempered by the unfriendly atmosphere around her. Soon after the wedding, she asked where she could find work to supplement my father's income. . . . She was given the address of a garment factory and the address of their apartment and put on a streetcar. Our dear flustered Mama clutched the piece of paper and managed to reach the factory where she somehow with gestures conveyed that she could do the work they needed.

To return home at the end of the work day, Mama had been told to board a streetcar at the same stop where she had got off in the morning, However, streetcars departed from the corner for various destina-

tions and Mama boarded the wrong streetcar. When she realized after a time that she should have reached home, she panicked and showed the conductor her address again. He . . . left her off at the next corner. Dazed, she looked around trying to determine what she could do. A kindly woman noticed that she was troubled and helped her find her way home. And after that trauma, she had to worry about whether the family would believe her. . . . That experience must have had a very strong, lasting effect on her because many times in her lifetime, she went out of her way to be helpful to new immigrants who found themselves in similar circumstances.[4]

In 1917 my grandfather sent for his wife and the daughter he had never seen. With money in hand, Alexandra Shukas and her seven-year-old daughter walked the several days it took to cross the Albanian border. [Although ethnic Greek, Alexandra Shukas spoke only Albanian.] They then made their way to the Greek port of Patras where passage was secured for America. . . . [they] arrived in Chicago . . . with no inkling that my grandfather—now in the army—would not be able to meet them.[5]

After three weeks in third class, the brides, yellow from seasickness, unable to wash themselves properly, afraid that no one would meet them, arrived in Ellis Island. They survived the interrogation by Greek-speaking interviewers and the physical examination. Most often they were directed to trains and with tags tied to their lapels began their journeys to New York City, Chicago, Grand Rapids, Atlanta; to cities and towns throughout the alien country.

All through the day birds swooped down to the arid earth and soared into the unbounded blue sky. Jackrabbits streaked away from the roar of the train. A coyote, tossed to the side by a passing train, lay swollen and stiff. Crows exploded from the carcass at the engine's noise, but greed brought them back, huge black maggots continuing their feast. Somewhere she would be forced out of the car, Emilia knew. A man resembling the dark, mustached Anti-Christ on church icons would be waiting. Pain struggled in her skull. The people about her blurred. She leaned her head against a grayed napkin, and darkness fell before her.[6]

The eagerly waiting grooms and their friends stood on railroad platforms, at times with a small band of Greek musicians. In western mining towns, Italian bands were hired to greet the brides. With strains of "O Sole Mio" and operatic arias in the air, the brides, hard put to look presentable after three weeks on board ship and days sitting in a coach car, stepped down to meet the men chosen for them.

The pictures the brides and grooms held did not always match the young women and men facing each other. Chicanery ruled: a younger, prettier sister's picture; a photograph of a better-looking friend with a full head of hair, or of the handsome American movie actor Rudolph Valentino, brought dismay. Nothing could be done; *filotimo* on the men's part decreed that they should accept what fate had sent them; and having nowhere to turn, the women sighed over their fate and the wedding took place.

Most couples accepted their lot as fated: the women, who otherwise would have remained unmarried and a servant to their relatives; the men because they would again have the comfort of wives to cook Greek food, to wash their clothes, and to celebrate their name days appropriately. They expected to return to Greece soon with a young family and savings that would enable them to become shopkeepers or owners of property and rise above their birthright as laborers.

The engagement and wedding traditions of *patridha* were absent. There were no girls singing while the bride's hair was washed; while the groom was shaved; while the decorated horse or mule carried the dowry to the house of the groom's parents; while they sang of the groom as an eagle, his bride as a dove or partridge; while the bread for the wedding dinner was baked in the parents' ovens; while the bride hesitated at the door of her new home—all were missing. Parents, brothers, sisters, the clan were needed to fulfill the centuries-old rites. The brides at least were spared having their wedding-night sheets displayed in the light of day.

In their old age women related the "homesickness that has no cure" that they had suffered, alone in a strange land, strangers for husbands, tears they cried when the autocratic men were not around, the ache to be back in the familiar villages with their own people.

True immigrant life began. The cramped city apartments and the three- and four-room mine and mill company houses were better than the huts and rock homes they had come from. At least there were privies outside, whereas in Greece they were almost unknown; people relieved themselves at the edges of the garden. Also in Greece, women and girls had to carry water from village wells or walk a long distance to streams and rivers. Most unusual, in America all women wore hats, the prerogative in *patridha* only for those in the middle class and above. Village women came wearing head scarves, a sign of modesty for wives, but immediately they put on hats at their husbands' insistence, so they would not look like peasants. The women happily accepted this release from custom, but they retained everything else that was possible in this *ksenitia*. It gave them a security that the world had not been completely turned upside down.

At night houses were lighted by the faint glow of vigil lights burning before icons. Each bride now became mistress of her house. A Greek proverb proclaims, "The mother is the column *(stylos)* of the house." Although Greek culture gave her a subordinate role, she was free to take charge of her domain. To reach this supremacy women since antiquity have given themselves worth by taking over the entire responsibility of home, children and their discipline, and religious duties. The supremacy was won at enormous emotional costs: the mother became the scapegoat for the inevitable crags in family life; the illness of a child was vaguely her fault; as children struggled against old-country values, a lack in her was exposed; and on her was laid the failure of her husband to progress.

Wherever the women found themselves—in Greek Towns, in apartments, in small houses with backyards where they planted gardens and tended them with the wonders of America (plenty of water with the turn of a tap, and often an outdoor domed oven for bread-baking)—they transplanted their Greek village culture to the new land. They relied on dream books to tell them what lay in store for them. The woman who could read was held in esteem and favored above all others.

Mothers were not demonstrative toward their children. They showed their love for children by their extreme concern over their eating enough, their being strong to fight off the childhood illnesses that killed so many of the young in villages. Food and the mother were inextricably bound. The Greeks knew, as if instinctively, that sharing food had an emotional value, not found in all cultures: "the first step in understanding mothers is in understanding the special place which food has in a family."[7] Food was more than a Greek family ritual or social occasion; it was a bond. In America, too, mothers had more available than the food of the poor—corn, beans, and squash.

Mothers taught their children that bread was holy; it was not only for sustenance, but with wine consecrated in the chalice, it became the Body and Blood of Christ. "No one would think of speaking profanely with bread in hand."[8] If a piece of bread fell, mothers told the child to kiss it, make the sign of the cross, and eat it; if it were dirtied, the bread was burned; it was never thrown into a garbage pail.

A page from one of the ubiquitous dream books, this one belonging to the author's mother. A camel has many meanings for a dreamer, signifying an enemy plot in court cases; a well-loaded camel means future wealth. Author's collection.

Κάμηλος. —Ἐν βλέπῃς κάμηλον εἰς τὸν ὕπνον σου, εἰς δίκας καὶ εἰς κρισολογίας θέλεις περιπέσῃ, ἔτι δὲ καὶ ἐπιβουλὴν ἐχθρῶν σημαίνει ἡ κάμηλος. Ἂν βλέπῃς καραβάνιον ὁλόκληρον καμήλων, πορευόμενον εἰς τὴν ἔρημον, πλούτη μέλλοντα νὰ προέλθουν ἐκ τοῦ ταξειδίου ἢ ἐκ μελετωμένης ἄλλης τινὸς ἐπιχειρήσεως. Ἐὰν κάθησαι ἐπὶ καμήλου, ματαίαν πολυτέλειαν καὶ κενὰς ἐπιδείξεις ἐπιζητεῖς, διὰ τὰ ὁποῖα θέλεις ἐπισύρῃ τὴν χλεύην καὶ τὸν μυκτηρισμὸν τοῦ κόσμου. Ἐν γένει ἡ κάμηλος σημαίνει ἐπιβουλὰς ἀδυνάτου ἐχθροῦ, ὠφελοῦντος μᾶλλον ἢ βλάπτοντος· προσέτι δὲ καὶ κέρδη διὰ πλεονεξίαν καὶ πολλάκις δηλοῖ βλάβην εἰς τὸ γόνυ ἢ τὸν πόδα, ἣν θέλεις ὑποστῇ ἕνεκεν ἀπροσεξίας.

Although meat was cheap and available in the new land, mothers would not cook it on Wednesdays and Fridays, when parishioners may receive the Eucharist.

Immigrant mothers kept intact the attitudes they had learned in Greece: boy babies were more valued than girl babies (girls would be married off to strangers and their loyalties would be transferred to their husbands); the oldest son had a special place in a family (he would take care of the parents in old age); the youngest child, whether girl or boy, would be pampered; boys had a responsibility for their sisters; and godfathers and male relatives would be given special attention.[9]

The mothers spoke in proverbs, adhered to the superstitions they had learned from their mothers, especially the incantations for dispelling the Evil Eye, which afflicted children with fevers and malaise.

When she [her baby] was three months old . . . we stopped to see a woman who lived nearby [the post office]. . . . She kissed it and hugged it and said so many complimentary things about the baby's beautiful eyes. . . . By the time we left, the baby was stiff and burning with fever. . . . Dr. Slopansky told me double pneumonia, but the baby did not have pneumonia. Her skin was yellow like a lemon. The doctor told me to stop nursing the baby and Mrs. Felice, an Italian neighbor, nursed the baby until my aunt, Mrs. Kisamitakis, came with her children and

Among the earliest of Greek American children, 1904. Photographed in New York City by Jacob Riis. By permission of the Museum of the City of New York.

stayed a month to nurse the baby and take care of it. [She] knew how to dispel the Evil Eye. . . . First of all she would say, "In the name of the Father, Son, and Holy Spirit." . . . Then she said a prayer half secretively . . . about devils and nereids [the beautiful and dangerous phantasms]. And then she measured the baby. Took the baby and measured the baby. Took the diaper and measured the baby from the elbow to the fingers and did this several times. If the diaper did not reach to [the] fingertips, it meant that the baby had the Evil Eye. She did this three times because the number three [for the Trinity] is a holy number to the Greeks.—Athena Kissamitakis Pallios[10]

Other traditions had difficulty surviving in the new land. In Greece, custom and the shortage of arable land forced the disinterment of bodies. America's wide spaces did not require disinterment and no one knew whether vampires had possessed the dead or not. They did, though, conjecture about it.

In the Mountain West during the early 1900s, young Greeks gathered in a coffeehouse to discuss the funeral of a compatriot who had been killed in a mine accident. They talked about vampires and wondered if they existed in America. As a trick they appointed a braggart to go to the graveyard at midnight when vampires tried to enter the graves of the newly buried. At midnight the miner reached the graveyard, not knowing that the men had dispatched one among them to be at the grave covered with a sheet and with a burning miner's lamp on his head. When the miner began walking toward the grave, an apparition arose from the gravestones moaning horribly, its yellow "eye" bright in the blackness. Pulling a gun from his belt, the miner fired at the yellow eye. The apparition fell to the ground and the miner ran back to the coffeehouse shouting, "There are too vampires in America! I just killed one!"

In the fatherland, also, witches *(maghisses)* could put death spells on people; subterfuges were required in America. Two brothers from a mountain village in the Peloponnese were in business together and lived with their wives in the same house. The older brother began to lose weight and doctors were unable to find a cause for it. Soon the patient became bedridden. His wife feared a curse had been put on him and suspected her sister-in-law. She wrote to the village from which she and her sister-in-law had emigrated and learned that a curse did exist. The sister-in-law had cut a small piece of her brother-in-law's underwear and sent it to the village witch. The witch then traced the outline of the cloth on a piece of soap. Each morning with incantations, she poured hot water on the soap to melt it. The older brother died within days after his wife received an answer to her letter.[11]

Voices from the Virgin and saints warning villagers of pending loss or needing watchfulness that were common in Greece disappeared once the immigrants landed. America was not holy land. "Did Christ cross the ocean?" they asked.

The mothers fasted for forty days before the great church days; husbands "worked hard" and were exempt. Mothers prayed before the family icons; each day they tended the votive light, adding olive oil to the glass of water and a fresh taper to float on it. As they crossed themselves, they addressed the deity: "*Panaghia mou* (my Virgin, specifically All-Holy)"; *Hristos ke Panaghia* (Christ and the All-Holy)"; most often they prayed to *Hristouli,* the diminutive word for Christ. On leaving the house and entering it, they made the

A New York City baptism, 1922. The guests are wearing small baptismal medallions. Courtesy of Olga M. Coucourakis.

sign of the cross and they tried to avoid unnecessary household tasks on Tuesdays, the day the holy City, Constantinople, fell to the Turks.

They grew basil plants in abundance. Basil was not used in cooking. It was a sign of friendship; it was holy, recalling the spot where the scent of basil growing in the barren Holy Land led the Empress Helen to the True Cross, the day commemorated as the Exaltation of the Cross. Priests dipped small bunches of basil in holy water to sprinkle believers on Epiphany, when during Christ's baptism by Saint John "a voice came from heaven, 'Thou art my beloved Son, with whom I am well pleased.'"[12] Priests immersed basil in holy water to sprinkle, cleanse, and bless houses and new ventures.

The mothers baked bread for liturgies, pressing a wooden stamp on the risen dough with the carved acronym for Jesus—IXTHUS (IHTHUS), Greek for Jesus Christ Son of God Savior, also the ancient Greek word for fish, another symbol of Christ, the fisher of souls.

Greek women could not rest until their infants were baptized. Although Orthodoxy says little about deaths of the unbaptized, mothers were inconsolable when one died, haunted by the child's burial in an unconsecrated grave, mourning that the child would not meet God. At baptism the baby would have been submerged three times for the Father, Son, and Holy Spirit and three wisps of its hair would have been cut by the priest and dropped into the baptismal waters as a gift to God. Since ancient times a person's hair was his prized possession.

The Christian fish symbol, in Greek IHTHUS (fish), is also the acronym for Jesus Christ Son of God Savior. The acronym for Jesus Christ Conquers is carved into a wooden disk which is stamped on the dough before the bread that will be consecrated with wine for communion is baked. Author's sketch.

When an infant or a child died, mothers and godmothers dressed the baby in white, placed a wedding crown on the small head; a miniature gold band on the ring finger of the right hand, the hand that makes the sign of the cross; and sat at the side of the coffin and sang the *mirologhia*, the laments for the dead.[13] They railed against jealous Hades, god of the underworld, a deity unrecognized in any form by Greek Orthodoxy: "If Hades had two children and one was taken from him, then he would know how I feel." They keened:

> Where are you going, my little pigeon, to make your nest?
> If you make it on the mountain, snow will ruin it,
> If you make it on the seashore, a wave will ruin it,
> And if you make it underground, snakes will ruin it.
> Where did you go, my little pigeon, to make your nest?
> And withered my mouth and burned my heart?[14]

Cretans brought an unusual custom for children's burials. At baptism a godfather tied the baby's hands and feet with a ribbon connected to him. The ribbon was saved; if the child died, its hands and feet were again tied with the ribbon during the liturgy for the dead. Before the final closing of the casket the ribbon was cut.

The night after burial, the mother of such a child dreamed that her little girl was still bound hand and foot and could not play with other children. She would not rest until the grave was dug up and the casket opened.

The ribbon, as she had dreamed, had not been cut. The ritual was then completed.[15]

Because many unmarried laborers were killed in accidents, in cities and towns women noted for keening the *mirologhia* sang the laments as the men lay in their caskets, dressed as bridegrooms. The ancient custom of breaking the vessel used to wash the body had no opportunity to become established in America; funeral attendants took over the old, vital duty of preparing the dead for burial. After washing the body, the attendants wrapped it in a shroud, the *savanon,* of four or six yards of muslin, as mourners had instructed. New clothing was put over the *savanon,* unless the dead person had asked to be buried in a previously worn suit or dress. If he was unmarried, a wedding crown was placed on his head. If he had been married, what was to be done with the wedding crowns, the *stefana,* in glass boxes next to the family icons, depended on the *topos* from which he had come. They were the property of the widow. She could cut the ribbon uniting the wreaths and place one at the side of her husband's body; she could burn both; or she could keep them in their case and have them buried with her when she died. A widower depended on women to tell him what should be done with the wreaths.

The women performed all other rites of mourning: burning frankincense on coal stoves to purify the house, placing coins on the dead person's closed eyes, and breaking a plate before leaving his or her house. In ancient days the coin was to pay the ferryman taking the dead to the underworld, but the women did not know the reason for this custom or for breaking the plate: "That's how it has always been done."

On the day of the funeral, someone was left in the house to prevent the dead person's soul, which was unwilling to begin its journey, from entering. Relatives and friends followed the casket to the church and to the cemetery. For a few years in America, men followed custom and attended services without shirt collars and unshaven, reminders that in the presence of death attention to appearance was vanity.

Following the burial, mourners assembled in the dead person's house, or in a Greek boardinghouse for bachelors. A fish dinner was served in remembrance of Christ. The funeral dinner was called *makaria* (feast of blessing) or *parigoria* (consolation). A few days later the room the dead person had used was thoroughly cleaned and all the bedclothes and articles in it were washed. Often the clothing was burned. Immigrants from the area around Sparta also burned the mattress. A priest was then summoned to purify the house with incense and holy water.

After forty days of deep mourning, during which widows did not leave their houses, family and friends attended a memorial service held with the

Young mothers and un-married women, dressed as brides, were buried in Death Wedding ceremonies. The wife of George Dokos, Pelopon-nesus, in her wedding dress. At her funeral she was buried in this dress, her veil, and a wedding crown. Courtesy of Andrew G. Dokos.

Sunday liturgy. Over a mound of wheat called *kolyvo* or *kolyva*, the priest asked of God that the soul of the dead be like the good wheat that is sown and grows again. The requiem for the dead commemorated the forty days that Christ wandered the earth before ascending to Heaven. The dead had now met God. Memorial wheat is made of boiled, sweetened wheat, nuts, raisins or currants, Jordan almonds, pomegranate seeds, and parsley. Wheat, nuts, especially almonds, and pomegranate seeds are symbols of immortal-ity; parsley represents the greenness of the other world; sugar or honey sig-nifies its sweetness.

Eating the *kolyvo* was done in remembrance of the dead and in mutual forgiveness if the dead and living had wronged each other. Memorial food has come down from pagan times. Aristophanes' Lysistrata mocks an old deputy: "What do you mean by not dying? . . . . I myself will knead you a honey cake at once."[16] *Kolyva* was and is prepared and commemorated in yearly memorial services. Services may also be held six months after death, on the third anniversary, and on the Saturday of Souls.

Young mothers in the new land rarely had older women relatives to help them with marriages, births, baptisms, and deaths. In the cities and towns, *mamis* (midwives) delivered babies and saved the women from the ignominy of having a male doctor attend them. The midwives were most often unlettered and had learned their profession from older women, usually their mothers. Mothers in Chicago and later in Milwaukee were fortunate to have the services of a professional midwife. Maria Krommyda was one of nine midwives listed in a 1922 Greek business directory; seven practiced in New York and two in Manchester, New Hampshire. In 1906, she left her village near Delphi and went to Athens, where she earned a diploma. After a seven-year practice in Greece, she came to America, married, and had four children, two of whom survived. She continued delivering babies and wrote a manual for mothers and children. Her husband tore up the manuscript and burned it. Krommyda rewrote it secretly and had it published. It went into four printings.[17]

Wherever Greek women had others nearby to help with their births and childhood illnesses, nostalgia for their villages was somewhat tempered. Many women, though, found themselves alone in hamlets, mining camps, and small towns. They pined for their villages and for the sound of a Greek voice.

> *I was the only Greek woman in the railroad town. I was so lonely that I baked cookies and sat on the porch waiting for the school children to come by. I had them eat the cookies and didn't understand what they were saying, but at least I heard the sound of human voices.*—Thelma (Anastasia) Triandafels Siouris, Vitina, Province Ghiortinia[18]

Although it was common for Greek women to have their husbands' brothers and cousins living with the family, those in the Midwest and West had an additional burden in their young years. Mine and mill owners at first had no intention of providing housing for the thousands of incoming immigrants. The responsibility for housing them rested on young wives—so their culture told them. Fatigued from baking bread in earthen ovens and tending gardens, from sleepless nights with sick children—families of eight children were common—they sighed and carried out its dictates. Mothers had time only for the basic care of their children. In Greece, grandmothers and great-grandmothers did much of the child rearing. Few of them had come to America, so children were not lulled to sleep with the *yiayias' nanourismata* (lullabies):

> Sleep, who takes the little ones, come and take this one
> small small I bring him to you, return him big to me
> big as a tall mountain, tall as a cypress,
> its branches to reach east and west.
> Sleep, sleep, sleep, sleep,
> my little baby should.
> Come, sleep, take him
> and sweetly lull him to sleep.[19]

Eleni Papoulis Koulouris of Mavrolithari, Fthiotis Province, Roumeli, recalled: "[My sister-in-law and I] boarded forty men. We had to go to the river for water. We had two chairs. We had to eat standing up."[20]

Argyro Koustourakis Georgelas of Lekokitinora, Crete, remembered:

When the men brought me their clothes to wash on their way to work, I had them drop them by the fence. Then I would lift them up with a long stick and drop them into a tub of water boiling over a fire in the yard—because they were crawling with lice.[21]

Just as men were saved from loneliness, nativist hostility, and injustices in their work, women found solace in handiwork. Late at night, as they sat under dangling light globes, their hands "flew" as their tired bodies relaxed and their thoughts concentrated, not on crying babies and demanding husbands, but on the beauty that evolved as they worked. Women with some education, especially those who had had a few years' schooling under French nuns, did intricate solid cutwork, tatting, delicate embroidery, and crochet. Less-educated women relied on embroidery and crochet. They had come to America because they did not have a dowry, the *prika,* but they did bring the small dowry, their *prikia*—tablecloths, sheets, pillowcases, and other hand-woven pieces of beautiful artistry. "A Greek woman could marry a Greek man in the US without a prika, but without her prikia she could not make a home. . . . I could see that embroidery, lace, and woven textiles offered in some cases the only thread women had leading them through the labyrinth of time passed and geography crossed to homelands left behind."[22]

While women were bearing children and their husbands easing out of labor to become owners of small stores and restaurants, the world beyond

Greek immigrants took their Greek and American flags everywhere: weddings, baptisms, communal celebrations, and picnics. Ca. 1915–20. Courtesy of Thalia and Katherine Papachristos.

Greek Towns pressed in on them with invectives and demands that they "go back where they came from." Mothers seldom ventured out of their Greek neighborhoods, and when they did, they took their small children with them as translators and for security; for who, they thought, would accost an immigrant woman with children? However, they felt the contempt of sales clerks who pretended they could not understand what the mothers wanted. Speaking the few words they knew, mothers had to contend with the widespread hostility toward people who were not American. This hostility continued through the decades. In an application to Harvard, a young Greek American woman wrote:

> There is not another place [other than the South] where life is so deliberately slow, rhythmic, and oddly beautiful. I love it. . . . My father was raised in New York in a Greek family and my mother moved to the United States in her twenties. The South seems to have a problem with foreigners. I hate the way my mother is treated. I have encountered a few-too-many genteel ladies in the supermarket who coyly ask her, "My what an interesting accent, where are you from?" and grin patronizingly as they wait for an answer. I have lived my whole life in Georgia and am still trying to discover in which locked attic the Southerners have hidden hospitality.[23]

CHAPTER 21

STRIKES AND STRIKEBREAKERS

The nationalism of Greek immigrants was only one target for American hostility. Americans expected immigrants to leave their language and customs at Ellis Island, and it was especially galling to them that the immigrants sent money back to their families. The anger filtered down to children. An essay written by a Utah fifth grader was published in a local paper in 1912: "In our mining camps, we can, if we will, stop the Greeks and Japs from their work, and give our own men and boys a chance for work, giving them the money instead of others, who send it to Greece, and Japan, and other places, we might be rich now."[1]

The American press complained that the "unassimilable" immigrants took money from the country but gave nothing in return. The cheap labor they supplied for America's burgeoning industry and the role of employers who sought their brawn were ignored. When immigrants realized that laborers could strike for better living and working conditions and higher pay, the Greeks were ready to join the great push toward unionization. They began tentatively at the end of the first decade of the 1900s. By the second decade they were deeply involved in strikes throughout the United States. Greeks went on strike in the New York fur district,[2] in the Chicago railyards, in the New England mills, and in industrial enclaves throughout the Midwest and West. Their participation in the Lowell cotton mill strike in the early 1900s gave rise to a militancy that until then had been ineffectual, suppressed by their culture's acceptance of employers' rights over their employees.

In Lowell, Massachusetts, in 1910, Greeks as well as many other immigrant groups—Portuguese, Poles, and smaller numbers of Lithuanians, Russians, Turks, and Armenians—were working in the cotton mills, where jobs were plentiful.[3] Lowell's Greek community was the third largest in the country (after New York and Chicago). Lowell also had the greatest number of the new immigrants, those from southern Europe and the Balkans. Their numbers and cohesive bond greatly influenced the labor activism of the early 1900s. "[Beginning in 1903, for nine years] non-unionized workers waged a series of sporadic, partial strikes. . . . At times, the Greeks fought for higher pay; on other occasions, they waged narrow protests that called for management to rehire a Greek operative or fire a weaver who had worked on the Orthodox Christmas."[4]

Because of the large number of Greeks in the mills, labor leaders needed their support. When the mill workers walked off their jobs, the Greeks sought the help of their respected representative, Dr. George Demopoulos. The physician was afraid that alignment with the radical unionists, the Industrial Workers of the World (IWW), would bring censure to the Greeks and spread to their Market Street colony. "The sense of ethnic identity was especially strong among the Greeks. . . . Despite regional differences, the Greeks' Orthodox beliefs and strong nationalist sentiments added to their identity as a group apart."[5]

The Greek strikers held their own protest meetings and refused relief from the strike committee, taking charge of welfare needs themselves. They also decided against joining the IWW, which mitigated concerns of officials that the Greeks would revolt.

> While the UTW [United Textile Workers] was willing to settle [the strike] for less than a 15% increase, its members would not return without an explicit offer from the mills. . . . Demopoulos blasted the mayor as a hypocrite who had campaigned as the workers' friend but betrayed them when they needed support. Angrily denouncing the proposal as an insult to the workers' intelligence, the physician told the Greeks, that "you have been working in the mills all your life and you know what is needed to live without giving it another try." . . . The strike committee rejected Demopoulos' proposal to challenge the speedup of machinery and the increase in number of machines tended by individual workers (the stretch-out); by requiring meetings over future disputes, however, the strikers created the framework for discussing such practices . . . five mills quickly came to terms. The Hamilton's agent, Stephen Whittier, balked at meeting with his striking employees but, faced with Demopoulos' ultimatum that no mill would reopen unless the Hamilton settled, Whittier capitulated.[6]

On 20 April, children holding IWW pennants and wearing red IWW sashes led a parade of more than ten thousand marchers, celebrating the strike

George Miamis, a Greek spinner, Merrimack Mills, Massachusetts, ca. 1903. From *Labor's Heritage* 8 n. 2. Lowell Museum Collection/Lowell Historical Society.

victory. The Greeks followed, several thousand of them with their Lowell Cadet Band. In October, Demopoulos and several hundred Greeks left for the Balkan War; by then their connection to Local 436 was severed.

The Lowell strike was peaceful compared to those in the American West. In Grays Harbor, Washington, in 1912, Greek timber workers went on strike under IWW auspices. The combination of a union, Americans, and Greeks was called "Reds, Whites, and Greeks."[7] "Consider the conduct of the "Greek strike" of 1912 which took place under IWW auspices in Hoquiam, WA, a major timber products center. . . . Its resolution offers some

Greek lumber workers, Big Creek Logging Company, Knappa, Oregon, early 1900s. Courtesy of Thomas Doulis.

insight into the relationship of class to nationality in the U.S. and into the significance of race in the great Northwestern woods."[8]

Until 1900, Americans made up the labor force in the mills, augmented by an increasing number of Scandinavian immigrants entering the timber country. Although the Scandinavians were treated with contempt because they did not speak English, "ethnic impulses often drew Scandinavians into nativist alliances with other 'white' workers. A racial construction binding 'Anglo-Saxon' and 'Nordic' workers into a common tribal stock produced powerful alliances against workers of other 'races.'"[9]

Union workers were a minority. When R. F. Lytle, president of the Hoquiam mill, fired the union men, they were replaced by Greeks. When the IWW opened membership to non-English speaking people, the Greeks joined. The strike was then disdainfully called "the Greek strike." Mill owners countered that from then on they would have dealings only with Americans and American citizens. The ISWUA [International Shingle Weavers' Union of America] realized the risk as well as the potential of reaching out to the immigrants, who had been readily welcomed into the IWW: "What was the real complaint against the Greeks when they came here five years ago? . . . Why they lowered wages . . . they made "white" men work for less. . . . BUT these very Greeks are leading the fight for higher wages and better conditions. . . .

And business men blindly take up the old cry when the occasion for the old cry is gone and when the Greeks have learned enough to demand better working conditions for themselves and their fellow workers. . . . The Greeks are fighting for the best interest of Hoquiam."[10]

All the mills in Aberdeen closed, and the strike reached into Raymond and South Bend. Greeks were said to be arming themselves with revolvers. This propaganda inspired one hundred people of Hoquiam's middle class to form a "special police force." The vigilantes armed themselves with shotguns, rifles, revolvers, and clubs; they met at the Lytle mill and arrested any worker who said he was not going to work. They were then packed into boxcars on the Northern Pacific railroad tracks. Fifty Finns and one hundred Greeks who refused to report for work were deported. The vigilantes continued, though, to persecute the Greeks, Slavs, and "Red" Finns. The mill owners' proposal appeared in the *Daily Washingtonian* on 6 April with the headline, "Hoquiam Is to Be a White Man's Town." The proposal included a wage of $2.25 per day for "white" labor.

The campaign singled out the IWW, which citizens had come to associate with the "racially undesirable" Greeks and the "un-American" Finnish Socialists.[11] Most mill hands returned to work at the higher wage of $2.25 per day, but they also had been influenced by the employers' racism. In the mayoral elections that followed, the immigrants had no say, since they had not yet become citizens. The ISWUA immediately returned to its nativist position: "The Greeks had been embraced for short-term tactical reasons but clearly not from a committed sense of worker internationalism."[12]

The initial role of Greeks in the Intermountain West as strikebreakers quickly metamorphosed into that of strikers who would have to face the mine companies' and the National Guard's machine guns. They joined strikes and led them, even though they would lose wages committed to dowries and family mortgages and risked being blacklisted in mines throughout the area. Whenever they found that they were being paid less than Americans, or that they were being cheated on the weighing machines, or when they saw a chance for escape from paying bribes to *padrones,* the Greeks struck with a tenaciousness that astonished workers and brought them abuse in newspapers and the contempt of Americans. In small strikes the men were almost all from the Greek mainland. The unique characteristic of the big strikes in coal and mineral mines, however, is that they were led by Cretans. A 1912 copper strike in Utah and Nevada became one of the most important in the metal mining industry.

In 1912, the Western Federation of Labor called a strike in the Bingham, Utah, copper mines; McGill, Nevada, would follow.[13] The federation had tried to interest the Greeks in unionization for several years but had been unsuccessful. The Greeks still intended to return to the fatherland. Their only interest in labor was to get out of it, each to become his "own boss." It was important to the Western Federation to have the support of the Greeks, the largest group of workers. In saloons and boardinghouses, the labor organizers, called Bolsheviks, Wobblies, and agitators, made a pact with the Greeks: if they became members of the federation, a condition of the strike would be the firing of Leonidas Skliris as their labor agent. The Greeks in a body, twelve hundred of them, signed at once, and jubilantly ran up and down the streets of Bingham, Utah, shooting off guns.

Fifty National Guard sharpshooters, on order of Governor William Spry, and twenty-five deputy sheriffs from Salt Lake City were sent to the town. Gambling halls were closed, and mines and railroad crossings were floodlighted. The strikers took blankets and guns and barricaded themselves on the mountainside. This tactic harked back to insurrections against the Turks. (In the "Greek Strike," a year earlier in the Utah coal mines, Cretans took food, blankets, and guns and established themselves behind boulders, sagebrush, and junipers on a high mountainside. They splattered bullets around the American workers walking toward the mine for the day shift. Heavily armed mine guards returned fire and waited for the Cretans to use up their food, water, and bullets. The strikers held out unaccountably: fellow Cretans from twenty or more mining camps in nearby canyons were climbing over the mountains at night and bringing supplies.)

The union spoke of wages, but the Greeks, almost all Cretans, "famed as men who, when the spirit moves them to fight, are difficult to control" made the firing of Skliris their first goal. The Cretans were supported by the Greek-language newspaper published in Salt Lake City, *O Evzone,* named for the white-kilted Greek palace guards.

A Greek priest, Father Vasilios Lambrides, wearing his black robes and *kalimafkion,* climbed the mountain to exhort the men to refrain from violence. The Greeks took off their caps in respect to him but became enraged when the Utah Copper manager, R. C. Gemmel, steadfastly upheld Skliris. Strikebreakers were brought in, most of them unemployed Greeks sent in on Skliris's orders through his connections with Greek labor agents in Pocatello, Idaho, and Denver, Colorado. The strikebreakers were from the Greek mainland; enmity between them and the Cretan strikers never healed.

Gunfights among strikers, deputies, and strikebreakers erupted, killing two Greeks and wounding many men on both sides. The strike caused intense suffering among the union members and their families; business and transportation were seriously affected throughout the county; and ore production

Louis Tikas, the "Martyr of Ludlow" (second from right), with John Lawson, United Mine Workers organizer (second from left), 1913. Courtesy, Colorado Historical Society F6693.

fell drastically through the inefficiency of the strikebreakers. The strike gradually ended with the union unrecognized. However, it broke the power of Leonidas Skliris.

In 1913 a strike was called in the southern Colorado coal mines. When a Cretan came to Bingham looking for strikebreakers, several former strikers returned with him to Trinidad, Colorado. The Colorado Coal Strike of 1913–14 began in mines owned by John D. Rockefeller, Jr. Seventy-two people were killed.[14] Again Cretans became leaders; among them was Louis Tikas (Elias Spandithakis) from the village of Loutra near Rethymnon, Crete. He had arrived in the United States in 1906. As a coffeehouse owner in Denver, Colorado, he was known for befriending countrymen needing shelter, speaking with American officials on their behalf, and writing letters to their villages. Tikas became an interpreter and then an organizer in the northern Colorado mines.

When the United Mine Workers called the strike on 23 September 1913, hundreds of miners left their company houses. They loaded children, rickety furniture, straw bedding, and cooking utensils into wagons, and made their way during an early snowfall down the muddy roads of Delagua and Berwind canyons. Many miners pulled top-heavy carts. Eight to ten thousand miners followed into the tent towns put up by the union, the largest of which was Ludlow. Louis Tikas became the leader of the Ludlow colony.

A report to the governor of Colorado said: "The most forceful portion of the colonists were Greeks. We do not know that they outnumbered the other nationalities in the colony, but we are positive that they dominated it. The will of the Greeks was the law of the colony. They were the most aggressive element, the fighting men. . . . Such was their position and authority that although many of the nations had leaders of their own, the Greek leader [Tikas] was the master of the tented city."[15]

Clashes between strikers and mine guards, and later National Guardsmen, brought in ostensibly to keep the peace, continued throughout the winter in the mining camps surrounding Trinidad, Colorado, killing guards, strikers, and children. The Cretans were acknowledged for their cunning. As some of them had come from the Balkan Wars, rumors spread that their strategy had been learned on the battlefield and that they had brought a good supply of Greek-made bullets.

On 19 April 1914, Greek Easter (Julian Calendar), Tikas and his Greeks barbecued lambs and danced old native folk dances, several of the men in Cretan *vrakes*. The next day, the Colorado National Guard moved against the colony. The guard said later that the day was chosen because word had come that the Greeks were planning an assault as part of their celebration. The Cretans maintained that the soldiers expected the Greeks to be dazed from drinking wine and unprepared for attack.

In the early morning, guardsmen fired on the Ludlow tent colony, killing five men and a boy. The strikers ran to their stations and began firing across the road at the soldiers. In many of the tents, holes had been dug and covered with planks as hiding places for women and children during gunfire. Tikas tried throughout the day to lead women and children to a deep, dry river bed for safety. By afternoon he was able to bring small groups to the *arroyo*, while the noise of strikers' bullets and the guards' machine guns increased and came closer.

The tents caught fire; two women and eleven children hiding in the dugouts suffocated. Seeing the impossibility of getting all the women and children to the river bed, Tikas raised a white cloth of truce and approached a National Guard officer, who broke a rifle over his head. Then Tikas and two others were pushed into the crossfire of strikers and guardsmen. Tikas fell, riddled with bullets, and would become known as the "Martyr of Ludlow."

His coffin covered with flowers, had headed the procession for the dead women and children. Then it was brought back to the mortuary to await the arrival of Father Paschopoulos from Denver. . . . Ragged, weary men file[d] by Tikas' body all day, their eyes glassy

The funeral of Louis Tikas, Trinidad, Colorado, 1914. Courtesy, Colorado Historical Society F6711.

from lack of sleep. They touched Louis' forehead, then crossed themselves and muttered a prayer. . . . On the twenty-seventh Father Paschopoulos, gray bearded, in a white robe shot through with silver and gold, prepared to chant the service for the dead. . . . A Greek in overalls and corduroy coat chanted and swung the censer in front of the improvised altar.

There is a special pathos in all this, Tikas had died unmarried. He had fathered no children to live after him, had continued no line. In the Greeks' eyes, he had died unfulfilled. Had this been the Old Country they would have buried him in the bridal crown and regalia of a groom, for Death was his bride now, the tomb his marriage bed. The laments the women would keen would be filled with these images of loss. And yet the death of Louis Tikas had been, in its way, a fortunate one, and the chants that rose up from that crowded hall were filled with the joy of rebirth. For Louis Tikas had gone to his death cleansed. He had died during the Bright Week of Resurrection and, the tradition had it, even if he had not given satisfaction for his sins, in falling then he still had been granted pardon.[16]

In immigrant-led strikes, Greek women were absent. "Big Mary" Septek was a militant leader in the 1897 National Anthracite Coal Strike. Italian women marched on city streets; they hid Mother Jones from the authorities during the Utah Coal Strike of 1903–04; they followed her down the muddy western mining-camp roads to support their men during the Colorado Coal Strike of 1913–14. Twenty years later, Serbian, Croatian, and Slovenian women in the Utah coal fields became leaders.[17]

There were no Greek women in the Ludlow, Colorado, tent city. Greek women in the United States were few in the first two decades of the 1900s, when immigrant strikes became common, but they could not have joined other women in support of labor wars. Greek culture prevented their marching, demanding, rallying. They would have needed their husbands' consent, and a wife who aspired to anything beyond the demands of home and children was an affront to her husband's masculinity. The Turkish conquest affected other peoples besides the Greeks, with their extreme views of women's subjugation, but the Greeks continued the cultural pattern of women having no participation in life outside the home. If they had to work, it would have to be in a factory among many women or in a family business. The fear of the ancient seigneurial edict that an employer could satisfy his sexual impulses with women dependent on him had been brought to America.

In New England factories and cotton mills, Greek women stood at the giant machines that turned thread into fabric. In her novel *Gold in the Streets,* Mary Vardoulakis tells of Cretan women in Chicopee, Massachusetts, following the example of Polish women who stole fabric from the mill to make sheets and tablecloths for their dowries.

> "That's more of it, eh?" asked Barb'Anastasi. "Do you know where the girls got the linen, Mrs. Bakos?" he asked her respectfully. . . .
>
> Mrs. Bakos looked disconcerted. "From the mill, where else?" she answered seriously, after a minute. "There's so much cloth there. Do you think they'd miss a few yards which a poor girl can use to good advantage?"
>
> Meliotes looked at his aunt astonished. "Didn't it occur to you that there would be trouble?"
>
> "There's no trouble," she answered. "We rolled the cloth under our coats and walked out."[18]

PART THREE

Americanization

CHAPTER 22

DISORDER AND
WORLD WAR I

Americans looked on at the ever-increasing numbers of Greeks in la-
bor-union ranks and their participation in strikes as unpatriotic
and insulting: "Biting the hand that feeds them." A dangerous nativist reaction to immigrants escalated when a Serbian student, Gavrilo
Princip, assassinated Grand Duke Ferdinand of Austria in 1914, precipitat-
ing World War I. When Germany entered the war against Serbia to bolster
Austria-Hungary, the status of Germans in the United States changed.
Once looked upon as sober, industrious people who would be an asset to the
country, they were suddenly vilified as Huns and *boches* (thick-headed persons). The virulence directed against the Germans spread to southern and
eastern Europeans. The tirades in foreign-language newspapers upholding
their native countries' positions in the spreading war was the final undeni-
able proof that the immigrants had not melted into the American pot; they
were still tied to their countries of birth.

The South Slavs gave their loyalties to opposite sides: the Serbs to the
Allies; the Croats and Slovenes to the Austro-Hungarian Empire, which
had incorporated them centuries before. The Greeks divided vociferously
into two camps: the Venizelists, followers of the premier of Greece Eleftherios Venizelos, and the royalists, who upheld King Constantine. The
Venizelists wanted the Greeks to join Britain and France; the royalists
wanted Greece to remain neutral. Soon Greece sent out a call for reservists
to return. The men gathered in American railroad depots to retrace their
journey back to Greece.

When America entered the war on 6 April 1917, many young Greek immigrants were reluctant to enlist. Few were American citizens; they still considered themselves sojourners who would return to their country with their
savings after years of working in *ksenitia*.

The Greeks knew what powerful nations had done over the centuries to their small, vulnerable country and feared its being again divided among them. A Greek, who later volunteered, wrote a newspaper article entitled "Why the Greeks Don't Volunteer." He extolled Greek bravery throughout history and said the Greeks would not commit themselves until they were told what would happen after the war to the Greek provinces "now under the yoke of the Turks, English, and Italians. Will the Greeks take part in war to help big nations steal Greek lands? The allies must make themselves clear first. Greeks hate the Kaiser but can't fight him for national reasons."[1]

The hostilities between the Venizelists and the royalists escalated into warfare. Church board members quarreled with each other with such intensity that churches were closed. Beatings and killings occurred. The Great Idea was given new life: the possibility of Greece's regaining its lost lands. Newspapers took immediate, iron-clad positions: the *Atlantis* backed King Constantine; the *National Herald* Venizelos. In Chicago, seventy-five policemen were dispatched to a Venizelist meeting to prevent a battle. A committee of 225 Venizelists was stationed to prevent royalists from entering. "But the inevitable occurred . . . as the opposing forces met, the policemen were unable to tell a Venizelist from a royalist: "It was all 'Greek to them.' " . . . According to a sympathetic account, "the committee gently picked up the Royalists from the ground as so many dolls and set them aside." . . . In time two-hundred Cretans in military formation reached the scene followed by hundreds of other Greeks . . . "and fell upon the poor Royalists like hounds."[2]

Some Greeks answered draft calls, and others enlisted. Although the feud between the royalists and Venizelists continued, the Greeks were committed to an Allied victory. The number inducted is disputed, from Nicholas Casavetes's 60,000, which he cited in *Everybody's Magazine,* to Seraphim G. Canoutas's 22,090, based on a letter he received from the adjutant general's office. The exact number will never be known: Greeks coming from Turkish-occupied lands in Asia Minor, Thrace, Macedonia, Epirus, and several islands were counted as Turks in the census of 1910.[3]

Oral histories abound on the experience of Greeks in the American army. Many were afraid they would be unable to understand orders: they had learned little English on all-Greek labor gangs and in Greek restaurants and in Greek Towns. Some returned to Greece to fight because their comrades would be Greek. "Pretend you're dumb and don't know English and they'll put you to tending the cavalry horses," was the advice given to a Greek drafted into the American army and who later served honorably in France.[4]

As America mobilized, a great show of patriotic fervor for their adopted country swelled in the Greek communities. Greek and American flags were tacked on the walls of coffeehouses and stores. Greeks led flag-bedecked parades. In western mining camps, Greek miners held "Get out the Coal" rallies. The Greek consul, G. A. Papailion, traveled throughout the United States, to cities, towns, and mining camps to urge his fellow Greeks to support the war. Greek-language newspapers exhorted them to remember they were descended from the ancient Spartan warriors.

Increasing numbers of Greek immigrants came forward to put their savings into war bonds, and the young mothers found that America's once available butter, meat, flour, and sugar were being sent to the army. "My mother told us children this story about the war years. My father had been able to get a bag of sugar and told my mother that she had to be careful to make it last, but our Greek Town neighbors came to the door with empty cups and she could not turn them away. She said she was glad when the sugar ran out."[5]

From Greek candy stores, war songs wafted out to the streets: "It's a long, long way to Tipperary / It's a long way to go"; "Nights are long since you went away / My buddy, my buddy"; and "Jeanine I dream of you in Lilac Time." And especially a song that grade-school boys sang for years after the war ended:

> Mademoiselle from Armentiers, parley vou.
> Mademoiselle from Armentiers, she never
> wore any underwear. Hinky dinky, parley vou!

Along with Americans and men of many nationalities, young Greeks fought in the trenches; some died, many were wounded. They suffered from trench foot, lice, the unceasing sound of bombs and machine guns that shattered their minds—it was called "shell shock." Among them were heroes. A twenty-two-year-old Greek, George Dilboy (Zilboy) from Alatsata in Asia Minor, was the first Greek immigrant to be awarded the Congressional Medal of Honor. His family had fled Turkey to avoid persecution during the Balkan Wars of 1912–13. They settled in Keene, New Hampshire, and later moved to Somerville, Massachusetts. Four years later, at the age of sixteen, Dilboy joined the National Guard, Company H, First Infantry Regiment. In 1917 his company was sent to France and fought in the Champagne-Marene and Aisne-Marne battles. He was killed near Belleau, France, on 18 July 1918.

His citation described his accompanying the platoon leader to reconnoiter the ground beyond a railroad embankment. An enemy machine gun fired from one hundred yards away. George Dilboy, standing, returned fire, but the machine gun continued rattling. With his bayonet fixed, Dilboy ran forward through a wheat field toward the machine gun. Twenty-five yards away, he fell, with his right leg almost severed and several bullet holes in his body. He continued to fire, killing two enemy soldiers and scattering the rest of the crew.

Bethlehem, Pennsylvania: Parade of Balkan War Veterans in support of the United States' entrance in World War I, July 4, 1918. Courtesy of Andrew Paspalas.

The remains of George Dilboy were removed from France to his birthplace Alatsata, Asia Minor. In 1922 while Dilboy's remains were still lying in state in the church, Turkish soldiers seized the city. They entered the church, seized the American flag from the hero's coffin, scattered his bones and proceeded to desecrate the Church. . . . This incident became an international issue with the U.S. demanding an apology and reparation. The Turkish authorities conveyed to the U.S. government an official expression of regret. . . . On September 7, 1922, at Chesmeth, southwest of Smyrna, to which the body of Private Dilboy was brought, an American detachment landed and was saluted by a Turkish guard of honor drawn up beside the coffin, which was covered by an American flag. The coffin was then formally delivered to the American officials and carried on board the *Litchfield,* full military honors being rendered by both detachments.[6]

Newspapers regularly listed the names of men killed in the war. To these were added great numbers of victims of the virulent Spanish influenza, which raced throughout the world in 1918. Civilians suffered also; entire families died or were left disabled. No drugs available at the time could help. "Yoryis met Nick on Main Street. Nick was shivering, his breath reeking of whiskey and garlic. 'Go to your hotel and get in bed,' Yoryis ordered. 'I'll

George Dilboy (Zilboy), the first Greek American awarded the Congressional Medal of Honor for bravery in World War I. Courtesy of Chicago Hellenic Museum.

send a doctor.' 'No, if I go to bed, I'll die. With whiskey and garlic I'll make it.' "7 By the time the Armistice was signed, eight and a half million men had been killed, more than twenty-one million wounded. In the United States alone more than half a million people died of influenza.

During the war, attacks on immigrants escalated. In Utah, two Greeks were saved from lynching when their countrymen arrived with guns and knives.8 Returning soldiers found an America bent on forcing immigrants to become Americanized immediately. Under the "Red Scare," massive arrests and deportations of purported radical immigrants began; the Chicago Palmer raids were the most significant. In the "Red Summer of 1919," lynchings of blacks increased: in 1917 there had been forty-eight; in 1918, sixty-three; and in 1919, seventy-eight—ten victims were veterans, several were in uniform when they were burned alive.9

Except for the Japanese, immigrant soldiers were granted instant citizenship. The foreign-born veterans became members of the American Legion, which was established in March 1919. The Legion led the Americanization fight with stinging attacks on all immigrants. A capricious attitude toward the immigrant servicemen characterized the American Legion. A national commander reviled immigrants, oblivious to the ethnic veterans listening to him. Yet a number of immigrant and American servicemen formed lifelong friendships. Greeks found it best to form their own American Legion posts in certain areas.

The American Legion resolutely drove its campaign against immigrants. During strikes it unleashed its most formidable propaganda weapon: striking was un-American. The immigrant strikers were called Bolsheviks and I-Won't-Work (IWW) slackers, and cries grew that they be deported to their native countries.

The Legion spearheaded the doomed compulsory education program. The majority of immigrants refused to attend the classes, saying they were too tired in the evening. Some had had no early formal training; others had rudimentary reading and writing skills in their own languages and feared that they would be humiliated in trying to learn English. The Greek veterans who did become students had come to America at a young age and had benefitted from some American schooling, before going on to become teachers, physicians, and attorneys.

> Ioannis A. Lougaris arrived in the United States in 1907, and ten years later, when he was 30 years old, volunteered at Oakland, Calif., for the army going to France. A corporal, he was wounded at Chat-Thyierry as the Americans blocked a German offensive the summer of 1918. His wound was complicated by tuberculosis and the doctors advised him to find a warm climate to live his remaining six months or year. They said, "and have a good time before you kick the bucket." . . . He opened a fruit stand in Carson City [Nevada]. Studied law by correspondence before entering school and . . . became an attorney, April 5, 1927. . . . His first application for the bar was turned down because he had no grammar or high-school education. Fair enough he studied some more. . . . "He's the only living American to have a VA hospital named after him—by an act of Congress."[10]

CHAPTER 23

THE KU KLUX KLAN AND THE AMERICAN LEGION

The Eighteenth Amendment to the United States Constitution, ratified in 1919, declared the making and selling of liquor illegal. Considerable attention was given to immigrant bootleggers, although a greater number of American-born dealers also found it lucrative. Greek owners of restaurants and candy stores feared having the "Feds" walk through their doors and were vigilant lest they should plant a bottle of whiskey and arrest them. *Bootlekkers* (bootleggers), *stool pigeon,* and *shyster* were new American words added to the Greek vocabulary. Although the Feds were zealous in their pursuit of bootleggers, in many areas of the country little was done to them after arrests were made. Money often changed hands among bootleggers, judges, and the Feds. Legends grew out of Prohibition. Sons and daughters of early immigrants recall such stories. The author wrote of the patriarch in her railroad-mining town:

> [Barba Yiannis (Uncle John)] had *harisma,* charisma. The sick and grieving felt better after he visited them, although he merely sat and said little. [A sheepman, the first Greek in town,] he delivered all eight of his children: "It's no different from a ewe and a lamb," he said. Pregnant women came for his verdict: "Would it be a boy or a girl?" Barely glancing at the woman in deference to her modesty and his, he made his pronouncement. Legend has it that he never made a mistake. For more than sixty Easters, he read the shoulder blade of the paschal lamb. Peering at the bone, feeling the bumps and demarcations, he foretold, accurately, it is said, what the coming year would bring. Uncle John also had a dream book, and many came to consult him about their dreams. With ceremony, while the traditional spoonful of preserves and *mastiha*

liqueur were served by his wife, he would put on his glasses and look into the worn book. If Uncle John did not like what he read, he gave his own interpretation.[1]

Those are the attributes his fellow Greeks respected in Uncle John. The Americans respected him for a wholly different reason — making the best liquor in the state. "You could trust it," Bracken Lee, a former governor of Utah, said, referring to deaths and blindness caused from drinking adulterated whiskey and wood alcohol.[2] Uncle John's sons delivered whiskey bottles, wrapped in Greek-language newspapers and tied with string, to the town's "leading citizens." Uncle John was often brought before a tired judge, who asked him one time, "You've got a big family to support. Now, if I let you go, will you promise not to make any more whiskey?" After a moment's thinking, Uncle John said, "I don't know, Judge."

> *It was all right to make just enough wine for the family, but if you sold it, you got in trouble with the Feds. One day, snow had just fallen, and the word went through Greek Town, "The Feds are coming!" My godfather took his barrels out to the street and began pouring the wine down the gutter. The Feds followed the wine trickling through the snow to his house.*[3]

Shoeshine parlors were important whiskey supply stations for American doctors, attorneys, and businessmen. The long-established custom of having their shoes shined during their work day gave ample opportunity for respected men to learn where the "good stuff" was. By the 1920s, Greeks had completely taken over the shoeshine parlors, once the province of African Americans and Irish. They became conduits between their countrymen's bubbling stills and respectable, insatiable citizens. Former modestly dressed, diffident shoeshine owners began wearing monogrammed silk shirts and driving Cadillacs, some with chauffeurs. The Greeks thought America's liquor laws were foolish and paid little attention to them — except when bootlegging and prostitution were combined, an anathema to the immigrants. Wealthy bootleggers, though, who had fallen out of grace with officials could spend as long as eighteen months in McNeil Island in Washington State and in other prisons throughout the United States.

Although "leading citizens" drank bootleg whiskey, they also upheld the resurrected Ku Klux Klan. The KKK had arisen in the South during Reconstruction days to keep African Americans "in their place" by beatings, lynchings, and house-burnings. In the 1920s the Klan added immigrants to its hostile policies, and espoused such disparate principles as "protecting

Ku Klux Klan march in Long Branch, New Jersey, 4 July 1924. By permission of Brown Brothers.

American womanhood" and preventing forest fires. Newspapers gave sanction to the Klan in its hard-hitting campaign against aliens. "Scum of Europe a Menace to the U.S." and "Alien Influx is National Menace: Must be Stopped" were typical headlines of the early 1920s.

The immigrants were accused of being radicals who must become American citizens immediately—although many were still moving from job to job and could not fulfill the five-year residency requirement for first papers. The Klan demanded that the immigrants learn to read and write English and no longer publish foreign-language newspapers. Congressmen voiced their fears: "They are coming now at a rate where we can not sift them out, and the worst part of it is that a large percentage of the people . . . are radical . . . malcontents are being gathered and dumped on us" and "Another thing which would de-Americanize America would be . . . a hyphenated population. . . . The coming and going tides of human migration will change the races of men."[4]

White-robed masked Klansmen, many of them American Legionnaires, marched down streets, burned crosses, harassed immigrant businessmen, and rampaged through their candy and grocery stores and restaurants. American girls were warned not to work for immigrants. The Klan clamored against "foreigners who wouldn't let go of their customs." The Greeks were singled out for establishing Greek schools, sending large numbers of

money orders to their families in Greece, and reading Greek-language newspapers in coffeehouses. They angered Americans by speaking Greek on the streets. The Klan song was popular:

> When cotton grows on the fig tree
> And alfalfa hangs on the rose
> When the aliens run the United States
> And the Jews grow a straight nose
> When the Pope is praised by everyone
> In the land of Uncle Sam
> THEN—the Ku Klux Klan won't
> be worth a damn.

In the summer of 1924, the national pre-election campaigns recognized the KKK. In the small town of Great Rapids, near Grand Rapids, Michigan, a mob drove the Greeks out of their houses and to the town limits. From there, like old-country refugees, they made their way to the Greek community of Grand Rapids for shelter.

The author remembers a night during those years when her father was not at home. She stood with her mother and three sisters at a kitchen window and silently watched a cross burning on a mountainside. Across the narrow valley a circle burned. Many years later she would learn that

AHEPA Banquet, Columbus, Ohio, chapter 139, 1931. From its inception in 1922, the AHEPA expected formal dress for banquets. From the seventy-fifth anniversary (1987) The Annunciation Greek Orthodox Church Commemoration album.

Catholics and immigrants were answering the Klan with an *O* for the word *nought:* the Klan's efforts would come to nothing. She and her sisters did not go beyond their small yard for a long time.

Throughout the country children saw burning crosses. Niki Janus, fifteen years old, shared a bedroom with her little dog, Kukla (Doll), on the first floor in the front of the house:

> The flames from the burning cross literally lit up her whole room and Kukla went wild barking. Suddenly, Kukla jumped out of the window and attacked the nearest Klansman, hanging on to him with her teeth. Another Klansman began pouring kerosene all over Kukla who finally let go and started running away hurt and howling. Another Klansman went after her with a flaming torch and was about to set Kukla on fire when Niki, calling to her father and running out of the house, threw herself over Kukla and cried, "You'll have to burn me too."
>
> The next morning everybody in Montgomery knew the awful story. Niki wrote a letter to the local newspaper which later was used as a stirring sermon in the local church. She helped organize a town meeting protesting the Klan. . . . The Klan was not disbanded but there was no more cross burning or Klan parades.[5]

The Greeks responded to the Klan by forming lodges with the express purpose of counteracting the Klan's portrayal of them. AHEPA, American Hellenic Progressive Association, was organized in 1923 in Atlanta, Georgia; and GAPA, Greek American Progressive Association, was established in Pittsburgh, Pennsylvania, in 1924. The AHEPA espoused the English language and used it in meetings. The men wore white flannel pants and car-

ried canes, emulating American lodges. Their national conventions were elaborate affairs in expensive hotels with formal balls and reigning queens.

GAPA was interested mainly in preserving the Greek language and traditions. Its members were conservative. They dressed in dark business suits and shunned flamboyance. Their favorite gathering was a picnic on a mountain or in a park with lambs roasting on spits and round dances celebrating the *kleftic* days of their people.

Immigrants banded together. The excesses of the Klan brought disgrace and forced politicians and community leaders to disavow it openly. Hostility toward immigrants then became covert, but the cry for immigration restriction grew. The 1917 legislation that refused admission to illiterates over the age of sixteen had failed to stem the rush of immigrants into Ellis Island. In 1921 Congress passed the first restriction law. It limited immigration by nationality to 3 percent of the number living in the United States in 1910 and limited the number of arrivals from southern and eastern Europe to a total of 357,802. This reduced immigration from Greece to 3,063 yearly. These numbers were unsatisfactorily high to Congress, and, in 1924, immigration was further reduced by allowing only 2 percent of the number in the country in 1890. So few Greeks resided in the United States in that year that only one hundred Greek immigrants were allowed entrance under the new law. Later the number was increased to 384 a year.

CHAPTER 24

THE GREEK CULT
OF SUCCESS

A brief recession in the early 1920s affected the Greeks somewhat. Western sheep and cattle owners were forced to begin again with smaller herds. The nation rebounded and the frugal Greeks shared in the decade's prosperity. Many had left labor and had used their savings to buy property, and restaurant owners moved their lunchrooms closer to Main Street. There they became well-appointed dining places with white tablecloths and waiters in dinner jackets. Earlier names, such as Corinthos, Athenian, and Paradise on restaurant and candy store windows were replaced with new ones: Palace, American, and Eden.

Candy stores now had floors paved with white hexagonal tile, long mirrors behind soda fountains, reflecting glass bowls of fruits, and many different kinds of glassware. Each booth was upholstered in leather and had a box attached to the wall. When a nickel was inserted under the chosen number, a song burst out from a jukebox at the back of the store. Across from the marble counter were glass cases displaying a variety of chocolates, Jordan almonds, and Turkish *loukoum*.

In the back room, cauldrons of chocolate and caramel bubbled on big black stoves. At long marble-topped tables, immigrants turned candymakers, used wooden paddles to fold hot liquid caramel and chocolate into pliable masses. The sweet, hot scents floated over the booths and glass cases and into the street.

Windows no longer displayed the penny candy that had enticed steady little customers; now they featured artful, realistic looking ice cream sundaes in tall glasses, the scoops of ice cream made of painted cardboard, artificial syrups, cotton fluffs to represent whipped cream, and wooden balls painted red to represent maraschino cherries. In front of them were placards with the lettering: Mary Pickford Sundae, Banana Split, Chocolate Ice Cream Soda.

ΑΓΓΕΛΟΣ ΙΩ. ΠΑΠΠΑΝΔΡΕΟΥ
'Ηλικίας 4 'Ετῶν.
Υἱὸς τοῦ ἐν Fredericksburg, Va. κ.
'Ιωάν. Παππανδρέου, ἐκ Θεσσαλίας.

ΔΗΜΗΤΡΙΟΣ ΘΕΟΧ. ΠΕΡΑΤΗΣ
'Ηλικίας 3 'Ετῶν.
Υἱὸς τοῦ ἐν Los Angeles, Calif. κ. Θε-
οχ. Περάτη, ἐξ 'Αφθόνης Μαρμαρᾶ.

ΔΗΜΗΤΡΙΟΣ ΝΙΚΟΛΟΠΟΥΛΟΣ
'Ηλικίας 4 'Ετῶν.
Υἱὸς τοῦ ἐν Mexico City, Mexico
κ. 'Ιωάννου Νικολοπούλου.

Immigrant children.
Prometheus
Publishing.

In the West, the Greeks increased their flocks of sheep and herds of cattle and were soon among the most prosperous of stockmen. Everywhere, Greeks made payments on properties that they expected to sell someday when they returned to Greece. *Kali Patridha* (Good country) they toasted each other, meaning "We'll see Greece soon."

Weddings, baptisms, and lodge affairs became ostentatious affairs. Cretans could not celebrate them properly without Harilaos Piperakis and his musicians, who traveled throughout the United States to perform old and contemporary favorites.

They bought cars.

The emigrant sons now sent even more money back to their families and large donations to gild their village churches. As the immigrants prospered, memorial wheat was elaborately prepared by Greek confectioners. It was mounded, thickly covered with powdered sugar, and decorated with green gelatin fir trees (a sign of immortality) and silver-coated dragées forming the name of the dead.

A landmark in the Mountain West, the Politz Candy Store of Salt Lake City, Utah, in 1921. Steve Sargetakis Collection, used by permission, Utah State Historical Society, all rights reserved.

The Elias Varessis Garden Fruit Store, San Antonio, Texas. Grocery stores metamorphosed from small, crowded shops to tiled, well-stocked, brightly lighted stores with bounteous displays of fruits and vegetables. By permission of the University of Texas Institute of Texan Cultures at San Antonio.

Ball sponsored by the Cretan organization Omoghenia, a word for fellow Greeks in a foreign country. Central Opera House, New York City, 1920. Courtesy of Olga Koukourakis.

Isadore Nackos family. Salt Lake City, middle 1920s. Courtesy of Konstandinos Kambouris.

The gilded iconostasis in the village church, Klepa, Nafpaktias, Roumeli (birthplace of the author's father). During the prosperity of the 1920s, immigrants sent home money to gild their church icons, bishop's thrones, and altar doors. Author's collection.

Memorial wheat, kolyvo or kolyva, is a mixture of boiled, sweetened wheat, nuts, currants, pomegranate seeds, and parsley. It is eaten on the fortieth day after burial and at other times in memory of the dead.

CHAPTER 25

AMERICA SWALLOWS
THE YOUNG

ndustrial accidents regularly killed laborers. Three of the largest occurred in the Intermountain West. In 1904, two trains collided and exploded near the Lucin cutoff, a shortcut across the east end of Great Salt Lake. Black powder on one train spread to dynamite on the other and set off the explosion. Of the twenty-eight dead, sixteen were Peloponnesian Greeks.[1]

On 22 October 1913, about a hundred of the 263 men killed in a coal mine explosion in Dawson, New Mexico, were Greek.[2] On 27 April 1917, the Hastings, Colorado, mine exploded, killing 121 miners, seventeen of whom were Greek.[3] The official report on 8 March 1924 listed fifty Greeks killed in a Utah coal mine explosion, leaving nineteen widows and forty-one orphans.[4] Three Cretan widows returned to Crete with their children. The rest of the women remained, knowing that life in the homeland for widows and orphans would be almost intolerable. At least in America, they said, their children would get an education.

The outcry over the explosion provided the widows with six dollars a week for six years. Only one widow married again: the old tradition of but one marriage for life persisted in America as it had in Greece. The widow's new husband, an older man, was praised for performing a *psyhiko,* an act good for the soul.

An anecdote still told about the explosion graphically portrays the immigrants' feelings about their *topos,* their ancestral place. News of the explosion was instantly relayed to Greek Towns in the West. A Wyoming coffeehouse owner telephoned the Cretan owner of the Stadium Café in Salt Lake City and asked how many of their people were killed. The café owner replied, "Forty-eight of our boys and two Greeks."

The death of a father was a horrendous tragedy that left his wife and children without any means of support. In industrial accidents, death

169

Hundreds of men were killed in mine explosions, by collapsing coal, by molten ore, and in rail-road accidents. Courtesy of Ernest Benardis.

benefits from management and from Greek lodges were small and quickly dissipated. A mother was helpless to provide for her children. She dyed the window curtains, her clothing, and the children's clothing black, turned mirrors and photographs—objects of vanity and pleasure—toward the wall. She could not leave her house to work for others and flout custom; she could wash and iron for other women in her home for a pittance. If her husband had a male relative, he would occasionally give her a ten-dollar bill and bring a bag of flour. Often churches provided some help. Greeks at times took up a collection to send a widow and her children back to her native *topos*.

The death or incapacity of a mother was both a tragedy and a calamity. Fathers were helpless, unable to take over a role custom had not allotted them. Relatives raised orphans, and if there were none, the oldest girls became the mother substitute. The author knows of two nine-year-old girls who washed, ironed, cooked, and tended siblings. One of them took the baby to a Greek neighbor before going on to school; the baby died within a few months. If the father had no one to help him, he resorted to either orphanages or social services. The grim, cruel fate of children in foster homes of that era is chillingly portrayed by H. L. Mountzoures in his fiction.[5]

Fifty Greek miners were killed in the Castle Gate, Utah, explosion of 1924, leaving forty-one orphans. Several are shown here, including Steve Sargetakis, the baby held by a girl in the top row, center. Sargetakis became an important collector of immigrant photographs. Courtesy of Steve Sargetakis.

The 1920s posed a paradox: within the American environment of hostility, the Greeks enjoyed the best years of their American experience. Many had established themselves in businesses; the pushcart had given way to the modest grocery store.

> There's a fruitshop down our street,
> It's run by a Greek,
> And he sells good things to eat,
> But you should hear him speak,
> When you ask him anything,
> He never answers "No,"
> He just yesses you to death,
> And as he takes your dough he tells you:
> Yes! We have no bananas.
> We have no bananas today . . .
> [We] have all kind of fruit . . .
> But yes! We have no bananas,
> We have no bananas today!
>
> Things were going well with him,
> He wrote home to say,
> Send me Mike and Pete and Jim,
> I need them right away.
> When he got them in the shop,

> There was fun, you bet,
> 'Cause when you asked them anything,
> They answered in quartet. Oh,
>
> Yes! We have no bananas,
> We have no bananas today![6]

A small number of immigrants had enrolled in universities, including medical schools; others, though, were still working in mines, mills, and on railroad gangs. Americanization was going on without the immigrants realizing it.

> Like most Greek immigrants, my father had originally intended to make his fortune and then return home to lead a leisured and respected life. Again like most of his fellow immigrants, circumstances did not work out the way originally planned. Although life in America could be hard, it did have its compensations. My father partook of the amusement parks and Lake Michigan cruises of 1920s Chicago. Introduced to baseball by black shoe shiners, he became a Cubs fan. He liked American dancing and was a habitué of the great ballrooms of that era, the [Greek-owned] Aragon and Trianon. He enjoyed big city life.[7]

The immigration laws forced immigrants to travel to Canada, Cuba, or Mexico to meet their picture brides. Brides from cities and provincial towns were less strict in demeanor than village women. Many were daring, modern women with short hair.

In "To Alanaki" (The gadabout), Tetos Demetriadhes, the leading Greek popular singer in America, sang that he wanted to spend his life like a magnet and a gadabout:

> That I may not be eaten with bitterness,
> To roam with *manga* [street-tough] friends!
> Out with poverty!
> Short-haired woman, my, my, my . . .
> That I might spend all night, my, my, my
> With her every night. My, my, my.[8]

Erene Frangopoulou Marino of Seattle, Washington, was born in the village Bouyiati, Gortinia, Arcadia. Compared to earlier picture brides, she was cosmopolitan. Bobbed hair on women surprised older immigrants. Courtesy of Zoe Marino Fidler.

CHAPTER 26

REFUGEE SONGS
FOR SOLACE

A horror coincided with passage of the immigration restriction laws. In 1922, the Greek army under the banner of the Great Idea, invaded Asia Minor, land lost to the Turks in 1453. It brought disaster to both the Greeks and the Armenians.

> On 8 September the Greek army evacuated the city [Smyrna], which the Turkish army entered the following day. Initially the Turkish occupation of the city was relatively orderly but on the evening of the 9th outbreaks of killings and lootings began. This was followed by a full-scale massacre of the Christian population, of which the Armenians suffered the greatest casualties. Some 30,000 Christians perished.[1]

> In the ensuing bloodbath . . . Archbishop Chrysostomos of Smyrna was hacked to death after being handed over to a Turkish mob, meeting a martyr's death a century after the execution of Ecumenical Patriarch Gregorios V. . . . Panic-stricken refugees [jumped] into the water [of the bay] to escape the flames and . . . their terrified screaming could be heard miles away. In such an ignominious fashion a 2500 years Greek presence came to an abrupt end. The vision of the Megali Idea, or Great Idea, was to be consumed in the ashes of Smyrna.[2]

A forced Armenian march from the interior followed the Greek defeat. Turkish soldiers went on a frenzy of looting and killing Armenians and Greeks. In Smyrna, the Greek and Armenian part of the city was on fire. Christians ran to the quay and tried to reach the ships for help. The ships flew the flags of many countries but, afraid of Turkish retaliation, they re-

'Η Στρατ. Δικαιοσύνη
Άγιόν-Καραχισάρ. 1922

A postcard sent to a Greek immigrant in Beaver Falls, Rhode Island, during the 1922 Greek military campaign to regain their ancient lands. The Greeks were routed by the Turks and both Greeks and Armenians were expelled from Turkish lands. Courtesy of Peter Chronis.

fused to take the refugees on board. British and Greek ships were able to save a quarter of a million refugees.

Ernest Hemingway sent dispatches describing the muddy "never-ending, staggering march [of] the Christian population of eastern Thrace . . . jamming the roads towards Macedonia. The main column . . . is twenty miles long. . . . They don't know where they are going."[3]

The Greek army's humiliating defeat resulted in 1.3 million Greeks being forced out of their ancestral homes and becoming refugees. Refugees from Russia and Bulgaria raised the number to 1.5 million. In exchange, four hundred thousand Turks in eastern Thrace, Greece, were sent to Turkey.[4] Many of the refugees who had lived for generations in each other's countries created an anomaly: most of them did not know their own ancestral languages. Greeks spoke only Turkish and Turks spoke only Greek.

We were unable to get on the ships, but many people were left behind and they had hoped to get on ships but they never did because the Turks had them completely surrounded and none could get away. . . . We were on the island [of Limnos] for 24 hours under quarantine. We had nothing to eat other than some moldy bread and no water. . . . Later, we found a barracks and fixed it up and lived there in Salonika for three years.—Efrosini Karagheorghiou Cozakos, Kios, Asia Minor[5]

We could not believe the Turks would harm us. Then we saw their soldiers coming over the mountains and we hurried and got on board the ships. In Thessaloniki, my grandmother became ill and we took her to the hospital. Then we fanned out, everywhere that we thought we had relatives, hoping for help. When we returned our grandmother was not in the hospital. By mistake she had been sent to Adrianopolis. My brothers went there and could not find her. My mother wept for her every day of her life.—Efterpi Tsallas Filis, Pringipis, Turkey[6]

Laurence Durrell describes the refugee quarters in Greek cities "with its earth street and minute houses constructed out of petrol tins and shattered sugar boxes. He hears snatches of old-fashioned Greek—fragments of Doric that were once carried up to the shores of the Black Sea, and that have now been washed down here to this barren littoral of history . . . song split suddenly into quarter tones speaks of Smyrna, the streets with their huddled cafes, bubble of narghiles, red fez."[7]

The ties to the homeland, *patridha,* had never waned for the Greeks in America. They responded with an unparalleled generosity. During this period, the unrelenting conflict between King Constantine and the liberal prime minister Eleftherios Venizelos increased. In America, coffeehouse fights over Greek politics led to beatings, arrests for disturbing the peace, and killings. "Thus Greece, exhausted by three wars, and after having given hospitality to refugees following the Cretan revolts against the Turks of 1867 and 1897 and the Balkan Wars of 1912–1913, now found herself faced by the problem of supporting and settling a mass of immigrants equal to a quarter of her population [5.5 million]. . . . Greece received a golden stream of remittances from her thrifty emigrant sons. The high point occurred in 1921, when the remittances totaled no less than 121 million dollars."[8]

The women who came to the United States as refugees were far different in education and privilege from the earlier village brides. Their families' property had been confiscated by the Turkish government, leaving them without dowries. Many married laborers with inferior education. This drastic displacement was surmounted by most of the women, who brought a cosmopolitan air to the communities. Some taught Greek school and took part in plays. Several wrote poems that were published in the *Atlantis* and other Greek-language newspapers. They made brave attempts to temper what had happened to their people and to themselves. "The Asia Minor Disaster of 1922 changed overnight the character of modern Greek culture and society. . . . The Greek people suffered an ideological, social, and emotional dislocation that changed the course of modern Greek civilization."[9]

Again the pattern of nostalgia for the homeland was repeated, and for many refugees it was nearly unbearable. In "A Song of *Ksenitia*," a woman keens for her lost homeland.

> Anathema on you, *Ksenitia,*
> You and your blessings.
> Neither your wealth did I want
> Nor your burdens. . . .
>
> Death is a consolation . . .
> But the live separation
> Has no comfort.[10]

For years following the disaster, songs of pining and longing for the Asia Minor homeland were being composed and sung:

> Mothers weep, girls weep, the *rajah* [Turkified Greek] weeps.
> They weep, they weep. The bells of Saint Sophia weep.[11]

In the song "Konstantinoupoli" (Constantinople), a singer laments that he must leave the city with its great beauty, but he will return to wander on her cobbled streets.[12] A song sung for years after the disaster tells of a child refugee turned musician playing the stringed *outi:*

> I'm a little refugee, *achh* I tell it,
> They chased me out of Smyrna, miserable one,
> Sometimes poverty, sometimes riches, I learned to play the *outi,*
> In the Café *Aman* (mercy). *Ach, aman, aman.*[13]

During the 1920s, nostalgia for the homeland caused approximately 196,000 Greeks to return to it.[14] "My uncle went back to Crete to live in the early 1920s and he took plans for a flush toilet with him, the first in the entire island."[15]

When repatriates who became disillusioned with the static life in their native *topos* attempted to return to the United States, they were listed as new immigrants. This calls into question the 40 percent figure given for repatriates. If they could not enter the country under the quotas of the new restriction laws—even though they were citizens—they were forced to remain in Greece. A man who went back to visit his family and had not given three years of military service to Greece before leaving for America was in a dire predicament. He had to either serve the three years, pay two hundred dollars to absolve himself of duty, or pay someone else to take his place.

When Gus and I went to visit his village Nestani [Province Mantinea], he was forced into the army. There I was alone in his village. I didn't know Greek and his family didn't know a word of English. Gus was frantic. He hurried back to the village every Sunday and it was two months before he found someone to take his place. I taught his mother and sisters to make French fried potatoes.—Minnie Blackman Theodore[16]

CHAPTER 27

STRADDLING TWO CULTURES

Many immigrants became citizens, but they were indelibly Greek at heart. "The Greek immigrant was more consciously Greek than the average Slovenian, say, or Pole was Slovenian or Polish," Louis Adamic writes.[1] The Greeks were still young; their children were small, dutifully following Greek customs; picnics were held regularly on Sundays with one or two men in the Greek national costume, the *foustanella* (white pleated skirt), and both Greek and American flags flanking the gathering. In church basements men played *lyras, clarinos,* and *laoutos* for communal gatherings and lodge celebrations.

Lodges proliferated. The old Philhellenic Unions had been disbanded, and in their place, immigrants from each province in Greece established lodges. An immigrant could belong to several lodges connected to his village. A villager from the village Klepa could be a member of the Klepaiotes, the Nafpaktias Province lodge, and the Roumeli organization. Almost every week one or another lodge held festivities. March 25, the commemoration of Greece's revolt to gain independence from Turkey, and the great feast days of the Orthodox church—Christmas, Easter, and the Dormition of the Virgin—were celebrated with fasting, liturgies, and traditional festive foods.

Greek school programs were staples of the commemoration: dressed in ethnic costumes, children proclaimed their love for Greece and extolled their heroes. With their parents, they sang Solomos's great "Hymn to Liberty," which had sustained the Greeks during their revolt. The piping of children was overpowered by the fervent booming of their fathers:

I know you by the blade
of your dread sword,
I know you by your eye

Alexander Karanikas, educator and author, as a small boy (right). His father, Stephen, traditionally holds in his mouth crosswise the knife used to butcher the lamb. Goffstown, New Hampshire, 1919. Courtesy of Alexander Karanikas.

Quickly surveying the world.
Risen from the bones,
a hallowed Greek Trail,
and valiant as of old,
Hail, O Liberty, hail![2]

In their homes, the fathers still sang the songs of the table, of Markos Botsaris:

And when the Romaioi heard the news
And when they heard the tidings,
They dressed themselves in clothes of black
They dressed themselves in mourning
They're taking Markos to the church
They're taking Markos to the grave

Twenty bishops go ahead
And sixty priests behind.

They sang of the old dying *kleft* who asked his men to dig his grave wide enough for two so that he could stand, take aim, fire, and reload, and with a window at one side to let the swallows of spring fly in and out.[3]

The old songs had overwhelming competition—the ever-increasing numbers of phonograph records and piano rolls, bought from specialty stores in cities or ordered from the Atlas catalog by those in small towns. Phonograph records of the comedic Karagiozis were available in America. "Karagiozis in America" has him still getting the better of pompous Greeks, but now, also, innocent Americans. "Karagiozis on the Telephone" shows him trying with malapropisms to locate a trunk that should have arrived in America. In another episode Karagiozis asks a friend who speaks a little English to help him woo an American woman.

Kondofarthos and Zanetos was a popular comedy routine written and recited by Titos Demetriadhes. Kondofarthos (Short-wide) was the inflated president of the Watermelon Society of America, a sly joke on immigrants who formed lodges left and right. At church celebrations Kondofarthos gives long, excruciating orations on the March 25 anniversary of the Greek Revolution. The Greek that comes out of Kondofarthos's mouth is a mishmash of demotic, dialect, and academic *katharevousa* blunders that is grating to listeners.

Kondofarthos is in love with Elsie, an American woman. One night he serenades her with the traditional Greek love song "Evangelio." All the singer asks from Evangelio is a glass of water—a sign of his interest in her. The neighbors in the apartment house oblige Kondofarthos by dousing him with water.

Zanetos, newly arrived from Greece, comes to Kondofarthos's office and introduces himself. He tries to kiss his cousin, who rebukes him, saying he is too great a man, the future leader of Greek society in America, to be offended by a peasant who would attempt to kiss such an important personage. Zanetos is suitably cowed, and Kondofarthos uses him as a lackey.[4]

Barba Yoryis (Uncle George), from Roumeli, rasped out his experiences as a village bumpkin in the big city of Athens. He ties his mule to the back of the train and takes a seat inside. When he reaches Athens, he cannot understand what has happened to his mule. All that is left is a frayed rope. Such records show much about the Greek immigrant personality in exaggerated, but believable form.

The popularity of the comedy records reflected a buoyant well-being among the immigrants: they were sharing in the country's prosperity; miseries of the early days were now memories for most of them. When they gathered to celebrate name days, *kefi* (joy) took over. They often sang *"Pos to Trivoun to Piperi"* (How pepper is ground) while the singers' fists began a circular motion, which then spread to their noses, their elbows, and their shoulders, and ended with the singers (men, not women) sitting on the floor and swiveling their hips to much hilarity.

Besides the comedy records, traditional love songs, and the old *kleftika*, the guerrilla songs, Greek records were made with strange translations of popular American songs: the sweetly sentimental love songs "Ramona," "Jeanine, I Dream of Lilac Time" and "My Blue Heaven" became recriminations—"You filled my heart with poison," "I believed in your oaths and your innocent look." "I Kiss Your Hand, Madame," "Little Spanish Town," the Spanish "La Paloma," and the Italian "O Sole Mio," all peculiarly translated and renamed, were also available from the Atlas Company. "Kato sto Ghialo" (Down at the seashore) turned into "Down at Coney Island."

Women's independence, though, was sung (although it was illusionary for most Greek and Greek American women) in "To Sigareto"—"I inhale it and don't care what people say"—and in "Patzames" (Pajamas) in defiance of attacks on women wearing trousers.[5]

Rebetika were songs of the underclass of Greek life, with roots in poverty and despair, especially following the forced removal of Greeks from Turkish lands in Asia Minor. They told of drugs, free love, and loss of *topos:* "We lived for six months in someone's yard like dogs." The *rebetika* became popular, though, because "the *rebetis* was a man who had a sorrow and threw it out."[6]

The Smyrna refugees brought their own kind of song, called *Smyrnaica,* which was different from that of the Piraeus underclass. The educated Greek middle class could spurn the *rebetika* and *bouzoukia* as low-life music and look down on the *tekes* (cafes), where the musicians sang and improvised as they went along, calling out "Aman, Aman" (Mercy, mercy), but the hard existence they recounted appealed to the immigrant Greeks because they, too, thousands of miles away, knew poverty and trouble.[7] Rosa Eskenazi, a refugee from Smyrna of Jewish parentage, was famed among Greeks for her singing of the *rebetika.*

Yiorgos Katsaros, "last of the Café-Aman singers," described the scene from 1915 on: "The time I coming to the United States, I find here every [city] San Francisco, Salt Lake, Utah, Chicago, Detroit, Cleveland, Philadelphia, Boston, New York . . . it was more than fifty bands a Greek musicians, you know six, seven together . . . in Chicago in those years it was eleven twelve cabarets every night . . . and dancers, Armenian, Turkish girls . . . and Egyptian. . . . Play Turkish music, play Arabic music, play Greek music, everything. Those musicians they got to be experience."[8]

Several Greek *patriotes* had become celebrities in the 1920s. Nick the Greek (Nicholas Andreas Dondolas from Crete) became a United States citizen in 1902; he was eighteen years of age and sold figs on the streets of Chicago. "He disdained roulette and blackjack, considering the house odds against a player too high, but he was probably the best ever at dice, and almost as good at poker and handicapping horses."[9]

Three rebetis, *musicians who sang of despair and loss of their Asia Minor homeland, playing cards, the 1920s.*

Jimmy Londos, the "Golden Greek" wrestler, a native of Theophilo, Greece, came to America at the age of twelve or fourteen—in villages births were often not recorded. At the age of seventeen, he won the California light heavyweight and heavyweight championships. He went on to become the world's heavyweight champion by defeating "Strangler" Lewis, seven times in all.

Four men in the theater business—Alexander Pantages and the Skouras brothers—exemplify the Greeks of the 1920s who ventured beyond the typical restaurant, shoeshine, and grocery businesses. Pantages, born on the island of Andros, worked as a cabin boy on tramp steamers. In Marseilles, London, and South America he visited music halls on ship's leave. In Panama, he found work with the French company that was trying to dig a canal through the isthmus; he handled a pick and shovel and ran a donkey engine. After an attack of tropical fever, he was put on a ship for San Francisco. He was twelve years old. In San Francisco he worked around theaters and became acquainted with vaudeville entertainers. Next, hearing of gold

Rosa Eskenazi, a Jewish singer, famed for her rendition of the rebetika.

strikes in the Yukon, he contrived, because he had no passage money, to get past the Canadian mounted police. He made his way to Alaska, where he again worked with a pick and shovel, then in a bar where he realized prospectors would squander their money on entertainment. After further adventures, he opened a theater. With a projector, which enabled him to show the new moving pictures, and a vaudeville act, he launched his amazing career. He bought out theaters in the Northwest and Canada, and after the 1907 fire he bought six theaters in San Francisco. Eventually he owned or had stock in eighty theaters. During the Depression, he sold them to Warner Brothers and Radio-Keith-Orpheum in return for stock in their companies.

Charles Skouras, the oldest of the brothers, arrived in New York from Skourohorion (Skouras Village) in 1908 and worked in a restaurant for fifty cents a day plus meals. He then moved to St. Louis; after three years he had saved enough money to bring his brother Spyros to America. Spyros had been studying for the priesthood and learning English and accounting, but in St. Louis he became a bus boy. In the evenings he studied English and business law. A third brother arrived, and the three bought a theater with the four thousand dollars they had saved. They sold tickets, ran the projector, and cleaned the theater. In 1917, Spyros and George joined the United States Air Force and were honorably discharged at the end of the war. They added thirty-seven theaters in St. Louis and had interests in Indianapolis and Kansas City movie houses. In 1931, Spyros operated theaters in the East for Paramount. He then became head of Fox Metropolitan Theaters. By 1942, there were 563 theaters in the Skouras brothers' chain. A year later Spyros became head of Twentieth-Century Fox. In contrast to Alexander Pantages, the Skouras brothers were nationally known for their philanthropy.[10]

Well-known Greek success stories, like those of Pantages and the Skouras brothers, did not impress the average American. While newspaper cartoons derided the Greeks and songs satirized them, the immigrants clung to their communal gatherings for assurance and reminder of their Romiosini. A popular vaudeville song of the early 1920s was titled "The Argentines, the Portuguese, and the Greeks":

Columbus discovered America in 1492
Then came the English and the Dutch
The Frenchman and the Jew.
Then came the Swede and the Irishman
Who helped the country grow.
Still they keep a coming and now
Everywhere you go
There's the Argentines, the Portuguese,
The Armenians and the Greeks.

One sells you papers, one shines your shoes,
Another shaves the whiskers off your cheeks.
When you ride the subway train
Notice who have all the seats
And you'll find they are held by
The Argentines and the Portuguese and the Greek.

There's the Ritz Hotel and the Commodore and
The Vanderbilt and the rest.
All of them are classy, up-to-date hotels
They boast accommodations of the best.
When you ask a clerk for a room and bath
He looks at you sarcastically and speaks
Why we're all filled up with the Argentine
And the Portuguese and the Greek.

There's the Oldsmobile and the Hupmobile
And the Cadillac and the Ford.

They are the motors you and I can own
The kind most anybody can afford.
But the Cunningham and the Mercury
And the Rolls Royce racing free
Ah, they all belong to the Argentine and
The Portuguese and the Greek.

There are pretty girls, there are witty girls,
There is every kind of girl.
Some you like a little, some a little more,
But none of them will set your heart a whirl.
When you really feel you've met your ideal
A girl with spark and cheek
You will find she belongs to an Argentine or
A Portuguese or a Greek.

They don't know the language,
They don't know the law.
But they vote in the country of the free.
And the funny thing, when we start to sing
"My country 'tis of thee"
None of us know the words
But the Argentines, the Portuguese, and the Greeks.[11]

This peculiar song was typical of the ethnic songs of the vaudeville circuit. Such songs were usually comedic, often slightly risqué, such as one sung in a pseudo-Italian accent with the refrain "Push a push a push." That Argentines, Portuguese, and Greeks who shined shoes and shaved off whiskers could afford Cunninghams, Mercurys, and Rolls Royces was ludicrous. Although by then most Greek immigrants were setting up their own shops, few were rich. Nor did the Argentines, the Portuguese, and the Greeks acquire the "ideal, a girl with spark and cheek." The women the immigrants met worked alongside them in the cotton mills, waited on tables, and clerked in stores. A few of the "ideal" girls did marry already established Greek business or professional men, but Americans held virulent prejudice against Greeks marrying "white" girls. "Intermarriage with foreigners was considered as bad as death. [Girls did marry Greeks] in spite of their peculiar traits . . . and were despised more than Greek women."[12]

The song belied the reality of the immigrants' world. Greeks still thought of themselves as sojourners and expected to return to Greece, even those who had established young families in America. In lodge halls, with a

Greek flag at one end and an American flag at the other, they boomed out the Greek "Hymn to Liberty," the Greek national anthem, but few sang "My Country 'Tis of Thee," except children who had learned it in school.

Why was this curious song composed in 1920, while the American Legion called foreigners the "unassimilable flotsam" thrown on American shores? Greek laborers and businessmen were acutely aware of the hostility beyond Greek Towns. On every holiday, they displayed American flags and took part in parades to show their loyalty to the United States.

Their wives felt safe within the Greek Towns as long as their husbands were home at night. Sheepmen's wives, though, had to contend with their fears and responsibility for children when their husbands were away for long periods during lambing and shearing, and trailing sheep to the mountains in summer and to the desert in fall.

Late at night with the icon light glowing in children's bedrooms, mothers sat in kitchens doing handiwork, anxiously wondering about those *ksenoi* who did not like them. Many of these women had an innate intelligence, but culture gave little heed to it. Illiterate mothers could look at a complicated piece of crochet at a neighbor's—they would not ask for instructions, they might be rebuffed—then return to their homes and replicate the pattern perfectly.

Outside their ethnic enclaves, the immigrants met daily difficulties; inside they had problems among themselves. The acrimony over who should be the archbishop of the Americas had continued, as had the quarreling by factions supporting King Constantine against those upholding the liberal leader Eleftherios Venizelos. The events in *patridha* were as vivid to the Greeks in the United States as they were to those in the homeland, and Greek-language newspapers in the United States added to the turmoil.

During the 1920s, some churches offered liturgies intermittently. Many priests omitted the name of King Constantine when asking God to "be mindful of him." Father Vasileos Lambrides told his congregation in the Saint Sophia Church in Washington, D.C., "I would rather die than pray for a man [King Constantine] who was proved a traitor to his country. If I am ordered to commemorate Constantine and to approve his return to the Greek throne, I shall prefer not to celebrate any longer in any church, rather than betray my conscience and the head of the Orthodox Church."[13] Eighteen hours later, Father Lambrides died "from a broken heart." His magnificent funeral was widely reported in both American and Greek-language newspapers.[14] Utah Greeks remembered him as he had been when they were new in the country. He had climbed a mountain to convince Greek strikers to come down to settle a copper strike.

Notwithstanding the upheaval caused by political and church affairs,

The Reverend Father Vasilios Lambrides, who left the priesthood rather than ask God to bless King Constantine as the liturgy required. Courtesy of Daphne Ross.

the immigrant Greeks in cities, towns, hamlets, and mining camps had the Atlas catalogs to supply their every need. Their catalogs had a greater variety of goods for the Greeks than did those of Montgomery Ward and Sears Roebuck for rural customers. A social history of Greek immigrant life could be written by the offerings of the Atlas catalogs of 23 Madison Street, New York City: dreambooks, medical books for laymen, the Bible, Greek-English dictionaries, novels, both contemporary and classic, in Greek and in translations: Victor Hugo's *Les Miserables,* Daphne Du Maurier's *Rebecca,* Tolstoy's *War and Peace.* Victrolas cost from fifteen to one thousand dollars; phonograph records featured prominent singers and instrumentalists performing *kleftic* ballads, *zebekika, rebetika,* and hymns: Rosa Eskenazi, Maria Papagika, Koula, Yiorgos Katsaros, S. Stasinopoulos, Maria Smyrnaias, Tetos Dimitriadhes, and others sang for the Greeks in this country they called "exile."

Records of American symphony orchestras and world-renowned singers were featured, as well as European waltzes, polkas, mazurkas, schottische, and tangos. The old favorites "Samiotissa" (Woman from Samos) and "O Ghero Dhimos" (Old man Demos) were advertised along with "Stoma me Stoma" (Mouth to mouth) and "Sfikse Me" (Hug me) for the more cosmopolitan. Piano sheet music and pictures of banjos, guitars, mandolins, *laoutos,* flutes, clarinets, and accordions took up several pages.

"Nothing will be missing for the wedding," the 1927 catalog exclaimed, as it offered invitations, silver trays, embroidered and beaded veils, and beribboned white candles, priced between twenty and seventy dollars. White Jordan almonds, the *koufeta,* in individual bags or boxes, and the octagonal glassed boxes in which brides displayed their wedding crowns were listed at various prices. Godparents could order complete baptismal clothing that sold from twelve dollars to the "Super Special" at fifty-three. They could also choose baptismal medals commemorating the event for guests, crosses for babies, and colored Jordan almonds as favors.

The all-important *brik* pans for making Turkish coffee came in nine sizes, a necessity for homes and coffeehouses. Narghiles, water pipes for coffeehouses, no doubt, continued to be advertised long after the Greek men discarded the habit of smoking them.

The Atlas Company did a profitable business with postcards, as is evident from the survival of many. Cherubs; suitors with bouquets in hand; pretty women, handsome men with the Greek words for "I Hope and Wait" across the bottom of the card; Christmas, New Year's, Easter, and nameday greetings, all showed the influence of contemporary America.

The Greeks had accommodated to America to survive and had begun to prosper, but the hostility against immigrants, particularly those from southern Europe, grew. They could never be Americanized, newspaper editorials asserted. They were still bound to their native countries. They refused to learn the English language. "The local Greek priest has been in the country twelve years and cannot speak or understand a word of English. . . . If he doesn't

Page from the Atlas Catalog, *1927–28.*

ΕΙΣ τὰς ἑπομένας δύο Σελίδας βλέπετε τὰς φωτογραφίας τῶν εἰς τὸ κατάστημά μας πωλουμένων Σὲτ Στεφάνων, τὰ ὁποῖα εἶναι τὰ τελειότερα ὅλων. Τὸ κυριώτερον χαρακτηριστικὸν τῶν ὑπὸ τῶν Καταστημάτων «Ἄτλας» πωλουμένων Σὲτ Στεφάνων εἶναι τὸ ὅτι ὅλα τὰ χρειώδη διὰ τὴν τέλεσιν τοῦ Μυστηρίου εἶναι συγκεντρωμένα καὶ καλλιτεχνικῶς τοποθετημένα ἐντὸς κυτίου. Ἕκαστον κυτίον περιέχει τὰ ἑξῆς: 1ον. Ἕν ζεῦγος στέφανα ἀρίστης ἐπεξεργασίας. 2ον. Μίαν καλλιτεχνικωτάτην γυρλάνδαν. 3ον. Δύο Νυμφικὰς Λαμπάδας, πλουσιώτατα ἐστολισμένας μὲ ἄνθη λεμονέας καὶ πολυτελεῖς ἐκ μετάξης ταινίας. 4ον. Δύο Λαμπάδας ἄνευ ταινιῶν διὰ τὸν Ἱερέα καὶ τὸν Κουμπάρον. 5ον. Ἕν πέπλον ἐκ μετάξης ἀρίστης ποιότητος καὶ ἐπεξεργασίας. 6ον. Δύο μπουκέτα ἀνθέων διὰ τοὺς μελλονύμφους. 7ον Τρία μάτσα μπρίλλιες διὰ τὸ στόλισμα τῆς Νύμφης. 8ον. Ἕν μεγάλου μεγέθους ἄνθος διὰ τὴν κομβιοδόχην τοῦ Κουμπάρου. 9ον. Ἀνθάκια μικροῦ μεγέθους διὰ τοὺς πλησιεστέρους συγγενεῖς τοῦ Γαμβροῦ καὶ τῆς Νύμφης. Προμηθευόμενοι ἕν Σὲτ Στεφάνων ἐκ τῶν Καταστημάτων μας ἐστὲ βέβαιοι ὅτι δὲν θὰ σᾶς λείψῃ τίποτε κατὰ τὸ στεφάνωμα. Ὅλαι αἱ παραγγελίαι συσκευάζονται ἐπιμελῶς καὶ ἀποστέλλονται αὐθημερὸν δι' ἐξόδων μας.

want to learn the American language so that he can converse with the local people, he should go back to where Greek is the national language."[15]

The intense pressure brought by the American Legion on the United States Congress that resulted in the immigration restriction laws had two

Page from the Atlas Catalog, *1927–28.*

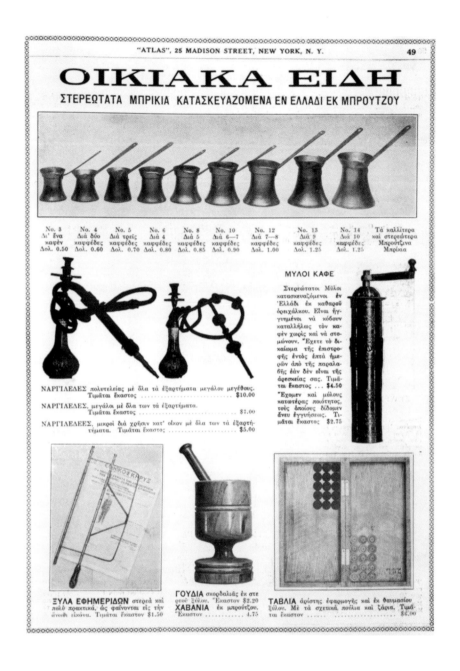

good effects. It brought an end to the *padrones'* hold over labor, and it freed women in the Midwest and West from running boardinghouses. Old-country culture, though, continued to rule. Parents watched over their daughters with paranoid obsession: a girl's glance toward a young man brought punishment:

> *The mill workers used to pass by our house after work. We were just about the only Greek girls, teenagers, you know, in Greek Town and*

Page from the Atlas Catalog, *1927–28.*

the men used to look into our front yard. Dad painted the windows with gray paint so they couldn't see inside, and, of course, we couldn't see out.—Wilma Mageras Klekas[16]

I was seventeen when I got married. . . . We eloped. . . . My father was a Cretan and had been taught that you're supposed to marry a Cretan. I married a Spartan . . . in 1920. [The couple lived in Tulsa, Oklahoma, for five years until it was safe to return.]—Katherine Zolintakis Jerifos[17]

In the prosperity of the 1920s, children attended Greek schools after public schools. In cities the classes were held in church basements or in public schools. The teachers held diplomas from Greek institutions. In small towns without churches, the children met in private homes or empty rented buildings. The teacher was often a man or woman who had one or two years of schooling beyond the four years of grade school that had been considered sufficient for men in Greece.

Because children were attending public schools with other ethnic and American children, parents increased their efforts to provide a Greek milieu for them. That the children would lose their language, their religion, and their very culture in the new land was a constant threat to parents. Orthodoxy was imbedded in Greekness and not in great peril, but the Greek language was assailed by the public schools, by the play of ethnic children who used English to communicate, and by the children themselves as their first language, Greek, was being superceded. Mothers shouted to children to speak Greek in the house, and overly zealous parents punished them physically. Fathers throughout the United States spent enormous amounts of money

Sts. Constantine and Helen Greek Orthodox Church, Washington, D.C., middle 1920s. Courtesy of George Koutras.

to bring teachers to their communities and to provide them with amenities. When teachers left for more lucrative positions, crises developed until replacements could be found. Teachers avoided the West, the "Siberia for Orthodox priests and teachers in America."

Children began their studies with primers written in the *katharevousa,* the language of the Greek courts and universities, a language they would never hear spoken. Baffled, they looked at a sketch of a nose and under it the word *rhys;* they had grown up hearing the word *myty* for nose. Under a sketch of an ear was the word *ota,* not *afti.* Whether the *katharevousa* or the peoples' demotic was taught depended on who was in power in Greek politics, the conservatives or the liberals. At the time of the epic migration to the United States in the early 1900s, the conservatives were in power and the *katharevousa* was preferred.

Teachers in Greek schools had the authority to punish students, and they did so with a thoroughness that would be called child abuse today. Some teachers inspired the children by praise, but most of them taught with negatives. The author's fifth-grade reader from the 1920s lectures: "I don't see you going to school with that determined desire and the shining face that is wished. You still go without desire."

In public school, the children were taunted with slurs of "dirty Greek," "Dago," "Wop"—the insults did not distinguish between ethnic groups. Their names were arbitrarily changed by their teachers—Panaghiota became

Greek school in the copper mining town of Bingham, Utah, mid–1920s. Courtesy of Peter C. Dimas.

Bertha, Peggy, Penny, or Josephine! (the author's sister); and no possible logic turned Alcibiades into Walker. Greek children sat struggling with the artificial language while outside, their schoolmates were playing catch or marbles or hopscotch. More passive according to cultural dictates, girls often excelled in Greek schools; it was preferable to what awaited them at home—housework and tending smaller siblings. Boys were often openly recalcitrant:

> One reason I hated Greek school was because it gave me little time to play or do the things I wanted to do as a youngster. Imagine a grade school youngster coming home from public school in the late afternoon, then having to ready himself for a school he had no desire to attend, and which he attended often under protest, haunted with the thought he would be reprimanded by the teacher for coming to school unprepared, taking with him often a chunk of bread or some other edible to curb his growing appetite, often sitting in bleak, uncomfortable, and sometimes cold surroundings totally different from what he knew in the public school, and forced to have a late supper, sometimes between 7 and 8 in the evening. The disciplinary problems at times reached unbelievable dimensions . . . during its existence the system was a scourge and a terror to pupils.[18]

A student writes of her 1920s school experience in New York:

> The Greek-American Institute of New York was founded in the year 1912 for the purpose of teaching English, as well as Greek . . . and for

Greek school play in Minot, North Dakota, early 1930s, on March 25, the anniversary of the Greek Revolution of 1821 against the Turks. Courtesy of William Kandas, center, between two girls.

the preservation of the Greek traditions. . . . It accommodated approximately two hundred and fifty students. Instructions, in both languages, were by well-qualified teachers. . . . The English teachers, although good disciplinarians, were far more understanding and gentle in their punishment than the Greek teachers, who were extremely strict, using the same disciplinary tactics that had been used on them during their learning years.[19]

Visiting clerics, newspaper reporters, or anyone who considered himself important gave pompous orations while the children sat listening to the droning. Language and history were one. The Turkish occupation was the ever-present subject—that the Turks had conquered all of the Balkans was never mentioned; what they had done to the Greeks was drilled into the students. On March 25 the obligatory *kleftic* play was put on with teachers, parents, and, yes, children, proud and enthusiastic.

Few small towns had churches and a great many children of immigrants either did not attend church, except when visiting priests arrived for Holy Week Easter services, or went to the Episcopal church if one was available. Holding the Nicene Creed in common allowed marriages and baptisms when a Greek priest was unable to officiate. Others attended Protestant Sunday schools.

YMCA Sunday school attended by the author and many Greek immigrant children in the railroad/mining town of Helper, Utah, middle 1920s. Used by permission, Utah State Historical Society, all rights reserved.

Papa Yiannis was of the church with his faded robes, tall priest hat, and beard; and Mr. Shepherd, ascetic and lean, speaking of Jesus lovingly, without even a clerical collar, was the man who ran the YMCA. But whenever we sang in the YMCA basement, a poignancy held me, sentimental as the words were about the kind, all-loving Jesus who forgave and understood and would lead us to Heaven. Not the words but the sad sweetness of the music brought me close to tears for something I could not comprehend.

> I come to the Garden alone,
> When the dew is still on the roses,
> And He walks with me and He talks with me,
> And He tells me I am His own.[20]

Anastasia Soteropoulos, the first Greek child to arrive in Fort Smith, Arkansas, came with her parents in 1907 at the age of two. A Greek church was not established until 1951. Once a year a priest came to administer Holy Communion to the ten members. During this long period, she kept in close touch with the Presbyterian church and other denominations by displaying Greek treasures and speaking of her faith. "I would describe Anastasia as a mystic for she has dedicated all her life to God and she gives credit for all her learning to Him and the study of the Bible."[21]

Eva Topping, classicist and author, attended Baptist Sunday School from the age of six to eighteen in Fredericksburg, Virginia:

> I am the daughter of two immigrants from Thessaly, Greece. A Greek Orthodox priest traveled by train from Washington to baptize me. (Automobiles were rare in those days.) Since he did not bring a proper baptismal font with him, an ordinary washtub was used for the sacrament. . . . We were never more than two or three families. We had no church. It was not until the memorable, truly pastoral visit of Archbishop Athenagoras to Fredericksburg in the early 1930s that the priest came from the church in Richmond to conduct services once or twice a year for our tiny Greek flock. . . . Having grown up singing Baptist hymns, it is no surprise that I still remember many of them. . . . My husband and son always smile whenever I burst out singing:
>
> > Yield not to temptation! For yielding
> > is sin. Each victory will help you
> > Some other to win. . . .[22]

Writing in 1926, Joakeim, bishop of Boston, sounded an alarm and expressed profound pessimism regarding the future of the Greek identity in America. He decried the decline of Greek as a spoken language, lamented the growth of mixed marriages, and pointed out the prevailing conditions conducive to assimilation and the disappearance of the Greek identity in the United States.[23]

For parents, Greek identity meant not only language and religion but the continuation of their native country's customs in America, burdensome and frustrating though they were, especially to American-born daughters. Daughters learned early that they should be *semnes* (modest) and careful in dress, speech, and manners. Sons were only superficially instructed in propriety. An anomaly developed: girls often gave exaggerated attention to "refinement"; their brothers were as often guilty of boorishness.

Mothers placed great importance on manners. Children who forgot to stand up when an adult entered the room or spoke to an older person in the familiar demotic, instead of the polite Greek of *thee* and *thou,* felt the sting of "eating wood," meaning a beating. If they forgot their mothers interminable warnings of "What will people say?" and "What goes on in the house must never go beyond," they were treated as pariahs. Children of immigrants, now old men and women, remember their terror of the *zoni* (belt) and the *blasti* (a cut-off broom stick used to roll out *filo* dough): "I was grown before I stopped having nightmares about 'getting the belt.' "[24] Another reports, "Father had complete control of our lives, over our thinking; we had no right to voice an opinion, or make a decision, often being fearful to even pose a question. We had, many times in the past, been subjected to severe physical punishment, often for little or no reason at all."[25]

Greeks were not the only people to exact hard punishment. "Spare the rod and spoil the child" and its variants are universal proverbs. Greek immigrants believed that a good parent must use hard discipline to help the child become a credit to his *soi* (clan). In America, they raised their children as they had been brought up. Forty or more years later, an essay on family patterns in Greece reveals a change in attitudes toward children.[26]

Boys could accept the culture without much struggle because, unlike the girls, they had little to do with everyday life. They also knew instinctively that they had a more important place in the family than did their sisters.

> *Everything was for my benefit. I was the favored one. My sister was never consulted about anything. I was the one to get an education. And she never once held it against me.*[27]

> *We were five girls and three brothers in the family. When a brother walked into the room, our mother would say, annoyed at our remaining seated, "Get up and give your brother your chair." If the family was going out to a church function or some kind of gathering and one or the other of our brothers hadn't come home, one of us sisters had to stay behind to heat the food and serve him. One of my brothers married an American woman and he scrubbed her kitchen floor. My father made out his will giving everything to my brothers because, he said, "That's how it was done in Greece and brothers took care of their sisters"—it didn't happen that way.*—Mary Pappas Lines[28]

Girls were raised to become good *nykokires* (housewives). They were trained to proffer the hospitality tray to visitors with the same care for the ritual as Japanese American girls were taught the tea ceremony. The tray most often belonged to the mother and had held the candles and *stefana* (crowns) at her wedding. The white embroidered doily, the napkins, the best water and liqueur glasses (carefully filled and with the moisture wiped off the outside), the cherry preserves, sugared orange rind, baklava or other pastry—all had to be flawless. The demitasse of Turkish coffee should be properly prepared with just the right foam. Then the oldest daughter presented the tray with the

The hospitality tray is set on a cutwork linen scarf which belonged to the author's mother. Photograph by Allan Smart.

polite language of the hospitality ritual and answered a modest thank you when the visitor took a sip of the liqueur and said, "To your wedding crowns."

Boys could dally after Greek school, but girls had to return home immediately. They were lectured about their conduct, loud talking and laughing, being teased by a boy, even when they had not invited such notice. Anything that brought attention to them was censured because coffeehouse habitués would report to their fathers, or neighbors would lose no time in bringing the news to mothers. In Greek villages any adult could admonish a child; in America, adults carried out this responsibility by telling parents of pranks and misbehavior. Anything that sullied the family's *filotimo* had to be taken care of, no matter if the messenger was a bootlegger, a card player, or a person who "didn't know why he was living," a common expression about ineffectual people.

Growing up Greek in an American environment in immigrant days placed responsibilities on girls beyond the all-important attention to manners.

> *When my mother was a teenager, her godfather came to the house one day and, of course, she immediately brought out the tray. He refused to let her serve him because she had polish on her nails. She had to go into the other room and remove it.*—Steve Kogianis[29]

> *One day at American [public] school in the restroom one of my friends plucked my eyebrows. Afterwards, I was so scared my parents would notice that I was afraid to go home. I really got it bad.*—Toula Kalikakis[30]

My mother sewed our dresses. She was a good seamstress, but she made the sleeves long and the collars buttoned up. She wouldn't let us go to the movies, because she had gone once and the actresses "were half-dressed, smoked, and gave men the eye."—Goldie Papailion[31]

After school I was not allowed to socialize with non-Greeks. . . . All of us were forbidden to. We never asked why. . . . Sometimes you would want to go out and play with some of them, or when you were invited to their houses, you would want to go. I was once invited to a birthday party. It still sticks in my mind. I was told by my mother that no Greek children she knew were going there, so what did I need to go for? I never brought it up again, she was so angry.[32]

It was as if [my parents] were talking about [Americans as] a whole uncivilized group of people. . . . I believe my parents' picture of an American was of eating cold pork and beans out of a can, and wiping their mouths on a dirty T-shirt . . . not having any feelings or emotions about their families. . . . I don't know where they got their opinions and judgments.[33]

The family always had to be together. Every Sunday, Thanksgiving, Christmas, Easter, name days we sat around our mother's dining room table. There was no such thing as going to the park with friends on Fourth of July or attending a Christmas party. This continued even after we married and had children. We all crowded into our parents' house regularly. There was this feeling that we would be disloyal if we didn't. My husband and I never developed close friendships and I lay the blame on those family dinners.—Marina Daskalos[34]

In addition to Greek schools and church and lodge celebrations, the immigrants established auxiliaries for their children. Although there was little interaction between the girls and boys clubs, parents believed they would be safely enclosed within the Greek life they were promoting in America. The clubs: AHEPA's Sons of Pericles, Maids of Athens, and Daughters of Penelope; the GAPA's auxiliaries, named after the ancient Greeks and 1821 Revolutionaries; and the many regional clubs, particularly the Pancretan Association, completed the circle that had begun with men's lodges.

The lodge picnics were exciting events for children: lambs roasting on spits; fathers singing the old guerrilla songs; mothers laying out their feta-cheese *pites*, eggplant *mousakas*, and honey-nut pastries and slicing enormous watermelons; boys playing catch and baseball; girls huddled together talking and laughing. The cool breezes and scents of pine and roasting lamb transported children from the everyday world and the burden of being Greek and American

The exodus from Greek Towns into more desirable areas was almost complete by the late 1920s. Children left the familiar neighborhoods for schools where they were often the only Greek Americans in their classes. Those who had not yet attended public schools in their old neighborhoods, went to new schools knowing only the Greek language.

> *My sister Magdalene and my brother were put in a class for retarded children because they could not speak English. The teachers mistook their silence for low intelligence.*—Kallie Souvall Politis[35]

If children lived far from Greek schools and would have to take streetcars—their mothers not knowing how to drive—they would drop out early and lose the comradeship of children like themselves. For most, not having to attend Greek school was a release, but they also lost the secure world of Greek Town.

Although the immigrants were spending great sums of money on Greek schools to sustain their language in a foreign country, English words increasingly crept in and produced the anomaly that the linguist P. David Seaman calls American Greek.[36] In an interview with him, a respondent used English words immigrants had appropriated and "Greekified," such as *tsekia* for checks, *banka* for bank, and English words among his Greek.

> [Transliteration] Lipon, simera imuna BUSY, ke xalasa pola tsekia, ke piga sti BANKA dio fores, na xalaso ta tsekia. FIVE-THIRTY, mu TELEFONAI, lipon, i sofia oti i maria ine VERY SICK, ke trexo, ke ti berno apo to spiti ke pao sto . . . DOCTOR GEORGE.
> [And so, today I was very busy, and cashed many checks, and went to the bank two times, to cash checks. Five thirty, Sofia telephones me, and so, that Maria is very sick, and I run, and take her from the house and go to . . . Doctor George.]

The respondent's daughter, who attended a Greek school sponsored by the church, showed Seaman a picture of a family opening Christmas presents and described it in the Cretan dialect.

> [Transliteration] Edo ine enas andras pu dini this jinekas tu ena PRESENT sto CHRISTMAS MORNING, ke ta pedja tu ine sto BACK-GROUND AROUND ena megalo CHRISTMAS TREE, pu ine oreo me OR-NAMENTS AND EVERYTHING, ke pezune ta peja me ta TOYS, kanun OPEN MORE PRESENTS, ke . . . kine WRAPPINGS ke . . . EVERYTHING ALL OVER THE PLACE.

[Here is a man who gives his wife a present on Christmas morning, and his children in the background around a big Christmas tree, that is beautiful with ornaments and everything, and the children play with the toys, they open more presents, and . . . the wrappings and . . . everything all over the place.]

Children of a Greek-immigrant father and an American mother belong to a special category. An Italian or a Yugoslav mother would immerse herself in Greek culture, learn to cook Greek foods, speak Greek, and send the children to the Greek church and Greek school, but American mothers usually stood on the fringes of Greek life and were often hostile to it. Many such children had no clear identity and eventually moved away from all things Greek.

If, though, the father had relatives, a child could weather this dichotomy:

I spent a hectic few years from 3 to 5 traveling a lot between Denver, Cincinnati, Ohio, and New York City, as my parents' marriage faltered. . . . I came under the Greek influence fortuitously. . . . [Visits to my father's brother] were wonderful as I remember his running an import delicatessen somewhere in the produce section of lower waterfront Cincinnati. There all the aromas delighted me. Open barrels of pungent cheeses, olives, olive oil, garlic, spices, and wood shavings on the floor. . . . An aunt, Efthemia, was caring and nurturing and made often, especially for me, kourabiedes, *baklava, and* glyko *that made up for all the deprivations. . . . [The aunt developed tuberculosis and could not take care of him.]*

An event occurred at age 6, when for logistical reasons, my father placed me in a "home." It was a facility run by a Christian church in Denver with dormitories for boys and girls placed there not as orphans, but from what is now euphemistically called dysfunctional families. He did this in a spirit of vengeance toward my mother, though she was in no better position to take care of me than he. My aunts Efthemia and Aspasia were angry at my father for placing me there and spirited me away for weeks at a time.

When I think of it, what I remember most of Greek homes, were the aromas that pervaded the whole house, not just the kitchen. When you entered there was the soft steamy awareness of meats or lamb with oregano, rosemary, thyme and maybe somewhere some incense burning, perhaps mastica.[37]

The immigrants were aging. Letters, bordered in black, telling of the death of parents began arriving from Greece with frequency. Emigrant sons and daughters spoke less often of a permanent return to *patridha*. Visits also presented problems. Businessmen complained: How could they leave their work to employees who would take advantage of their absence and rob them blind? And there was so much to be done in America and besides, they were still sending money for dowries and to help their families in Greece.

CHAPTER 28

ΠΕVER A ΠICKEL
FOR A DRIΠK

On an October morning in 1929, large black headlines in the newspapers numbed the country: Stock Market Crashes! In the following months people lost their jobs; 15 million were not only without work but had neither unemployment insurance nor other benefits to help them. Families who were evicted set up tents and shacks, nailed together with discarded planks and boards. Single men huddled around bonfires and scavenged in garbage dumps for scraps of food. Town marshals stood on guard for strangers and followed them to make certain they did not linger. People starved to death. Freight trains chugged through prairies, valleys, and mountains filled with hungry men, women, and children, all going toward California, where at least it was not cold.

Greek immigrants used up their savings; many became destitute. Relatives and fellow villagers could give little help, for everyone was in a precarious state. They were reliving their earlier village life of fight for survival. During this period, writers were employed by the WPA to interview Americans and immigrants. Elias Vlanton and Evangeline Vlanton Newton compiled the available Greek files under the title "A Lost Generation."[1]

Following the westward caravans, Greeks drove aging cars over dirt and gravel roads through the great desert and toward distant mountains, hoping to find *patriotes* who could help them.

On June 17, 1935, Dad loaded the . . . Model A Ford and a two-wheeled home-made trailer to capacity with all our possessions and we were off to California. Imagine if you can, Mom, Dad and seven children in a Model A Ford. It was so crowded that John had to sit on a bucket between the front and back seats. During the journey we ate things Mom had prepared . . . at the side of the road.

*The first overnight stop was at Elko, Nevada and through the im-
migrant network, Dad located some Greeks that owned a soft drink bot-
tling company who put us up for the night. Gus and John, sleeping on a
bachelor's bunk bed were very much frightened when they discovered the
bachelor had left his revolver under the pillow.*

*[In California, the family made stops on the way, staying with fel-
low villagers.] In Ceres, Mrs. Bollakis took mother, Pearl and Lovey to
Modesto's Sun Garden Cannery where they were hired for the apricot
season, followed by peaches and tomatoes.*

The ingenuity of the family overcame hardships. Seeing a farmer uproot his
vineyard, the father asked whether he could have some of the stumps. He
cut them into pieces and used the wood to heat the house in winter and fuel
the coal stove for cooking.[2]

*Our father never discussed a move that he was planning to take with ei-
ther our mother or us. He would bring home a stack of peach baskets
and tell us to pack. . . . We had few possessions, and virtually no furniture. In Paterson [New Jersey] we were evicted for not paying the rent.
. . . The peach baskets were loaded up. . . . our father was having a terrible time supporting us. . . . [He] would find temporary jobs at restaurants to bring home a few dollars. He sometimes won at cards at the*
kafenion. *He also sold* raki, *or* ouzo, *which he made at home. . . . He
was also a "runner" for the numbers gambling game . . . . he was desperate trying to provide for us.*—Mary Veronis Thompson[3]

*We never went visiting [in Modesto, California] without bringing
something, a few chicks, a bottle of canned fruit, a loaf of bread. We
never went empty-handed.*—Athena Kissamitakis Pallios[4]

*In Detroit in 1932 my father lost his business and then our home. We
went to Poughkeepsie, New York, where he worked for his cousin who
owned the Texas Lunch. From there we went to Seattle and my father got
work with his brother in his Golden Gate Café. In 1938 we were back
in Detroit. There was never a nickel for a bottle of pop or an ice cream
cone and when we did get one, it was a great treat. We were enrolled in
the Aid to Dependent Children program (ADC). [When the Roosevelt
programs took effect] Welfare gave us flour and staples and powdered
milk that I remember to this day how awful it was.*—Deno Pappas[5]

*I remember one Easter, our big family, three of us already married
with children, eighteen of us, could not get three dollars together to buy*

a lamb for Easter. Not to celebrate Christ's Resurrection with the Easter lamb! It was so awful. I can't forget it.—Melva Georgelas Kouris[6]

The Depression was real, real bad. They come to my store [a small grocery store in Salt Lake City that also sold imported Greek foods] and they come for a nickel to buy potatoes. One nickel. We tried to eat the bread and radishes and green olives for not to break the grocery store. I remember now. [Eat the food they could not sell.] For not to close the door. We do very economic of the food for not to go out of business.—Louis Lingos[7]

Jack rabbits are not good eating, but during the Depression groups of men and kids, including me, went out to the sagebrush desert and shot enough to fill the back of a truck. Then we came back and dumped them on Main Street of our [copper mill] town. People picked them up and took them home to eat them.—Nick Papanikolas[8]

As far back as I can remember, Mama always worked. Through the other Greek ladies, she found out about a factory [Chicago] which made women's better wear, and would allow women to take work home. This was illegal because the "home" workers were paid much less than the in-factory workers. . . . Later, when some of the more experienced women informed Mama that she could do better if she took a job in the factory, Mama couldn't do it because by that time my father had become an invalid and she was afraid to leave him alone. He had a heart attack and when he asked the doctor how long he had to live, the doctor kiddingly said, "Oh, I think we can get you through six months." My father who imagined he had all kinds of illnesses, took the doctor seriously and came home to announce he was dying! Since that day to his dying day, our home was more like a hospital than a home—we were always in mourning sadly awaiting for my father to die. He lived until the day before his 80th birthday!

. . . In those days, in the thirties and forties, the garment industry was notorious for its labor practices. Mama started out working for 5 cents an hour. [The owner] was a tiny, wiry, ogre of a woman feared by all the immigrant women who worked for her. . . . She always scolded, reprimanded the women and kept them in a permanent state of fear that they would not receive any more work if they displeased her. Most of the women never knew her name. She was called "Mrs." by most of them. . . . her demands were so unreasonable. . . . workers would have to toil through half the night to accomplish what she wanted. I know Mama did because she was afraid

if she displeased her, she might not give her any more work and then what would we do?—A daughter's biography[9]

Our Mothers Club had monthly dues of ten cents for married women and five cents for those who were having a hard time. Out of this small sum we bought coal to heat the houses, clothes for the children. We asked Greek farmers for potatoes and onions and they brought them by the gunnysack. We bought milk for the children. We were determined that the children would not go hungry.—Lela Ioannou Kannes, Argos, Argolidhos Province[10]

"Don't invite me to a eat lambs' heads. I got sick of them in the Depression."—Several sons of sheepmen

I was playing on the floor. I got up and asked my mother why she was crying. She told me, "I don't have any food in the house and no money to buy any." "Mom, watch me, I'll go get some money." I went downstairs and walked along the curb, and Lord behold, I found a nickel. I rushed upstairs. "Here, Mom, now we have money for food." She sent me to the grocery store, which was next door, to buy a pound of spaghetti. She put a pot of water on the stove, and we had spaghetti, no cheese or sauce, just plain boiled spaghetti with salt.—Stephen J. Paitakis[11]

In the mining towns of the West, the Depression forced Greek families to leave their company houses and go elsewhere, mainly to California, in hopes of finding work with countrymen in the grape region. Sheepmen saw the price of lambs fall from eighteen dollars a head to three dollars. The price of wool was so low that it was not worth the money to graze sheep. Greek sheepmen suffered the bitter experience of riding livestock freights with their sheep, unloading them, watering and feeding them, and finding no buyers in Grand Junction, Denver, Omaha, or Kansas City, finally abandoning them in the Chicago stockyards. In the jargon of the Depression, the banks "owned" the sheepmen.

Boys fared better in the Depression than did their sisters. Although their mothers continually harangued them that they must marry Greek girls, teenage boys attended high-school dances which their sisters could not. In old age many women remembered pressing their brothers' pants and shining their shoes for dates. Their parents were aghast at the American custom of dating. Parents who allowed their daughters to go out with men were "throwing them to the dogs." In Greece, women and men, even girls and boys, did not speak to each other unless they were related.

Except for a small number in factories, women did not work for others. Evangelia Glitsos Constantinides, born in Smyrna, Asia Minor, is pictured at the sewing machine of her husband's Progressive Hatters and Cleaners, St. Louis, Missouri, 1965. Courtesy of Jennie C. Vlanton.

Although the immigrants believed fervently in education for their sons, their daughters were brought up to be housewives. Those who had been allowed to work only in the restaurants, candy stores, and grocery stores owned by their fathers, uncles, and godfathers now found work in Kress, J. C. Penney, and other department stores. Their low wages were used for their brothers' college tuitions. When girls expressed a wish to continue their education, mothers had ready replies: "If you could keep house with pen and typewriter, but a house isn't kept with pen and typewriter."

Girls were still expected to arrive at home at an hour that would not permit any sauntering with friends. They were constantly aware of the scrutiny that the entire community gave them. If they argued that their mothers were mistaken in their view that American dating meant sex, daughters got sardonic answers: "It isn't the man who's going to push the baby buggy." Many children of immigrants became "reluctant participants" in their parents' Greek America.

Language, religion, old world customs and endogamous marriages were accepted indices of Greek identification and because of this any deviation by their children constituted a threat to their security, their self-image, their traditional roles, and their well-being. . . . Their children, the second generation, experienced their parents' definition of ethnicity as a liability. Despite this, the Greek Church, the Greek school, and the Greek language became integral parts of the

A March 25th play,
Holy Trinity Cathedral,
Washington, D.C., early
1930s. Courtesy of
Helen Anderson.

self-image of these reluctant participants. They became the hyphenated Greek-Americans bordering two worlds.[12]

Yet, during this dismal, painful decade, the Greeks survived with communal activities that brought momentary relief. Plays were put on for the
March 25 celebration of the Greek War of Independence and on other occasions. Many of the plays were the old favorites brought from Greece; others were written by Greeks in the United States. They were almost always
free. Growing immigrant children often had roles, and, because it was considered inappropriate for men and women to mingle, men were sometimes
made up and took women's parts.

Haralambos (Harry) Kambouris, from a village near Thebes, left the
only journal written in the early years of mass migration from Greece, de-
tailing his frantic search for work between 1912 and 1915, from Kansas to
Oregon and to Utah. He also wrote many plays that were produced by his
Star Theatrical Company in Salt Lake City.[13]

A 1934 play by Mimis Demetriou (James Demetrius), dedicated to his
"Dear Countrymen," was a highly successful tragedy. As the author described it:

> In America, this illiterate Greek worker . . . had to struggle. . . . Law
> abiding, conscientious, careful. Having one sorrow, a hidden pas-
> sion . . . to return home! To fulfill his beautiful, his good, his ideal
> intentions! To cheer, to spend Christmas and the Resurrection

among his own! . . . But alas! This pure, clean, white, honest person, the ideal family man, falls into the trap . . . and along with his dreams, his hopes sink, are destroyed forever! . . .

His downfall is a blonde woman.[14]

Mimis Demetrius also wrote a satirical comedy entitled *The Brooklis in Athens* (Greek Americans, whether from Brooklyn or not, were called "Brooklis"). The Brooklis had returned to Greece and is described as "Bold with a big mustache, gold teeth, a thick gold chain, rings, pens, pencils." He speaks Greek with bowdlerized English that his employees do not understand. He is officious and gives a bribe because he has neglected to get a permit for his store. This leads to more bribes and situations where his arrogance is properly taken care of.[15]

Greek radio stations also provided hours of music and comedy sketches in New York City and Chicago. They advertised olive oil, cheese, and other imported foods and gave news of the Greek communities.

Because many families could not afford to buy the traditional lamb for Easter, churches held the Sunday Agape dinner for the congregations. Local musicians played *lyras, laoutos,* and clarinets. The growing children danced the *syrto* and *tsamiko* alongside the adults. Music gave surcease to the immigrants in the gray years. At baptisms, weddings, and religious events, phonograph records spun when no performers were available. Nostalgia of the Greeks in *ksenitia* sang out from the records: the pining for the homeland;

the loneliness away from family and friends, from the eagle-topped mountains and the "incomparable waters" of their villages; and the old *kleftic,* songs of which they never tired. They spoke with dry humor of experiences in early immigrant days and with wrath over political events in both Greece and America.

Songs from Greek and other languages were carelessly translated, and often their themes were completely altered. The old folk song "Mother, the Curly Basil [plant]," translated by the author into English, goes:

> Mother the curly basil plant broad leafed and cool
> a shame it isn't watered, it isn't pruned.
> Mother let's water it, let's prune it
> And from much watering and pruning
> It sprouted branches and boughs and covered a neighborhood
> and it covered me also whose mother has but me.[16]

A dance manual translates the folk song as:

> Mother, this pot of basil green, broad leafed and moist
> with dew-drop sheen
> Who'll water it from day to day and tend it whilst my
> love's away?
> Oh, mother, care of it let's take and water it for my
> Love's sake
> And with the water cool and bright, the tender care
> both day and night
> The basil sprouted leaf and spray and half the village
> hid away.
> And in its shade I sit me here and wait for one I love
> so dear.[17]

The hard years of the decade were the subject of "Ti Epathe O Tsimis Me to Depression?" (What Happened to Jimmy in the Depression?)

> Ach, Tsimi, ach Tsimi, you poor fool.
> You haven't a cent left.
> What did the Depression do to you?
> You are no longer Tsimi, nor are you Demetrios.[18]

Many Greek Americans adamantly believed that President Herbert Hoover had caused the Depression. In "Hoover, What Have You Done to Us," the singer recalls the days when they took taxis and ate steaks; now they have empty pockets and must walk and eat hot dogs.[19] In "The Honorable

Worker," President Franklin D. Roosevelt's National Recovery Act is invoked: "Now with the NRA, I will buy you a *kanape* [couch]." This song was recorded in Greece, where the reference to NRA was omitted because the Greeks did not know what it meant.[20]

Greece also had a new leader, the dictator John Metaxas. Greeks in America feared for their relatives under his regime. The *Atlantis* accepted him as an old royalist; the *National Herald* attacked him for bringing a dictatorship to their country, but it relented when his reforms, much like Roosevelt's New Deal, brought Greece a change for the better. "A necessary evil," the *National Herald* said.[21]

CHAPTER 29

ARCHBISHOP ATHENAGORAS

For the Greeks, the 1930s brought a significant event. The Ecumenical Patriarchate in Constantinople sent Athenagoras, the Metropolitan of Corfu, to become Archbishop of the Americas. This appointment ended the civil war over Archbishop Alexander, who was deposed. Despite dire predictions of Greek Orthodoxy being in peril, the turbulence quieted. Athenagoras's long tenure was salutary for the Greeks in the United States. He was tall, six foot six without the stove-pipe *kalimafkion* on his head. His dignity and sincerity endeared him to the Greeks, especially those in the South and West, who seldom had an archbishop visit their communities. His memory was phenomenal. Years after he was called to Constantinople (Istanbul) to become the Patriarch of the Greek Orthodox, Greek Americans visiting the Patriarchate were amazed that he remembered both their names and where they lived, although he had seen them only briefly.

His tremendous memory of America remained intact. He enquired about the progress of GOYA [Greek Orthodox Youth of America] and was pleased to learn that GOYA had embarked on building a Byzantine chapel in memory of our immigrant parents at his beloved Holy Cross Theological School in Massachusetts—, which he had founded in 1937.

. . . But nothing stands out more vividly in my mind exemplifying this "apostle of love" on our last visit at the Phanar. It was early evening and we had gone to pay our farewell respects to the Patriarch. As we walked into his office accompanied by His Holiness, someone turned on the lights. His reaction was swift but kind. "Please turn off the lights and I will put on my light at my desk." This was done and he quickly proceeded to explain why. "I do not want to disturb or

214

Archbishop Athenagoras was sent to America by the Ecumenical Patriarchate in Constantinople (Istanbul) in 1931. He instilled order in Greek Orthodoxy in the United States. Postcard issued by the Greek Orthodox Archdiocese of N. and S. America on his twentieth anniversary on the throne of St. Andrew (1949–69).

frighten away a family that has been visiting us for some weeks now."
We looked up and saw that the light fixture was the nest of a family
of birds, which had come in from the open windows of his office.[1]

Myths surrounded the archbishop. One sprang up in both the South and
the West. On leaving the Salt Lake City church for McGill, Nevada, a small
copper mining town, the entourage was delayed and drove across the desert
at night. The car was low on gas and the driver stopped at a service station
that was closed. He pressed on the horn until a sleepy attendant came out.
At that moment, the archbishop in his black robes, with the *kalimafkion* on
his head, got out of the car. The station attendant looked up to the enormous, black-shrouded figure and fainted. The version in the South had an
African American as the station attendant.

> *Archbishop Athenagoras had recently come to America and came to
> Perth Amboy [New Jersey] for an AHEPA celebration. There was a pa-
> rade and a* horoesperidha *[evening dance]. I was a small girl, dressed
> in frilly chiffon, and very much impressed with my father's being the
> president of our church. When I saw the archbishop in his vestments, I
> said, "Why are you dressed like that?" The archbishop answered, "So
> that people will recognize me." I insisted. "My father's the president of
> the church and he should be dressed like that. Our priest wears black."
> He patted my head. Afterwards he told my father I was a spoiled brat.
> That night after dinner at my parents' house, he, my father, Governor
> Harold Hoffman, the owner of the Crystal Candy Kitchen, and the
> owner of a hat-cleaning and shoe-shining place smoked cigars and
> played poker.*—Stella Voylates Bosch[2]

> *Athenagoras was visiting the Greeks in an eastern Utah mining town.
> Barba [Uncle] Yiannis told him they would go to his house for some-
> thing to eat. Meanwhile Barba Yiannis's wife Yiannina was doing the
> weekly Monday washing. For this she always pushed the washing ma-
> chine into the dining room because there was more room. The door
> opened and Barba Yiannis entered with the archbishop. "Old woman,"
> Barba said, "fix something for the archbishop to eat." Yiannina began a
> tirade at her husband for not telephoning to give her time to prepare for
> his visit. When she caught her breath, Barba Yiannis said, "Ma kala,
> anthropos einai" [Now then, he's only a man].*—Penelope Koulouris[3]

> *All the women in Great Falls wanted to serve Athenagoras dinner. He
> said he would go to the family with the most children. My mother had
> the most and she was so happy. He was going to visit Butte, Montana,*

after his visit to Great Falls. So the symvoulio *[church council] decided that whoever had the newest car should chauffeur the Archbishop to Butte. My father had a 1940 Oldsmobile 4-door sedan. . . . My brother Rock was appointed to do the driving. Athenagoras, his deacon, and Father George Stephanopoulos, the father of Robert and Elias, were seated in the back seat. Athenagoras spotted a man on a horse and asked if he was a boycow. . . . My father-in-law said Hillfoot Boulevard instead of Foothill Blvd.*—Dina Demopoulos Argyres[4]

(Reversing compound English words was common among immigrant Greeks. Although the author's mother had learned to speak English, she had trouble with words such as *olive oil,* which she pronounced *oilvoil.*)

Archbishop Athenagoras regularly celebrated the Epiphany in Tarpon Springs, Florida, on 6 January. He threw a cross into the water and boys dived in to retrieve it. The boy who was successful received a blessing from the archbishop: "As Christ was being baptized by John, . . . the Spirit of God descending like a dove and lighting on him. . . . And lo a voice from heaven saying, This is my beloved son in whom I am well pleased" [Matthew 3:16, 17]. The language of the liturgy remained ecclesiastical Greek, but the immigrants were losing some cherished words. The word "Romios" was no longer used to denote a Greek—it was replaced by the words "Ellinas" and "Ghrekos." More English words mixed in with their Greek.

The dream of immigrants to return to the homeland faded completely with the Depression. Letters they received from their families told of extreme poverty. The median yearly income there per person was seventy-five dollars, and the money immigrants had been sending to Greece had been cut to one-fourth of what it had been before the Depression.[5]

They were deeply anxious about marrying off their now-grown daughters. Many immigrant sons had begun marrying women who were not Greek, ignoring their mothers' threats that they must not bring a *ksenoi* (strange) bride into the family. Other second-generation Greek men were reluctant to take on the responsibility of marriage in the worsening economy. For most second-generation women there was no choice: they had to marry older immigrant men.

Parents made inordinate financial sacrifices to take their daughters to the AHEPA, GAPA, and other regional conventions. Marriages were sometimes arranged at the conventions, to the parents' deep relief. Young women were bound by culture to accept their parents' wishes and commands; leaving home to become independent, if they dared defy parents, was impossible in the Depression years, when millions of people were out of work.

Archbishop Athenagoras in Tarpon Springs, Florida, on the day of Epiphany, blessing a boy who has retrieved the cross, in memory of the baptism of Christ. Courtesy of St. Photios National Shrine, St. Augustine, Florida.

In immigrant marriages, the husband was often ten to thirty years older than the wife, so many widows were faced with marrying off their children alone.

Perhaps the most important consequence of widowhood was the intense attachment it generated between mothers and their eldest sons. A Greek proverb I heard cited often states that Greek mothers cannot marry off their daughters fast enough and never want to

marry off their sons at all. This had a ring of truth in our Detroit microcosm. Although mothers developed great anxiety about daughters who approached their mid-twenties unwed, marriage for sons had a different framework altogether. While always on the lookout for a "good Greek girl" for "my boy," mothers were content to wait for the perfect match.[6]

"Mothers thought if they had a son, they had a golden egg."[7]

Marriages uniting people of two different generations usually meant discontent for America-born Greek women. Besides the wide difference in age and the American-school background of the wives, the women had acquired American ideas of romantic love from movies and popular magazines—ideas that were lost on immigrant husbands.

My mother screamed and yelled that if I didn't marry him, she'd die of a heart attack or something.—Toula Fanerou (pseudonym)

My whole family knew it, but I didn't have the slightest idea that I was getting engaged. . . . I was at that time in Michigan for the vacation and one afternoon I got a telephone call from my father telling me I was engaged. . . . My sister and her husband sat in the front seat and I sat in the back with Neoclis. . . . It was the first time I had seen him.[8]

I hadn't finished high school, but I said I'd marry him if he fixed my front teeth. Even if he was a Greek from the old country. I'd lost my two front teeth when I was a little girl and fell from a tree.—Mary Petros (pseudonym)

I wanted to get away from my mother so badly that I agreed to marry————. He was thirty years older than I was. He fooled me. He knew I smoked, secretly, of course, and he used to give me cigarettes when I came into his restaurant. After the wedding, when we were on the train going to California for our honeymoon, I took out a package of cigarettes. He reached over, took them, and crumpled the package. "You're married now, and you're not going to smoke anymore." Not only that, but he brought Koutsos [a nickname for a friend who limped] because Koutsos had never been to California and wanted to see it.—Effie Perounas (pseudonym)

We went on a three-day honeymoon, about a hundred miles away. I put my makeup case in between us on the front seat so I wouldn't be close to him. I'd only seen him two or three times at the church horoes-peridhes. *If I had known how kind and good he was, I would have enjoyed those days.*—Bessie Lamperis (pseudonym)

Do you remember————? She didn't want to marry Jim, but she didn't want to end up the rest of her life an old maid. After the wedding dinner, she was getting undressed and somehow swallowed the safety pin she used on her slip. She spent the night in the hospital eating mashed potatoes.—Stella Bakros (pseudonym)

A few Greeks still went back to Greece for brides. The men were usually forty-five years old or so with decades of savings; their brides were eighteen or younger.

Yes, he was thirty-five years older. I told him I would marry him if he took me to see Hollywood. We haven't gone yet.—Theofani Makrios (pseudonym)

The plight of Greeks returning to Greece with a little money was depicted by two highly praised singers, Tetos Demetriades and Petros Kyriakos, with mandolin and guitar accompaniment:

> Say, I'm never going back to Athens,
> because when I set foot in Piraeus
> My relatives who were dying of hunger,

were all asking me to lend them dollars.
Oh, dollar, whoever loves you,
should not go to Athens.
Because who ever sets eyes on you,
po po po, hey, what sorrow, will ask you for dollars.
And the girls would quarrel among them, who would
be the first to take me as a groom.
And so I spent six months living like a lord
and the dollars sprouted wings.
Heavy hunger set in.
And everyone was telling me,
"It's just your luck. That's all."[9]

Many aging immigrant men gave up the idea of marrying or of returning to Greece. They continued their routine, which had been established from their earliest years in America: work, boardinghouse or hotel, Greek restaurant, and coffeehouse. Even on Sundays, they were found in coffeehouses, talking, playing cards, and drinking Turkish coffee. Priests castigated them, and several attempted to have church boards close down the coffeehouses. A priest in the author's mining town took nails, hammer, and boards and barricaded the coffeehouse early one Sunday. One of the patrons died soon afterwards. The priest stood over his open casket and shouted at him, "Worthless coffeehouse *alytis* (bum)! You never gave a dime to the church. Spent all your time in the coffeehouse! And now we have to bury you!"

Immigrant fathers were grateful for part-time work with the New Deal programs. Once-proud men now raked the grass of official buildings and cleaned out storm sewers. Coffeehouses were filled with men who had no money, no work, and nowhere else to go, except to their sad houses or third-rate hotel rooms. Many Greeks who had been royalists in *patridha* and had continued their conservative views by joining the Republican party in America became Democrats during the Depression and championed President Franklin D. Roosevelt. When he died in 1945, memorial services were conducted in Greek Orthodox churches. Black wreaths hung above pictures of the president with the words *aionia e mnymy* (Eons [be] his memory) inscribed under them.

In the coffeehouses, the old records became scratchier, the one or two newspapers were read and re-read; the cup of coffee had to last, and the talk was one of laments for the 1920s and the election upheavals in Greece. Greek politics would continue to churn the immigrants' emotions until they died.

Ambridge, Pennsylvania. Arthur Rothstein photographed four boys in front of a Greek coffeehouse, 1938. Library of Congress, LC-USF34-26532-D.

When Hitler invaded Czechoslovakia in 1938 and Romania in 1939, Greeks huddled around their radios and read American and Greek-language newspapers with mounting unease. On 28 October 1940, Mussolini, Italy's premier, demanded Greek land for his use and for that of his ally Hitler. The Greek government refused, and the Italo-Greek War began. On the mountain faces in Greece the white-washed word OHI (NO) was the answer to Mussolini. The date 28 October would be celebrated yearly, not only in Greece, but among Greeks throughout the world in honor of this heroic resistance to the formidable Axis powers.

CHAPTER 30

THE END OF THE GREAT IMMIGRANT ERA

Greeks in America were angered by and scornful of the invading Italians. Sophia Vembo's recordings of "O Ntoutsis" (El Duce) and "Na, O Macaronas" (There's the macaroni eater); Nikos Gounaris's "Ntoutsis, Noutsis" and "Koroidho [Fool] Mussolini"; Dimitriadhes's "Mourgo [Bulldog] Mussolini" and "Tsimblari [Bleary-eyed] Hirohito" were played on phonographs to hilarity and ridicule in homes and lodge halls and at receptions.[1]

> The songs of Sophia Vembo will be forever identified with the Greek involvement in World War II. . . . The defiant Vembo used her voice and social station to protest and challenge the invading [German, Italian, Bulgarian] armies. When she finally made her American debut in 1947 she was given nothing less than a heroine's welcome. . . . When a talent scout from Athens accidentally overheard Vembo singing, he immediately offered her a contract. Surprisingly, Vembo was not sure she should accept the offer. Her strict family upbringing led the young woman to believe that any woman who went on the stage would be inevitably "ruined."[2]

With Germany's invasion of Greece, immigrants feared for their people. Reports filtered through of the destruction of the country, with the Nazi army looting, requisitioning crops, and driving off domestic animals for their own use. People died from hunger each day on the streets of Athens, in towns, and in villages.

> *My father came down from the village and walked towards Kseromero, looking for relatives to help us. We had no food. He never reached Kseromero. He died at the side of the road from starvation.*

World War II–era cartoon of Mussolini by Reg Manning. Courtesy of The Salt Lake Tribune.

Strangers buried him. We never found out where.—Ioanna Zisi-mopoulou Giovas[3]

No help could get through to Greece or to Crete. When the United States entered the war on 7 December 1941, the day Japan bombed Pearl Harbor, Greek American men registered for the draft. Old-country mothers lighted candles before the saints on the *iconostasion* (the icon screen that shields the altar at the east end of the church). They offered *tamas* to the saints, making pledges in exchange for their sons' safe return. The *tamas* were inviolable. They would have to be carried out, whether the promise was to build a chapel in their childhood village, to send money to a monastery, or for an act of complete humility, such as attending church services barefoot.

I wanted to join the marines, but my mother wouldn't sign for me. I was in my first year of college and wasn't of age. I joined the merchant marines and my mother signed the papers because she thought I would be safe on a ship. She prayed all the time, before I left, while I was gone, and when I returned.

I was lost. My first time away from my family and first time out of the state. I was trained to be a refrigeration engineer. We traveled the world, India, Australia, Africa. In Lourenco Marques and Cape Town, South Africa, I met many Greek immigrants. They were well-to-do and exported fruits, vegetables, and other farm products. We had to wear civilian clothes when we left the ship because Lourenco Marques was a neutral port. Ships from all countries, Allies and Axis alike, docked in the port. The Greeks were very hospitable and were surprised that I could speak Greek. One of them asked about a Greek living in Salt Lake — but I don't remember his name. I was on the ship for three and a half years. I was a different person when I came back. I had seen the world. I had a broader education. My mother and I and the rest of the family went to church to give thanks for my safe return.—Andy Katsanevas[4]

In Camp Hood, in Texas, 1943, some buddies and I walked into a restaurant. I said to them, "What I'd like right now are some lamb shanks." Wishful thinking. Two guys in the back heard me. The owners. One guy said, "Are you Greek?" I said yes, and he said talk Greek. So we did. He asked me where my parents had come from. I said from the Peloponnese, outside Tripolis, and I said, "And you're a Roumeliot." I could tell by his dialect. Well, he told us to eat as much as we wanted, anytime, and not pay for anything. When I got out of the service, I used to deliver to Greek restaurants and the old timers always said, "Sit down, have something to eat," and we'd talk.—John Chipian[5]

One Saturday night he knew he had to get off base or explode. The next morning he took an army bus to Los Angeles and then a city bus to look for the Greek church listed in the city directory. He had trouble finding the right street and had to walk several blocks asking people on the way for directions. He was eager to get there—he, who since becoming an adult had attended church only on Easter.

Not many people were in the church. Mothers and grandmothers were lighting candles before the icons and praying. Steve breathed in the incense, was soothed by the priest and cantor's intoning the liturgy, by the Greek words. He had to watch the women to make sure he was making the sign of the cross at the proper times. . . .

Outside he looked at the blue sky and felt calmed, yet he did not want to return to the base. . . . An old man approached him, peering at him with age-filmed eyes. "Can you speak Greek?" he asked in English. When he said he did, a smile came to the old man's purplish lips. "Come to my house. My wife she cooked."

The dining room was uncomfortably quiet. . . . The chicken needed salt, but Steve would not reach out for the shaker in front of him. . . . The three ate on as if they were eating a mournful forty-day memorial dinner for a dead person. . . . The old woman clapped her hands against her withered cheeks, got up, and hobbled into the kitchen. She returned with a bowl of boiled dandelions. "My boy, I forgot the dandelions."

"Ah!" Steve said, a little cry of pleasure that sounded strange in the quiet room. He took a large spoonful of the greens, poured olive oil on them, and then the juice of a half a lemon. He took a mouthful and ate, smiling. The old woman looked at him with kindly, faded eyes. He thought he would cry: dandelions, home, his own house, his own people.

Afterwards, he stood [with them] on the cement path of the bungalow house. . . . He knew the old people were following the ancient edict of Greek hospitality by bringing him [there].[6]

Increasingly, young men appeared in uniform at liturgies. Soon memorial wheat was brought to church for sons who had been killed or lost. Many soldiers were buried in Death Weddings, with wedding crowns, wedding bands, and flowers in their lapels. The author remembers the Death Wedding of a son of Cretan parents. He was dressed in his uniform, and *koufeta*, the white almonds tied with white ribbon given as favors at weddings, were distributed to the parishioners at the end of the Liturgy for the Dead.

In the Rocky Mountains, the 122d Infantry Battalion was established with Greek Americans and Greek nationals for the purpose of invading Greece.[7] Their commander was a Greek American, Major Peter D. Clainos of Manchester, New Hampshire, West Point Class of 1933. The motto of the battalion was "Liberty or Death," an echo of Patrick Henry in the American Revolutionary War and of the Greek guerrillas in their insurrection against the Turks in 1821–28: "One day of freedom than forty years a

The 122d Battalion of Greek Americans and Greek nationals being trained to invade Greece, then under German occupation, Camp Carson, Colorado, 1943. Courtesy of Angelo Pappas, a member.

slave." The number 122 was taken from the years that had passed since the 1821 revolt against the Turks. Three hundred members of the battalion were parachute troops. During the German occupation, they dropped from planes to dynamite and destroy strategic roads and bridges.

Greek American women also began enlisting in the armed services and in the Red Cross. Among the first was Angeline J. Geo-Karis, who had been born in Tegea, Greece, and had come to the United States with her parents when she was young.[8]

Immigrant mothers from large groups in Chicago, New York, and Los Angeles to smaller ones as in Salt Lake City, Utah, rolled bandages and pre-

The 122d Infantry Battalion, called the Greek Battalion, with a Greek priest, a guest on Easter. Courtesy of Angelo Pappas.

pared kits for the armed forces. Mothers also saved cooking grease, and children gathered scrap iron, tin, and rubber.

Most young men were in uniform. Women, including Greek Americans, were taking their places in grocery stores, restaurants, and war plants where the workers were saluted with the popular song "Rosie the Riveter." Greek Americans were proud of the half-Greek Andrews sisters, who entertained troops, singing such songs as, "Don't Sit under the Apple Tree with Anyone Else but Me" and "Chattanooga Choo Choo."

Immigrant widows with half-grown children also went to work; although they spoke poor English, they bettered their families' situations. This veering away from culture was intensified by a number of immigrant daughters who played baseball. After a nationwide talent search, "Chicago Cubs owner Philip Wrigley decided to form a professional women's baseball league which would keep baseball alive even if major league play was suspended." Anastasia Batikis said, "Father didn't like it at first. Later he thought it okay."[9] The unprecedented action of young Greek American women leaving the sanctuary of the home signaled a waning of the immigrant generation's influence and the coming to the fore of their children's fight for independence.

During World War I, immigrant Greeks had bought defense bonds in generous numbers. Their patriotism in World War II was even greater, for their children were in the services and America had become more than a second country. All Greek lodges supported the bond drives with the Greek War Relief Association (GWRA) and AHEPA leading the way. The GWRA was

Angeline J. Geo-Karis served as Lt. Commander with top-secret clearance in the U.S. Naval Reserves. Courtesy of Angeline J. Geo-Karis.

headed by Spyros Skouras, the president of the National Theaters Company, who raised ten million dollars. Ninety percent of the money collected, Skouras said, came from Americans of Greek descent; because of the overwhelming volunteer support, only 2 percent went to administrative costs.[10]

In a meeting of the Greek War Relief Committee, Charles Skouras said:

Charles Moskos, right, now a leading military sociologist, professor of sociology at Northwestern University, and member of the American Academy of Arts and Sciences, with his brother, salvaging rubber heels for the war effort in their father's shoe repair shop, 1942. Courtesy of Charles C. Moskos.

"Ladies and gentlemen, I am fifty-five years old. I have been in this country about thirty-five years. . . . [My brothers and I] are still in the movie business. I am married to a woman of German descent and we now live in Beverly Hills. I have, living with me, two daughters, a son-in-law and a mother-in-law. All these years, every time I went home, I felt like a man of no significance. Very little attention was ever paid to me by any of them, my mother-in-law, my wife, my children. It was evident from the news that the Greek Army was driving the Fascist Legions out of Epirus. I went home one evening, around the second or third of this month [November] and they were all standing in line bowing to me. Due to the heroic stand of the Greek soldiers they looked at me, and all Greeks, with new respect. I am grateful, and I can't help but think that every Greek American should be grateful for what they have done to elevate the Greek name throughout the United States and the whole world. There isn't enough that we can do to repay those people. They've made the American people realize that the Greeks of today are true descendants of the ancient Greeks."[11]

A Congressional Medal of Honor was awarded to a Greek American, Chris Car (Christos H. Caraberis) of Manchester, New Hampshire. His citation tells of his advancing ahead of his unit with a submachine gun, eliminating a German machine gun, taking prisoners, proceeding under heavy fire, weaving and crouching toward a second enemy machine gun, which he destroyed "with a nerve-shattering shout and a burst of fire," and advancing to two more machine guns. "By his one attack, heroically and voluntarily undertaken in the face of tremendous risks, Sgt. KARABERIS captured 5 enemy machinegun positions, killed 8 Germans, took 22 prisoners, cleared the ridge leading to his company's objective, and drove a deep wedge into the enemy line, making it possible for his battalion to occupy important commanding ground."[12]

After the war, Greek-born Americans wanted to return to Greece to help their families, but a civil war between those loyal to the government and Greek communists erupted with horrific cruelty. The devastated country had lost 500,000 of its population of 7 million through battle, starvation, and disease. Greeks killing Greeks! An unthinkable, unbelievable calamity! The best the Greek-born could do was send used clothing—new clothing was taxable to the receivers—and medicine, especially quinine for malaria, which "forced the [Greek] race to its knees."[13]

The civil war indelibly seeped into the psyche of the Greeks. To the present time, the work of poets, writers, and historians reveals the open wound. Yiannis Ritsos, one of Greece's many renowned poets, who include George Seferis and Odysseus Elytis, Nobel Prize winners, says in his poem "Romiossini":

> Listen!
> The bells will toll at any moment.
> This land is theirs, as it is ours.
> Beneath the soil,
> Between their two crossed hands,
> They hold the ropes.
> They await the hour.
> They do not sleep.
> They do not die,
> They await to sound
> the resurrection.
> This land is theirs as it is ours,
> No one can take it from us.[14]

Immigrant Greeks in the United States avidly read of the struggle of the leftists against the rightist Greek government. According to their liberal or conservative views, they upheld either the Communist guerrillas or the government in the murder of George W. Polk in Thessaloniki. An American correspondent in Athens, Polk had "relentlessly criticized players of both sides in the Greek civil war. He had called the communist guerrillas thugs, accused the Greek government of greed and corruption, branded a former minister of public order a gangster, and blasted Washington for supporting the repressive right-wing Greek government."[15] The government's attempt to blame the Communists for the murder was eventually discredited: a conspiracy was uncovered between high officials and accessories to the murder. Disillusion for their birth country affected many Greeks in America, but the strong anti-Communist fervor in the country also helped minimize for others the glaring facts of the political murder.

(Fifteen years later the immigrant Greeks again read of another political murder, again in Thessaloniki, and again devoured the news in Greek-language newspapers. "In May 1963 a sinister light was cast on the activities of the professional patriots of the extra-parliamentary right with the murder of the left-wing deputy, Dr. Gregory Lambrakis, who was struck down by the ultra right wing thugs at a peace rally held in Salonika."[16] All over Greece the letter Z appeared for *zie*: "He lives." The murder was dramatized in the movie Z. Although immigrants would never give up their love for *patridha,* repeatedly talk in those years touched on Greece's inability to govern as America did.)

Echoing General Makriyiannis's account of an insurrection against the Turks in the late 1700s, an almost illiterate Cretan, George Psychoundakis, wrote *The Cretan Runner,* a memoir of his exploits in the Cretan mountains to bring messages to and from the British, who had parachuted into the island to destroy German communication lines.[17] Manos Hatzidakis's and Mikis Theodorakis's compositions evoking life before the war and the tragic darkness of the Civil War that followed found eager listeners among the Greeks in America.

Translations of Nikos Kazantzakis's books became available; Greek Americans continue to read him above all other Greek authors. Greeks who would have turned from him had they studied his philosophy, honored and defended him. When he died in 1957, the Greeks mourned. Priests were forbidden to bury him, but a Cretan priest defied the authorities and performed the Liturgy for the Dead. A mountaineer picked up the casket and lowered it into the grave. Konstantinos Lardas tells of Ulysses-Kazantzakis's return, ill from Germany, and his wrestle with Charon (Death) in "The Burial of Nikos Kazantzakis":

Through you
the caique-born Ulysses
Drifted to icy regions of the North;
The fallen Charon stretching beside him
On the slimy floor,
Smiling, to touch, to take.

You,
Schweitzer kissed;
The church, the nation shunned.

Through you
Ulysses clasped
The youthful fisherman

Roving the shores of Africa
Preaching
Through you
A gnarled Cretan
Rose to exceed

Exhausted Charon's labors;
Stretching to touch, to take,
Your coffin in his arms.

Lifted on high,
Lowered into the earth
By strapping man,

So should all giants be entombed;
So should they leave
This earth.[18]

The works of other Greek writers became available in Greek America, and
Greek American academics with a good knowledge of Greek could choose
from a wide variety of Greek-language books.[19] A few Greek films also
reached the United States. *Never on Sunday* and *Zorba the Greek* were acclaimed by most Greek Americans and at the same time condemned by immigrant parents for giving a false impression of Greek life. The cheerful,
accommodating prostitute, whose camaraderie with the men who paid for
her services belied the Greek view of such women as debased, the lowest
members of society: "the film depicts Greek ethnocultural specificity as naive
carnality and unreflexive pathos."[20] Zorba's irresponsibility to his family

could not be condoned, no matter how entertainingly he was portrayed. A deeply stirring realism would come later in the films of Theo Angelopoulos, who fuses contemporary Greek life with its bouzouki music, Greek and Balkan history, the icons and rites of Byzantium, and the puppet theater.[21]

For those who survived the war, the United States government provided generous benefits under the GI Bill of Rights. Veterans were called GIs (government issue) and could attend colleges and universities and receive stipends for books, tuition, and housing; they could take out government loans to establish small businesses; they could buy houses with loans at low interest rates. Eight million houses were needed, and vast subdivisions such as Levittown, Pennsylvania, sprouted up. The GI loans transformed America, and Greek American veterans were part of it.

The war brought a loosening of ethnic restraints. Young Greek American men were taking over American customs and fads with alarming disregard of the propriety immigrant mothers expected.

> [My yiayia] simply could not abandon her culture, a thing my father, as a teenager, was eager to do. To make her beliefs clear, she destroyed his zoot suit—black with red dragons embroidered on the sleeves. . . . That suit represented to her the threats to their Greek culture. A culture that, in her home, echoed deeply in its Greek food and music. Every piece of tyropita [cheese pastry], every koulouraki [cookie], every time the platter of New Year's bread was spun celebrated that these were not "ordinary Americans" but Greeks in a different land.[22]

The war signified the end of the great Greek immigration epoch of 1900–40. Greek Americans in war services had traveled far from their homes and worked and fought with people of a multitude of ethnic strains. People at home found work in war industries and experienced a wider intermingling with various peoples than they had previously known. They were adults, many questioning aspects of their culture, particularly the funeral customs, with the keening of the dark *mirologhia*. Only an occasional family reverted to the prewar custom of bringing the body to the dead person's home, where the laments were sung. The old *traghoudhia tou trapeziou* (songs of the table), which fathers had sung after dinners with friends, the songs of the *klefts*, were seldom heard. Instead love songs and comedies became phonograph staples. Hardly a house was without "Droum, Droum, Droum, ta Vraholia tis Vrondoun" (Droum, droum, droum, her bracelets jangle) and "To Ghiadhoraki" (The little donkey). Among the Greeks a donkey is a beast of burden with no redeeming attributes; to call a person a donkey is the most scurrilous of epithets. In the song the donkey's owner laments his dead donkey as his listeners laugh.

The authority of parents over whom children should marry was loosening. Sons had begun marrying out of the Greek world before the war, and now such marriages increased, although they were not easily accepted. Parents usually knew that their sons were dating "American" girls, but when it was time to marry, they would, they believed, choose Greek brides.

> *Andy and I met on a blind date on the Fourth of July in 1946. (We had met briefly several weeks earlier, so you could say it was a "fixed up" date.) That was the beginning of our courtship and we started dating regularly. By September we were engaged. I was a nursing student at Holy Cross Hospital, and they did not allow married students, so we planned to marry a year later, after I graduated.*
>
> *Andy's mother was very opposed to our relationship. In those days Greek boys did not marry outside of their religion and ethnic background. She made Andy miserable that year and refused to meet me.*
>
> *On October 25, 1947 we were married at my parents' home. Andy's mother did not attend.*
>
> *Several weeks after our marriage, Andy's brother and his wife convinced his mother to meet me at a family dinner. It was "love at first sight." She took an immediate liking to me, and the feeling was mutual. We had a wonderful relationship from then on, in spite of the language barrier.*—Margaret Matson Katsanevas[23]

> *My godfather didn't like it that I had become engaged to an American girl. He came to the hospital where I had just had an appendectomy and told me, "Ted, if you marry the* Americanidha *your bill o'fare will come out of cans."*—Theodore Saloutos[24]

[Lou and Marge] were determined to marry. Then not telling Lou's parents (Marge wasn't Greek) they eloped to Bowling Green, Ohio. [Marge] continued working and lived with her aunt, while Lou was going to college and living with his parents. A year later when their son was born, that's when they told Lou's parents that they were married. The parents were upset but eventually the young couple and their baby moved into Lou's parents' house.[25]

The upheaval of the war on old-country values also affected a small number of Greek American women. For the first time these few actively defied their parents. This was a wrenching act, for the family was still the most important force in life.

Ann was reared in a Greek-Orthodox family. . . . One of seven children, she was brought up in a strict Greek home. So in 1943 it wasn't unusual for young Ann to think she had committed the most unpardonable sin. She had fallen in love with a non-Greek. . . . Ann didn't tell her parents about Frank because in 1943 Greek girls did not date non-Greeks. . . . Frank gave Ann an engagement ring on Christmas Eve. . . . Ann wore the ring only when she was with Frank.[26]

Marriages with *ksenoi* would increase; with the grandchildren of immigrants it would become prevalent. Marriages uniting Greek ethnics would be unusual.

The immigrant children were also establishing themselves in the business and professional worlds. The immigrant fathers gave them ready advice.

My father came to America from Megalopolis in the Peloponnese in 1906. When I was ready to go out into the world, he told me, "When you go into a new town, look around. If you don't see a Greek, a Jew, or an Armenian, keep going. There's no money there." —Dr. Bill P. Maduros[27]

CHAPTER 31

THE LOST NATIVE LAND

After the Greek civil war ended, leaving the Greek people even more demoralized and destitute, the Greek-born returned to visit their birthplaces. On the mountainsides, they saw the whitewashed word *OXI*, the answer to Mussolini. They saw the blackened fingernails of starvation. They visited graves, heard incredible tales of resistance—small children during the occupation "who risked their lives to do absolutely unnecessary things such as defacing Nazi posters, giving expression to their essential freedom."[1] The travelers returned to their isolated mountain villages, which could be reached only by bus on narrow deep-rutted roads. They often found their ancestral homes a rubble of rocks, because "they went to America and a house needs living people to keep it from crumbling." Many houses, though, of roughly cut rock, centuries old, remained just as the emigrants had left them.

They found many *gherondokoroi* (old maids) who had been left behind when the young men went to America and had been passed over when the immigrants had established themselves there. Almost every village had one or more "white widows," whose husbands emigrated to the United States and did not send for them. Often the men had disappeared, never to send letters. John Kallas met a white widow, his Aunt Mariyoula, on his first trip to his father's village in 1985.

> She lived alone in a small one-room stone house overlooking the Mediterranean and was waiting to hear from her husband, Vangeli, who left Greece in 1921. . . . [Vangeli] had promised her that he would return or send for her soon. After [Vangeli and his brother] split up in Colorado, Vangeli went to South America where he vanished. Like Penelope, Mariyoula remained faithful and spent her entire life waiting for her Odysseus to return.

A bus taking returning Greek immigrants to visit the isolated villages of central Greece where they were born, 1950s. Courtesy of Zeese Papanikolas.

I recently learned that after 65 years waiting, Thea Mariyoula received a letter from Vangeli, explaining what happened to him and asked her to forgive him. She did and died soon afterwards.[2]

Vangeli had worked in the coal mines for two years—"worse than being in hell itself." After his friend Stavros was killed in a mine explosion and two

The returning immigrants found a few of their centuries-old houses in rubble, although most had remained as they had left them. Klepa, Nafpaktias, Greece. Courtesy of Ginna Allison.

other friends left for South Africa, Vangeli went to Brazil. There he became ill with malaria. A Spanish woman nursed him, and when he recovered, he began living with her. They moved to a city, opened a grocery store, and worked in it eighteen hours a day. After six decades had passed, he wrote Mariyoula and asked her to forgive him.

The returned immigrants, now called the *Amerikanoi* by the Greeks, provided dowries for nieces, brought waterlines to villages, rebuilt churches, and gave suitcases filled with clothing to their relatives. The nostalgia for their early life vanished: they mourned the destruction of their homeland, but they had become accustomed to America. They decried, they complained, they criticized: "That broken step I left fifty years ago, was still broken"; "The young men sat in the coffeehouses and talked about which girl was getting a dowry from an uncle in America that was bigger than what another girl had received"; "They all want to come to America. They think we're all millionaires and can give them work."

Many words the returnees had been using for more than a half century had been struck from the Greek language, "to purify it." Relatives laughed at the obsolete words left over from conquerors, mostly Turkish and Italian. Grandchildren of immigrants had more difficulties with the language. A young man who visited his grandfather's village was perplexed when his elderly aunts asked him if he had *kolatsis*. Embarrassed, he assured them that he had, thinking that *kol* had something to do with the Greek word for buttocks and that the aunts were asking whether he had relieved himself. Again the aunts asked him, earnestly, and finally he realized that they were asking whether he had eaten breakfast.[3] An aging immigrant who returned to America said, "We do not speak the same language, my country and I." He was speaking of more than language.[4]

Many Greek-born Americans brought relatives to America. The 1920s quota of 384 had been abandoned, a symbol of American acknowledgment of Greece's heroic stand against the German army. From 1946 to 1960, more than fifty-six thousand Greeks entered the United States. Most men who had lived the bachelor life in America and commuted to Greece regularly, leaving their wives pregnant (graphically described by Nicholas Gage), brought their families to the United States.[5] Their children adjusted; the mothers less easily, fathers often expressing disdain for their wives' old-country ways, which were out of place in America.

The new immigrants went to cities and towns where relatives would help them find work. Unlike the Greeks who came in the first twenty-five years of the century, they often arrived with families.

We came from Chios, my father, brother, and I, on December 21, 1946. We left my mother and two younger children behind. It was very difficult to communicate. I went to school from January to June and then got a job sewing in a men's clothing factory. Only older women worked there. I had no friends. It was very hard. Home, work, home, work. Two years later we had enough money to bring my mother and the other children. My brother worked hard to support us. In secret my mother and my future husband's mother had arranged a marriage for us. I married just before I turned seventeen. I had two children and when the youngest was three, I went to work. Everything was very friendly. We lived in Flushing, Queens. We always went to church. It was our security. This country has been good to me.—Frances (Franga) Ritsos[6]

We lived in a town in Epirus, thirty miles from the Albanian border. My father was a government accountant in Yiannina. He came home on the weekends. A wave of Greek Albanians came to America hoping for a better life. The Catholic Church Charities helped us. We went first to Worcester, Massachusetts, then came to New York. In Germantown, Astoria. But it was not comfortable for us. My father found worked as a busboy and had a mental breakdown after two months. I was put in the seventh grade. There was no bilingual education. I kept getting promoted even though I couldn't speak the language. I learned English playing in the street. We worked and my younger sister was able to go to college.—Lily Katos[7]

My father had been in Tarpon Springs in 1927. He returned to Chios and remarried. He brought us children for a better life. We had gone through World War II, famine, and the civil war. We lived in a basement apartment in Corona, Queens. It was not a bad life. The Transfiguration Church was central to our lives. Marriage arrangements had been going on for me from the time I was fourteen. When I was eighteen a wealthy Greek asked to marry me. I refused and went to college instead. My stepmother opposed college. I worked my way through. My father loved the Statue of Liberty. He loved America. He always said it was the land of the free.—Irene Spanolios[8]

I was fourteen years old in 1946 when our family left the island of Samos and came to New York. We came on one of the World War II Liberty boats and slept on the soldiers' bunks. It was very hard. We had no one to receive us. The Salvation Army came and took us to the Armory and then put us in a hotel on 54th Street between 8th and 9th avenues. We were three girls; Aspasia was twelve and our little sister was five. Our father spoke a little broken English. Welfare came and took us to a cold-water flat on 10th Avenue. We stayed there through 1946 and 1947. We had no furniture. Salvation Army brought us beds. Father had known someone in 1912 who had been a busboy in the Pennsylvania Hotel. He found a job there; he was fifty or fifty-one years old. Mother heard of a woman who worked as a furrier and found a job herself as a sewer. I was sent to middle school, Aspasia to public school, and our little sister to kindergarten. When I was nineteen, I found an apartment for us in Washington Heights; the old railroad apartment rented for $21.00, the new one for fifteen more. I started at McGraw-Hill publishing company as a filing clerk and took night courses at Columbia in English, science, advertising, paying for them with the money I earned at McGraw-Hill. When I was nineteen, I met my future husband. He was a civil engineer from Cyprus. There was a bride chosen for him in Cyprus, but he didn't want to go back. We married eight months later. We have three children: one is a dentist, the middle one is a financial analyst for Farleigh Dickinson, and the third is a professor in the Columbia School of Dentistry.—Frances (Fotini) Psillakis[9]

A packet of smaller Greek Towns sprang up, and two localities, Astoria, New York, and Vancouver, Canada—so close to the United States that boundaries blurred—became thriving miniature Greek cities. Signs were written in Greek letters, the language of the streets and stores. Restaurants offered familiar Greek foods; and import stores were filled with books, religious articles, cooking utensils, and phonograph records of Greek popular and *kleftic* songs.

> In 1927 there were only seventeen Greek families living in Astoria with five children attending the Greek school. . . . Like most mythology, the Astoria idyll had a base in reality. In the half century following World War II, Greek immigrants and Greeks moving out of Manhattan have transformed areas of Astoria and adjoining Long Island City into the undisputed capital of Greek America. Nearly two hundred Greek community organizations are headquartered in Astoria as are the nations' two daily Greek language newspapers, Greek Orthodox television, and all manner of mass media.[10]

The sound of Greek music floated out to the streets. A Greek parochial school, Archdiocesan civic center, Greek parades celebrating the March 25 revolution against the Turks, and soccer teams, all gave Astoria a distinctive Greekness. Vancouver had a similar experience. "Since World War II most of the Greek immigrants initially moved to Kitsilano, the centre of Greek Town. . . . The area continues to be the centre for new arrivals and for many earlier arrivals as well. Thus a truly identifiable Greek Town exists at present [1976] in Vancouver and will continue to flourish in the future."[11]

In Kitsilano and in Astoria, the crafts and customs brought from Greece were intrinsically bound in the daily life of the community. Bakeries made prodigious amounts of *filo* for celebrating name days, baptisms, weddings, and the *parigoria* following funerals. Daily the scent of *souvlakia* and *gyros* added to other pungent scents in Greek Town. Stores imported the staples and delicacies of Greece: olive oil, Kalamata olives, feta cheese, *loukoum*, pastries, salted cod, and foods eaten during the forty days preceding Easter, when meat and fish were forbidden in remembrance of Christ's shedding His blood on the cross. Since dairy products came from animals, they were also prohibited. *Halvah,* crushed sesame seeds mixed with honey, and salted dried chick peas became staples. With Greek phonograph records spinning the old *kleftic* and contemporary songs, young people formed groups and performed dances from all parts of Greece, wearing the traditional dress of the various regions.

The new immigrants were better educated; schooling had become compulsory in Greece. Roads had made villages accessible; provinces were no longer isolated from each other. These latter-day immigrants did not meet the extreme prejudices the earlier ones had faced. Nor did they think it necessary to shorten their names, as the first Greeks had often been ordered to do by judges granting them citizenship or by employers who refused to accept their patronymics. Much had happened since the first days of abusive newspaper articles and real estate clauses that banned Greeks from certain areas.

A most important difference was the attitude toward women's working outside their homes. Greek immigrant women had been bound by custom to stay at home or, until they married, to work in factories alongside many other *patriotisses*. The women who arrived later almost immediately found work in candy and clothing factories, in lunchrooms, and as dressmakers. As soon as married couples had saved enough money, they established businesses for themselves, repeating the immigrant generation's obsession to be independent. Souvlaki stands proliferated.

Tensions rose between the old and the new immigrants. The older ones bristled at the newer ones' talk about the superiority of all things Greek, and they resented the ease with which the newcomers were helped to get work. "They found the table set," the old immigrants fumed. The unifying bond, though, was the Greek Orthodox church, even though the new immigrants objected to paying dues. In Greece the government paid the salaries of priests, which were augmented by small payments from parishioners for ceremonies. The new immigrants also resented the clamor for English in liturgies by children and grandchildren of the old immigrants. (English usage would be permitted in 1970.) They were repeating the forces of nationality, religion, and language that made up their Greek identity.

At the end of the 1940s, a vanguard of hyphenated Greek Americans began to show interest in their people's folk culture and the effects of Americanization. After Mary Vardoulakis's pioneering work, *Gold in the Streets,* other Greek Americans began publishing, and Elia Kazan enjoyed a brilliant career as a film director.[12]

CHAPTER 32

REBELS AND PILGRIMS

In the 1950s, against the background of the Korean War, black-and-white television, Rosa Parks's refusal to give up her bus seat to a white man, and Senator Joseph McCarthy making wild charges of Communist infiltration into American life, the oldest grandchildren of immigrants had become young adults. In the families of more recent arrivals, girls still had difficulty getting permission to date.

> *My parents had come from Asia Minor. They were so afraid of my dating. At a Greek church dance, a friend brought an "American" who paid attention to me. My parents wanted me married even though he was an American and I had just graduated from high school. I was barely seventeen when we married.*—Georgia Hall[1]

> *My mother is American-born and has a degree in music; my father was born in the Peloponnese and earned a degree in business from the University of California in Los Angeles. I started dating in high school in 1953–54. It was very difficult for my mother. I was not told I could not date, but there was little communication about it. There were belief systems in place that I would find myself in an uncomfortable position which caused me to rebel even more. Rules were so rigid. The deference to family, especially males, was stifling. Dating was not easy. Once a male acquaintance said in all sincerity, "For a Greek you're really not that hairy." A boyfriend said he could never take a Greek home to meet his mother.*—Amy Theodore[2]

Parents continued their efforts to keep their children within a Greek milieu that would be conducive to their marrying Greeks. Most parents now allowed young men and women to meet in each others' houses for food and

Ohio University Greek-American club. Courtesy of Jennie C. Vlanton.

dancing. College students formed informal organizations; girls, though, still had to face their parents' disapproval of college for women.

> Besides, as far as [my parents] were concerned, "nice" girls did not go to college. They would be spoiled for a family and marriage. To them the only goal in my life should be marriage and children. Nothing else would be considered honorable. A job, maybe, as a cashier at the local five-and-dime or a teller in a bank, something like that. But only until the right man was available.[3]

> I finished two years of junior college and told my mother I wanted to go to the university one hundred miles away to get a degree. She asked my brother who was a student at the university what he thought about it. My brother said, "Girls don't learn anything there except to smoke."[4]

Many daughters secretly smoked, but innocent mothers lost no opportunity to preach about the Greek way of life and equated American women's smoking with bad morals.

Mainly, young Greek American women adhered to their parents' warnings against marrying *ksenoi*. Matchmaking went on, but in a less open manner than it had in the immigrant parents' experience. The young people were brought together by friends and relatives, supposedly by chance at communal dances, weddings, baptisms, and lodge affairs. A small but increasing number of women began to defy their parents about marrying *ksenoi,* even though they were threatened with banishment from the family and warned that such mutiny would "kill" their mother or their father.

In the story "Amen" by Theano Papazoglou-Margaris, Tassie elopes with a Polish neighbor, Stanley, leaving her father, Stratos, to weep that she has "died" and her mother to cry that she has "poisoned" her. In Stanley's house, his mother mourns that the bride is not even Catholic, let alone Polish. "Two years later the situation has changed in both households. Stratos calls his grandson a *Polonezai* with 'Greek eyes.' To Stanley's mother now the Greeks are not barbarians. She worries a bit because the child calls her *yiayia*—grandmother—and she wishes the boy would learn a little Polish. What Stratos did not spend on the wedding he will gladly spend on the baptism and reception."[5]

In Cotsakis's *The Wing and the Thorn,* the American-born daughter of Greek immigrants does not want an arranged marriage like that of her cousin, who married a Greek-born man aged fifty-five. She falls in love with her father's godson and says she will marry him. She does not believe in the old Greek taboo of spiritual kinship and thereby incest: that by going through the baptismal ritual, her father and the baby had a tie deeper than blood because God had witnessed it. Not only does she marry her father's godson, she insists on a catered wedding dinner.[6] Such drama could not have taken place before or during World War II, but in 1952, when the novel was published, Americanization was rapidly changing Greek culture in the United States.

In the 1950s, more children of immigrants began traveling to Greece, along with thousands of other tourists lured by the travel industry to see the remnants of Greece's ancient glory. Writers from many countries continued to make pilgrimages. Often both groups were disappointed. They found backward villagers who knew little of their country's lost greatness and who lacked the beauty of statues uncovered by foreign archeologists.

Greek-born writers did not feel the burden of having to compete with the ancients. They wrote of contemporary life: the stifling of ambition in a desperately poor society; the onerous responsibility of families that required boys and men to sacrifice their personal lives to supply sisters and daughters with dowries, or to help parents tilling heavily mortgaged rocky soil; and the defenseless girls and women who were destined to live under the domination of fathers, brothers, and other males of the clan.

In the United States, Greek Americans were investigating their people's culture. Dorothy Demetrakopoulos Lee had been writing about Greek traditions in the United States since the 1930s. Lee is the first Greek American folklorist, a pioneer in the field. She recorded Greek beliefs remembered by the first immigrants in the Boston area, particularly about *vrykolakes* (vampires), a belief that did not survive in America. She also gathered stories of the pranks played on village priests and their wives, which were gleefully retold by immigrants throughout America. A typical story has villagers placing a live friend in a coffin. During the service the man sits up. The priest, thinking he is a *vrykolakas*, hits him with the incense burner, and kills him.[7]

Following Lee, James A. Notopoulos recorded folk songs in Greece and published a book of modern Greek poetry.[8] American folklorists, not of Greek background, became interested in the lore Greek immigrants recounted of their homeland. Not until 1960 did a Greek American, Robert Georges, delve into the field, with his study of five communities: Tarpon Springs, Florida; Savannah, Georgia; Wichita Falls, Texas; Cincinnati, Ohio; and New York City.[9]

Greek Americans, though, were writing and publishing fiction and nonfiction about their peoples' *topoi*, their regions in Greece.[10] Greek American academics became increasingly drawn to the political, economic, and social life of their ancestors' land; their work would be published in book form and their essays in such publications as *Accent* (University of Illinois), *Charioteer*, the *Journal of Modern Greek Studies*, and the *Journal of the Hellenic Diaspora*. The Onassis Foundation in New York City, the Basil Vryonas Foundation in Sacramento, California, and the Patriarch Athenagoras Orthodox Institute at the Graduate Theological Union in Berkeley, California, among others, brought a new era of intellectual inquiry and created archival collections.

In his seminal book, *Hellenes and Hellions: Modern Greek Characters in American Literature,* Alexander Karanikas gives a detailed account not only of Greek American writers but also of Philhellenes like George Horton, an American poet and diplomat. His affection for and knowledge of the Greek people are in contrast to their superficial portrayal by earlier Americans like Jack London and Stephen Crane. Horton's affection is tempered with gentle criticism: "A Greek cannot live without his vine or his flower pot and his view of the sea, but he cares nothing for the condition of his back alley."[11]

Karanikas lists, often with synopses and critiques, the writers who followed. He gives Theano Papazoglou-Margaris a deserved lengthy examination.[12] Because she wrote in Greek and only two of her stories have been translated into English, her reading public is small. She is well known in Greece, where her book of short stories about Greek immigrants in Chicago, *The Chronicle of Halsted Street* (1962), won a literary award given by the Greek government.

Theano Papazoglou-Margaris (kneeling between boys), Anatolian-Greek writer, actress, political activist, and journalist. Courtesy of Vivian Kallen.

Papazoglou-Margaris was one of the 1.3 million Anatolian Greeks of Asia Minor who were exchanged for four hundred thousand Turks living in eastern Thrace in 1922. Several of her stories are set in Constantinople and San Francisco, but Chicago's Greek community is the background for most of them. The very week she arrived there, she began to write. She acted in plays centered on social conflict, and she wrote for the weekly *National Herald* and other Greek-language newspapers. Her characters find sanctuary in an alien country, but the wealth and security they hoped for are denied them because of their inherent weaknesses and because of the overpowering events and cultural confines they can not control. Nostalgia for their homeland is a wound that will not heal.

Many Greek American writers had no patience with their parents' nostalgia for Greece. They had enough of being told by parents, priests, and Greek-school teachers how much better children were in Greece—they were respectful to elders, dutifully kept the rules of propriety, and always listened to their parents. Writers from the 1950s on wrote of confrontations with parents over American mores and about Greek American women who wanted higher education, the same as their brothers. "Within that fiery ring of Family—internecine passions, false pride, bitter resentments, pointless loyalties—in that magic area we were doomed to live, not to die."[13]

Karanikas's chapter "Growing up Greek-American" evokes the reflections and bitterness of many aging children of long-dead immigrants. It speaks of the Depression of the 1930s; bigotry toward Greeks; a girl's wish to marry a "non-Greek"; forced Greek-school attendance; revolt against all things Greek—"old-country," "old-fashioned"; Greeks who left wives in Greece and made a new life for themselves in America; and rage at families. Harry Petrakis, though, wrote on the elemental passions of human beings: love, hate, revenge, and duty.[14]

Children of immigrants began tipping the balance between their Greekness and their Americanness toward the latter. Events in the South— the murder of Emmett Till and the case *Brown v. Board of Education*—refuted the general idea that the 1950s were placid and silent. It was a decade of social change, and Greek Americans, like most Americans, wanted their share of the nation's prosperity. They felt they had earned it after living through the Depression and World War II.

CHAPTER 33

MARIA CALLAS:
A LOST CHILDHOOD

Greek Americans who had reached the heights of success were not generally known to others of their ethnic background, but two in the arts were: Dimitri Mitropoulos and Maria Callas. Never having forgotten the pejorative name-calling inflicted on them, young Greek Americans could look to these two artists with pride, for they exemplified Greeks' rightful place in American society.

Dimitri Mitropoulos was born in Athens in 1896.[1] He studied piano and composition at the Odeon there and finished his studies in Brussels and Berlin. He returned to Greece, taught at the Odeon, and became known world wide as a conductor. After guest-conducting with major European orchestras, he made his American debut in 1936 in Boston. In 1937, he became the conductor of the Minneapolis Symphony Orchestra; in 1949, he and Leopold Stokowski were conductors of the New York Philharmonic Orchestra, and Mitropoulos was the sole musical director from 1951 to 1957. From 1954 to 1960, he performed often as guest conductor at the Metropolitan Opera and in Florence, Milan, and Vienna. He died in Milan of a heart attack during rehearsals with the La Scala orchestra.

Mitropoulos was noted for understanding singers and working closely with them. When Marian Anderson finally agreed to sing at the Metropolitan—for years she had insisted on singing only in concerts because opera roles had been denied African Americans—she was diffident until Mitropoulos told her, "You don't know it [the opera] thoroughly. . . . When you know it, it will go."[2] It did.

The great Maria Callas (Kalogeropoulos, 1923–1977) believed that vocal troubles were always mental not physical.[3] "Only a happy bird can sing," she said. "It is not my voice which is sick, it is my nerves." Her mother had been determined that Maria would have the career she could not have had. She

Maria Callas (Kalogeropoulos) (1923–1977), who electrified the opera and concert world for twelve short years, in 1959. AP Photo. By permission of the Associated Press.

forced Maria to practice until late at night and enrolled her in radio contests. Maria had no dolls or other childhood possessions. "She reflected bitterly on this years later. 'There should be a law against that kind of thing. . . . They shouldn't deprive a child of its childhood.' "[4]

In 1937, Maria, her sister, and her mother returned to Greece, where Maria, not yet fourteen, was enrolled in the National Conservatory of Music in Athens on a scholarship. In 1939, a Spanish soprano, Elvira de Hidalgo, recognized the promise in the young girl's voice, and for five years she taught Maria the "dramatic sense and vocal technique" that would make her famous. Maria made her debut in 1940. After the war she returned to the United States; problems followed, but within two years she became internationally famous.

At twenty-three Maria married an Italian businessman twice her age; her career also became his overwhelming interest. "Theirs was a life based on 'Spartan domestic economy, rigorous self-discipline and hard work.' For a decade, her ambition, will power, passion for self-improvement were focused on her art."[5] "Callas's importance in the history of opera was based on two things. The first was the bel canto revival. . . . [She] more than anyone else dramatized and popularized it. The two [operas] that most attracted her . . . were Violetta in *La Traviata* and *Tosca*. . . . How Callas sang—how she sang and acted—was her other claim to significance."[6]

In 1958, Callas left her husband to live with wealthy shipowner Aristotle Onassis. A few years later he abandoned her to marry Jacqueline Kennedy. Callas's voice began to fail. She made films, went on a long concert tour, became a recluse, and died in Paris in 1977.[7] During twelve short years, Maria Callas's star had illuminated opera. For Greek Americans, especially for young women, she gave immense pride—that one of their own had reached unbelievable heights in an environment that was not conducive to appreciation of ethnic people's efforts.

CHAPTER 34

ANGUISH IN THE CONFESSIONALS

The 1960s were fruitful years for scholars of Greek culture. John Cuthbert Lawson published *Modern Greek Folklore and Ancient Greek Religion;* L. C. Stavrianos, *The Balkans since 1453;* Irwin T. Sanders, *Rainbow in the Rock;* and J. F. Campbell, *Honour, Family, and Patronage.* Greek American historians and sociologists entered the field. Theodore Saloutos's book *The Greeks in the United States* was published in 1964.

Although the Greek-born were immersed in Greek politics, they became vitally concerned by what was happening in their adopted country. As the upheavals brought by the nation's involvement in the Vietnam War enveloped the country, the immigrants, their children, and their grandchildren fought their own war. Immigrant grandfathers had become as nationalistic about the United States as they still were about Greece, and fathers had been involved in World War II, either as soldiers themselves or through having brothers or cousins in uniform, some of whom had been killed or wounded. They warred with the third-generation children who shouted obscenities against presidents Johnson and Nixon. Like others of their generation, many young men tried to avoid the draft by continuing their education. The elders thought this logical, but those who marched in anti-Vietnam parades and refused to acknowledge the "call to patriotism" flouted that call, had no *filotimo,* and disgraced their people.

It started out as a grand time. The Sturm *and* Drang *of youth vacillating from one crisis to another. The years from the early sixties and into the seventies were wild. There was the mundane challenge of voting out high-school officers, continuing the fifties' all-is-well optimism. The portable transistor radio carried everywhere our music of Buddy Holly, the Everly Brothers, the Beach Boys, the Beatles, and the hard rock of the*

Rolling Stones. Papou, *my grandfather, the patriarch, telephoned us every election and told our families to vote straight Republican. Then the first Vietnam jolt—the draft physical where classmates were all running around in their underwear feigning some type of injury.*

High school ended and college arrived to disperse vagabond friends traveling all over the United States to participate in Red Power, Black Power, Brown Power, Grey Power, Missionary Power. I followed College Baseball Power to avoid the draft via school deferment. In San Francisco I tried not to laugh at the flower-child culture and the Haight-Ashbury goings on. But it left me ill at ease as the California anti-war fervor spread among friends and family threatened by the draft. There were the periodic funerals of friends who did not have the political pull to get a deferment.

Every year my anger grew as the Kennedy-Johnson-MacNamara-Nixon machine kept escalating the war. I hid from it by entering law school where one was sued for using a gun. More and more of the expendable were called to serve, only to be derided on their return as baby killers by jaded flower children and as amateurs by the World War II veterans who knew what a real war was.

After dodging four draft notices, it was time to serve or take the consequences of avoiding the draft. My unit had street fighters from the Watts riots sentenced to the military. Muhammad Ali, the clowning poet-boxer, was now a symbol of the sacrifice of conscience and the target of the FBI. I was bitter at the lost opportunities as classmates more skilled than I at avoiding the draft took the good local law positions. I had deep feelings, still unsettling, at remembering goodbyes to family and friends, the insults while on leave wearing a uniform for an airline discount. Texans at Fort Hood knew, at least, how to deal with Jane Fonda encouraging the troops to desert.

We fought each other on the pretense of foreign conquests leaving the dead and walking wounded that haunt me still with unresolved anger. We had no business there! Decades later McNamara admitted they were wrong: the war could not be won and they knew it. What good was his apology!—Marcus G. Theodore[1]

Long-haired protesters, wearing thrift-store clothing and strings of beads, revolted at more than the war: sexism, racism, materialism, traditional mores, and manners. They alarmed older generations. Placards reading "Make Love Not War" and the casual smoking of marijuana clashed with the Greek culture of shame and secrecy. Parents could not avoid the truth and tried to hide from grandparents that their children had joined the hippie generation. The aging immigrant matriarchs sat in front of television sets, mesmerized, misinterpreting soap operas, aghast at blatant sex plots and especially at women wearing bikinis. The matriarch of the author's mining town condemned the bikini culture with pungent village oaths and said self-righteously, "I never saw my man without his *sovrako* [long underwear]!" They would not consider returning to Greece to live out their last years, but they could not understand America. To them America was a place where families with two cars could consider themselves poor; in America people didn't know what to eat first.

Priests heard anguished sobs in the confessionals. It was agreed: The world was ruined. Yet children continued to sit at the bountiful Sunday dinner tables. Mothers strained to guide conversation from dangerous territory, especially "homosexuals coming out of the closet." Fathers scornfully talked about "fruitcakes," "pansies," and "queers" and vowed if they found that a daughter was a lesbian or a son gay, the door would be closed forever. The women's liberation movement completely confounded the grandmothers. Many mothers who did not work outside the home were offended by the extreme activism of some women, meaning, mostly, lesbians, but also those who worked joined in the chorus of "Equal pay for equal work."

Added to the disorder of the times for the Greek-born was the rule of the "Colonels." On 21 April 1967, a group of junior Greek army officers took over the government with the excuse of an imminent Communist coup. The officers, headed by George Papadopoulos, took over all aspects of the peoples' lives. The junta inflicted the standards of their village culture on the hapless Greeks, who did not realize at first that their freedoms were being destroyed by a ruthless authoritarianism. The media were under their control, schoolbooks were rewritten, and college entrance depended on political tests. Stores closed on time, meat scales were rigidly inspected, women's clothing had to conform to the Colonels' views of decency, and a rigid censorship was imposed on the arts.

Greek Americans who visited Greece at this time heard heated recriminations against the United States for supporting the Colonels and for CIA involvement in Greek politics. An anti-Americanism erased the warmth the Greeks held for the United States' Marshall Plan, which had helped them rebuild their nation after World War II.

The junta used torture to silence critics. Thirty-four people, mainly university students, were killed and thousands were injured when the Colonels sent in troops and tanks to evict the students from the Athens Polytechnic building.[2]

The junta was deposed after seven years, but the new government had problems with Turkey over Cyprus. Turkey landed troops in northern Cyprus, leading to the partition of the island. Greeks were forced out of their ancestral homes in the north and into the south, the less-developed Turkish region. Turks in the south took over Greek properties in the north. This brought another group of refugees to America, many of them students, to repeat the cycle of immigration. Not only Greek-born Americans, but children and grandchildren had become affected by the rule of the Colonels and the Cyprus partition, which was still not settled in the year 2000.

> *Much of my Greek identity hinges on the Orthodox church, and I imagine this is true for most Greek Americans. So my most conscious sense of a break with my Greek past centers on the Church. With the coming of the Greek Junta in 1967, I began to find the need to take considered response to my heritage. I discovered that many of the most ardent supporters of the dictatorship in Greece as well as in this country cloaked themselves in the symbols of "Greekness"—just as Italian Fascists and German Nazis had cloaked themselves in such cultural symbols forty years earlier. And as American super-patriots were doing while the Vietnam war raged out of control. The silence of the Orthodox Church, whose young priests were among those being tortured by the Junta, was shameful. None of this made me abandon my heritage, but it led me to see that there was no automatic virtue in it, that its symbols could be used by both freedom fighters and torturers.* —Byron Z. Grivas (pseudonym)

The war in Vietnam ended; most hippies returned to school and nine-to-five work, except for a minority who had become addicted to the carefree ways of the movement. Life was not the same. With horror grandparents saw grandchildren living with people they had not married. They feared the church would die in America. They thought that all the Greek ways would be lost, but they were unaware of the young people who were drawn to Greek culture, especially the ecclesiastical. Chanting had a deep attraction for many of them, and superb chanters like Harilaos Papapostolou, a noted Byzantine musicologist, taught students his artistry. Jessica Suchy-Pilalis received her training in Greece and became the first Greek Orthodox woman chanter in America.[3]

Interest in ethnicity grew during the 1960s and Greek American scholars concentrated on their people's Romiosini roots. Constantine Manos caught Greeks in stark black-and-white photographs. Mary Vouras, the first Greek American ethnographer, continued her fieldwork in Greece. Collaborating with Constantine Manos and Sotirios Chianis, she inspired other Greek Americans and Philhellene scholars.[4]

Jessica Suchy-Pilalis, the first officially titled female psalti *(chanter), now head chanter in the Holy Trinity Church, Indianapolis, Indiana.* Courtesy of George Karahalios.

Scattered in Foreign Lands: A Greek Village in Baltimore, by Anna Caraveli, is a pioneering work on immigrants who arrived after World War II. The monograph describes the transplanted culture of Greeks from the island of Olymbos, which lies between Crete and Rhodes. It gives an account of a thriving ethnic community, and the photographs of the Olymbites in their new home are contrasted with pictures of those left behind in their ancestral island.[5]

Greek folk music had a true renaissance. Sotirios (Sam) Chianis followed Notopoulos with *Folk Songs of Matinea, Greece,*[6] and a few years later Theodore Alevizos produced a collection of his parents' Peloponnesian folk songs.[7] Ellen Frye's *The Marble Threshing Floor* and Gail Holst's *Road to Rembetika* added to the growing publication of Greek folk songs.[8]

Thalia Cheronis Selz traced the history of Greek and Greek American artists. On 6 October 1999, the Queens Museum of Art presented a show entitled Modern Odysseys: Greek American Artists of the Twentieth Century. The works of thirty-four artists from the 1920s to 1999 were shown. In

Mary Vouras, leading Greek American ethnographer, seated on a mule at the monastery of Aghios Stephanos, Thessaly, Greece, 1959. Courtesy of Mary Vouras.

the catalog essay, William R. Valerio, co-curator, says: "For these artists, as for most Americans, the experience of life is constructed out of an awareness of origins elsewhere—in this case Greece and a knowledge that one layer of identity is formed according to the varied manifestations, conscious and otherwise, of a Greek heritage."[9]

One of the old ways that was being contested was women's place in the Church. In the 1960s, Greek American women wanted an end to the old biblical injunctions of women's uncleanliness during menses and for forty days after giving birth, both of which prohibited their taking communion. They resented the practice of a baby boy's being taken into the altar area after the conclusion of his baptism, but of a baby girl's being held in front of the altar screen for the final prayers. The women's grievances deepened when the Greek Orthodox Archdiocese refused to support the Equal Rights Amendment (ERA).

In the 1970s, they joined women of other religious persuasions for a larger voice in church affairs. They wanted the ancient order of deaconesses, which Patriarch Athenagoras had established and which Patriarch Demetrios dismantled, to be reinstated. They startled ecclesiastics and lowly parishioners with their demand that women be allowed to become priests, even bishops.

Greek Orthodox and Anglicans (Episcopalians in the United States) had a common bond, but they were divided on the contemporary issue of

Immigrants, many of the post–World War II era from the island of Olymbos, at a wedding celebration. From Caraveli, *Scattered in Foreign Lands.* Courtesy of the photographer, Liliane de Toledo.

women's ordination. The headline in the church organ, the *Orthodox Observer,* 13 October 1976, "Episcopal Church Succumbs To Women's Liberation," shattered the bond. The Episcopal church was accused of an "uncharitable act . . . against the Churches of apostolic tradition . . . betraying the gospels. . . . This has been done to accommodate the world—in this case the so-called women's liberation movement."

The Vatican and the Patriarchate were adamantly against women's ordination, but a meeting between the Archbishop of Canterbury and Patriarch Demetrios "broke into public dispute on Sunday, May 1 [1977], over the issue of women priests. . . . The Patriarch quoted St. Paul: 'Let your women keep silent in the churches for it is not permitted for them to speak.'"

At the same time, letters to the editor in the *Orthodox Observer* brought responses both supporting and opposing the increasing use of English in the liturgy. For several years, the debate on women's ordination continued, with quotations from traditional, patristic writings and the usual explanation that Christ selected only men to become his apostles.

Yet Greek-Americans, both women and men, have held deep spiritual feelings for Christ and have established six monasteries: in Goldendale, Washington; Dunlap, California; Florence, Arizona; Hayesville, Ohio; Saxonburg, Pennsylvania; and Weatherly, Pennsylvania. Four are served by nuns and two by priests (Greek Orthodox use the term "monastery" for communities of both male and female religious).

Grave of the first Greek-Orthodox nun in the United States, Mother Thekla Makris. Tarpon Springs, Florida. Courtesy of Steve Frangos.

VESTIGES OF ROMIOSINI

One hundred years after the first immigrants arrived in America, a fourth and a fledgling fifth generation calls itself Greek, or specifically Greek Orthodox. They are mainly half or one-fourth Greek. In some areas, isolated from Greek communities, the number of intermarriages reaches ninety percent.

Many members of these generations have fallen away from Greek life, but most of them attend Greek churches and participate in activities connected with parishes. The once-important lodges do not attract the young as they did the immigrants and their children. The need for help and conviviality is no longer necessary; other avenues are available. GAPA lost in its emphasis on Greek culture, and few of its chapters remain. Although AHEPA is still influential in representing concerns of the Greek nation to Congress, it is mounting an aggressive campaign to gain new members.

Regional lodges continue to flourish for the social climate they provide. The newest of these, Asia Minor Hellenic American Society (AMHAS), was established in 1994 and has a large membership among refugees from Asia Minor, their progeny, and those whose families had roots in that Turkish-ruled land. In 1997, they commemorated the seventy-fifth anniversary of the end of the Greek presence in Turkey.

Associations are being formed to establish museums and preserve Greek culture; Salt Lake City and Chicago led the way in 1992. Only recently have Greek Americans realized the value of their immigrant parents' and grandparents' artifacts. Many souvenirs of early immigrant life, which would enlighten viewers on the joys and burdens of that era, have found their way into garbage dumps.

Greeks are prominent in politics. Michael Dukakis served as governor of Massachusetts for two terms, in 1974 and 1986, and was the Democratic nominee for President of the United States in 1988. Greek Americans have served and continue to serve as United States senators and representatives, as mayors, and in other official positions.[1]

A great number of Greek Americans are prominent in business, the arts (notably John Cassavetes in the theater and movies), law, medicine, engineering, academics, and religion. Their parents' backgrounds are almost always those of working-class immigrants with limited education. A worthy example is Tom Apostol, Professor Emeritus of California Institute of Technology, a childhood friend of the author in their eastern Utah mining and railroad town.

Tom Apostol's father had been an immigrant shoemaker. Professor Apostol is a world-renowned mathematician; his two-volume *Calculus* has been translated into many languages and is used in universities in the United States and abroad, including the University of Athens. He unravels ancient puzzles. One of these is the Tunnel of Samos, dug in the sixth century B.C. to bring water through a hill into the city. It was carved through solid limestone. Mathematicians sought to determine how workers from both ends of the island, using primitive tools, met with an error less than 0.15 percent of the tunnel's length. They concluded that the Greeks had used similar triangles, parallel lines, and addition and subtraction of straight lines to calculate the correct direction for tunneling.[2]

Until recently, scholarly Greek American journals showed little interest in publishing work on immigrant studies. Unexpectedly, scholars from Greece are finding the Greek-immigrant experience a fertile field of study, and many are enrolled in graduate work in Greek universities. Yiorgos Kalogeras, head of American Literature studies at Aristotle University, Thessaloniki, continues in the tradition of Alexander Karanikas. Two winners of the Yale Younger Poet award are Olga Broumas, for *Beginning with O,* and Nicholas Samaras for *The Hands of the Saddle Maker,* both of whom were born abroad. Other immigrants of the postwar era are finding adjustment difficult in the United States.

> *I was born in 1950 and I immigrated to the States in 1975. The reasons for my coming here were similar to those that brought the immigrants in the early 20th century. I came here to go to college but I ended up staying here. I have been visiting Greece every 2–3 years and am aware of the fact that it is not the country I came from anymore. At the same time I was too old when I came here in order to be absorbed into the American mainstream. For people who know me well, I am "Mr. Greece." I live in the past like so many immigrants. Of the many things that make me feel a foreigner here is the lack of respect for*

Tom M. Apostol, Professor Emeritus, California Institute of Technology, and world-renowned mathematician, a member of the Academy of Athens. Courtesy of Tom M. Apostol.

older people. The WASP family is a joke plain and simple. Dependents very often are little more than a tax deduction. What I still cannot believe is the treatment of the elderly. Often they see them as a burden that has to be disposed of. Real concern for their elders is what I appreciate in the middle-class Greek-American community of the American hinterland. These people may not speak more than a few words of Greek, but they are not cold people of north European descent.— Theodore Theodoratos [3]

Many second- and third-generation Greek Americans are involved in sports. Greg Louganis, holder of five Olympic medals in diving, and Pete Sampras, with thirteen major singles titles, are most prominent among many past and present athletes. Many Greeks have played professional baseball. [4]

Throughout America, collections of Greek memorabilia abound, including immigrant pictures, postcards, piano rolls, sheet music, and phonograph records. Church libraries house their histories and other books of interest to their parishioners, publications ranging from academic to popular topics. [5] Advertisements in Greek American newspapers and magazines promoting Greek vocalists and instrumentalists reflect the unflagging interest in Greek popular music. Over the years the names of Kokotas, Nana Mouskouri, and Dalaras became widely known.

Churches have survived and multiplied; both Alaska and Hawaii are served by Orthodox clergy. Greek American newspapers carry reports of

Pete Sampras, tennis legend with seven Wimbledon championships and thirteen grand slams, 1999. AP Photo/Fabian Bimmer. By permission of the Associated Press.

new churches. Histories are being written about the immigrant churches. The innovative architecture of Frank Lloyd Wright's Minneapolis church, though, has been replaced by traditional Byzantine style. The ranting, accusatory immigrant priests have long disappeared. American-born clergy are mindful of the competition posed by many different religions. Yet traces of the old clergy are seen, at times, in today's priests, who treat their parishioners as if they were wayward children.

Children walk down the church aisles holding pieces of *andidhoro* (consecrated bread) in their hands on the way to Sunday school. Most of their faces show the intermingling of Greek and other blood. Seldom do their names reflect the old tradition of being named after grandparents. The children are taught from prescribed materials, in the manner of Protestant faiths. On the first Sunday of Lent, the day commemorating the restoration of icons in A.D. 843, children carrying their families' icons form a procession inside the church. Although some houses of third- and fourth-generation Greek Americans and converts display icons, the latter-day Orthodox are more interested in Bible studies and retreats. Marilyn Rouvelas's book on Greek traditions and customs, particularly the religious, explains what immigrant mothers could not.[6]

Priests are ever vigilant about the loss of parishioners to other faiths. A letter to a Chicago newspaper reveals in a few stark words the anguish when a family member is drawn elsewhere:

The late Deno Pappas, Detroit, Michigan, collector of over ten thousand Greek single records of the early 1900s and consultant to scholars on Greek folk songs, rebetika, *and comedic records. Six thousand of his records are deposited in the Athens Museum for the Preservation of Intellectual Properties.*
Courtesy of Kathy Politopoulos.

Q. My sister (Greek Orthodox) now attends a non-denominational church in Texas. Is she still a member of the Orthodox church? (Concerned, Texas)
A. First, non-denominational faith groups are being established in every neighborhood. . . . Their clergy are self-ordained, meaning under no spiritual authority, teaching or obedience. Usually, you

Greek American school children in Astoria, New York, students at St. Rafael's Greek Orthodox school. By permission of Jenny Marketou, author and photographer, *The Great Great Longing: The Greeks of Astoria* (Athens: Kedros, 1987).

find no crosses or religious articles. . . . No sacraments, no sacred rituals. . . . Believe me dear friend; there is much more to the Christian Church than positive messages and feel-good religious productions of faith. Oh yes . . . they don't pray to our Virgin Mary, the saints, the Fathers and Martyrs of the Church. Enough said! . . . Your Orthodox sister has separated herself from the True Church of Christ. Urge her to return. . . . Your prayers will also be helpful.[7]

Psychologists and sociologists are vitally interested in what is happening to the present-day Greek family. They hold conferences to examine the cultural and historical aspects that mirror both mainstream American ethics and the still important ancestral roots of Greek Americans. A recent conference at Queens College, the City University of New York, discussed a variety of subjects from assimilation to homosexuality. In the introduction to the published proceedings, Sam J. Tsemberis writes: "Most European white ethnic groups were completely assimilated into the vast homogeneity of American culture by the fifth generation. The Greek Americans in the United States and Canada are rapidly approaching that critical period."[8]

Greek American dance group. Courtesy Ascension Historical Committee, The Ascension Cathedral, Oakland, California.

Expecting this critical period, the Church realized in the 1950s that it had to compete in the American way to keep children interested. National oratorical contests on the significance of Orthodox principles bring regional winners together. Activities for children of all ages give opportunities for basketball, field trips, retreats, and folk dancing. GOYA, established in 1957, conducts local, regional, and national conferences in which ethnic dances are an important part of the programs. The folk dances have become a national appendage of church life. Young people learn the dances of the Greek mainland, of Crete and other islands, and of Asia Minor. They perform choreographed dances in regional dress at Greek festivals that draw the public to taste Greek foods. The largest dance festival is sponsored by the San Francisco diocese. Bishop Anthony told the young people, "You may dance, but no hanky-panky." Notwithstanding, marriages have followed the festivals. "What began as a modest 39 dancers in five dance groups has now grown into the Olympics of Greek folk dance, where 1500 dancers in 80 groups come to test their mettle: and not just from California, but increasingly from a widening arc in the United States, Canada, and even Australia (where they discovered FDF on the Internet)."[9]

Ethnic sociologists and historians are well aware of the Greek Americans in the United States. The wider American public has learned about them through the nationwide Greek festivals that almost every Orthodox church presents yearly. The festivals have succeeded in two ways: as a bridge to other peoples and as a help in defraying church expenses—stewardship dues are low in comparison with other denominations.

We get up very early on Friday and put the lambs on the spit. We use

24 whole lambs and 125 legs

1,400 pounds kalamaria *(The Americans have learned to like them.)*

5,000 pounds chickens

3,200 pounds ground beef for pastitsio

2,400 pounds ghero *meat*

4,500 pork loin for souvlakia

1,500 pounds beef cubes

2,400 pounds butter

1,566 pounds feta cheese

967 dozen eggs

1,975 pounds flour

998 pounds filo

962 pounds honey

638 pounds coffee

300 pounds elbow macaroni

3,436 pounds flour

584 lemons

237 gallons milk

332 pounds almonds

464 pounds walnuts

1,793 pounds granulated sugar

27 gallons olive oil

262 gallons canola oil for deep frying loukoumadhes

16 barrels Kalamata olives (40 pounds per barrel)

1,180 gallon cans pearl onions

17 cases green onions

1,269 pounds dry onions

1,700 pounds rice for pilafi *and* doulmadhes

176 oranges for syrup

186 gallon bottles lemon juice

352 no. 10 cans tomato paste and sauce

70 gallons ghero *sauce*

336 ounces vanilla

66 gallons red wine vinegar

20 cases grape leaves

Crates and crates of lettuce, tomatoes, cucumbers
15 gallons burgundy wine. What's left over we drink.

By 4:30 Sunday afternoon we were out of everything, but I had an
extra 1,700 pounds of flour and I used fast-acting yeast and made enough
loukoumadhes *to last the night.*—John Chipian[10]

The church hierarchy contends with many troubling issues, including divorce, Greek American pressure for a role in choosing the archbishop of America, cremation, the problems of the Patriarchate within a hostile environment in Constantinople (Istanbul), the common date for Easter, intermarriage, and women's wishes for a significant role in church practices.

Both Eastern and Western churches follow the date established by the Council of Nicaea, which placed Easter on the first Sunday after the first full moon following the vernal equinox. For the Orthodox, it must also follow Jewish Passover. The Orthodox Julian Calendar places Easter thirteen days later than does the Gregorian Calendar, which other Christians use. Critics point out that Christmas Day was changed to correspond with that of other Christian churches, and Easter should also be celebrated on a common date to avoid the centuries of confusion that two dates produce.

The prevalence of marriages between Greeks and Mormons prompted a letter dated 14 February 1978 from the Patriarch to the Archdiocese stating, "a marriage of an Orthodox Christian with a Mormon is not permitted." This ruling was precipitated because Mormons do not believe in the Trinity; for them God, Christ, and the Holy Spirit are three separate personages. The criterion for couples wishing to marry has become: Does the church in which one is baptized hold the dogma of the Holy Trinity?

Women's place in the church has remained unchanged. A leader for equal involvement of women in church governance, Eva C. Topping, wrote recently: "With regard to women, our church has thus far failed to apply to itself traditional Orthodox discipline of self-examination. Had it done so, change would have inevitably followed, sparing Greek Orthodox women the cruel pain of oppression and alienation. We would be en route to the promised land of equality and full personhood where 'There is neither Jew nor Greek, slave nor free, male nor female.' (Galatians 3:28) Instead, in 1990 we are still in the life-crippling desert of gender-based discrimination."[11]

Nearing the second millennium, Greek Orthodoxy in America was faced with a crisis reminiscent of the turmoil seventy years earlier, when Archbishop Athenagoras became head of the church for North and South America. Intense campaigning on the part of the Orthodox Christian laity caused Archbishop Spyridon to be removed and replaced by Archbishop Demetrios. A movement for autonomy from the Patriarchate in Constantinople is gathering support; Greek Americans and converts resent the word *diaspora* in connection with the church in the United States—Greeks have been in this country more than one hundred years.

How Greek Americans relate to the Orthodox Church varies greatly. Some have no connection at all; others are "Easter Greeks," who pay dues, but attend services only during Holy Week; and for many others, the church represents the entire meaning of life, with Easter the great event of each year.

My grandparents on both sides were immigrants. My parents celebrated the church holidays, but they were not church-goers. They were involved with Masonic lodges and when they died they were given Masonic funerals. My sister and brother became seriously interested in New Age philosophy. I lean towards Buddhism.—Niki Georgeson[12]

Growing up Greek American, the three primary components of my cultural identity were family, historical continuity, and the Orthodox Christian faith. . . . The Greek family is tight knit with respect given to elders. . . . Family is an anchor of emotional, social, and spiritual stability. The historical continuity was best embodied in the Greek language (not dancing, music, and art, which did give me a healthy pride in a culture that expresses itself so passionately) and the Orthodox Christian faith. The faith shapes a world view characterized by love, humility, gratitude for all creation, and profound respect for mystery.

Several centuries before Christ, the Greek thinker Epicurus coined the word cosmopolitis—*cosmopolitan—literally a citizen of the world. The Greek culture with its curiosity over ideas and exploratory tendencies made me a citizen of the world. The Orthodox Christian faith gave me citizenship in the kingdom of heaven.*—Dean Athens[13]

For me the most wonderful festival in the church besides Easter, is the ceremony done the night before the Feast of the Virgin Mary. . . . I used to go every year no matter where I was. I would travel miles if necessary. I would find a church that was named for her and would go there to hear that service sung. . . . [The young priests] had these powerful, gorgeous voices. When it came time for them to all sing together, it was like listening to grand opera. I was immersed in the emotion of the experience, and in the beautiful words they were singing. The robes, the incense, the pageantry, all taking place in this little church that had been there, it seemed to me forever.[14]

The American, Greek, and Marine Corps flags adorn the gate of the Bakersfield, California, home of Charles Bikakis on Easter. A third-generation Greek American, Bikakis graduated from Annapolis and retired as a major from the U.S. Marine Corps. Courtesy of Charles Bikakis.

Although Orthodoxy is strong in America, Greek schools, synonymous with church-going in immigrant days, have a diminished enrollment. The students are mostly the grandchildren of the second epoch of immigration after World War II. Nineteen Greek American parochial schools in seven states teach more than four thousand students, but their deficits are large and they are "running on willpower."[15] Yet several cities are planning more schools, to present classes in Greek culture along with a regular curriculum. Denedin, Florida, near historic Tarpon Springs, is petitioning the Pinellas County School Board for a charter school to be called Athenian Academy.[16]

In 1971, the *Hellenic Chronicle* published an article entitled "Preservation of Greek Language Seen Hopeless."[17] Thirteen years later an essay in the *Ahepan* decried the loss of language. Byron Massialas blamed the adoption by Greek Orthodox Youth of America (GOYA) of English for deliberations and the Archbishop's proclamation in 1970 that local priests could use English in the liturgy at their discretion. The author suggested that AHEPA "ought to create an autonomous and independent center, a non-profit Hellenic Education Center with an endowment of between $100 to $150 million dollars, most of which should come from the Greek government. . . . unless we change accordingly, we will not be able to maintain our ethnic identity."[18]

The loss of language is a more passionate fear the closer a person is to his Greek birth and to the immigrant experience. This nostalgic wish, though,

The Easter lamb roasting on the patio of the Chares Bikakis home. Electrically powered spits have replaced the old hand-turned ones. Courtesy of Charles Bikakis.

cannot prevail against the tide of Americanization: the accommodation of the immigrant generation to survive, the opposite pull of two cultures on their children, and the complete Americanization of their grandchildren. Since Massialas made his proposal, another generation of Greek Americans has been born, making five since the pioneers of the early 1900s arrived in the United States. George Kourvetaris presents the reality: "By the third generation, a sharp decline of Hellenism and Greek cultural values takes place. Values such as family traditions, the use of the Greek language, Greek 'philotimo,' Greek hospitality, respect for the elderly, family loyalty, and kinship relationships lose importance as Greeks lose their Greek identity."[19]

The Archdiocese's yearlong study, "The Future of the Greek Language and Culture in the United States—Survival in the Diaspora," was presented on 27 May 1999. "The commission believes the greater use of English should be made at early stages to teach Greek heritage." The fervor of the early immigrants to maintain the Greek language is fading and interest in the preservation of culture is being transferred to the church.

> Orthodox church music for choir and organ is truly an American contribution to Orthodox church life, piety, and worship.
>
> But it was after World War II that professionally trained Orthodox church musicians provided musicologically-based choral music for the American Orthodox Church. The leaders of this movement have been Dr. Frank Desby, Dr. Tikey A. Zes and Presvytera Anna

Gerotheou Gallos. In 1976, it was fitting that Drs. Desby and Zes were conferred, *honoris causa* with the Ecumenical Patriarchal title of Lambardarius for their creative musical work. Unfortunately, Presvytera Anna Gerotheou Gallos was denied such recognition because of the Ecumenical Patriarchate's current anti-feminist sentiment, especially in the wake of the Protestant ordination of women.[20]

Enthusiasm for Orthodox choral music is growing. In the 1998 fall semester, the Patriarch Athenagoras Orthodox Institute of Berkeley, California, offered a course entitled "The Art of Byzantine Chanting: Theory and Practice of Byzantine Music." In the same year, a seventh-generation *psaltis* (chanter) was awarded a National Heritage fellowship by the National Endowment for the Arts. Harilaos Papapostolou was born in Agrinion, Greece, and was apprenticed with a traditional *psalti* at the age of five. He studied both Byzantine and Western music at the Athens Conservatory, at the same time earning a degree in theology from the University of Athens. In 1967, he became the lead chanter in Saint Sophia Cathedral in Washington, D.C., where he remained for thirty-two years. He accepted many apprentices and gave public demonstrations. The chanter, he said, creates, "the sound that facilitates prayer, that becomes the bridge between man and God, not a showcase for the performer."[21]

We have come now to a new century. The Romiosini culture the Greek immigrants brought with them has faded, as all immigrant cultures are wont to do. It began almost as soon as the immigrant men arrived and were forced to learn enough English words to survive. The diminution of wedding rituals was the first casualty to culture. Picture brides came, almost always, without families. Dowry contracts did not exist in the new land; the centuries-old customs of singing at every step of the weeklong activities that preceded the Sunday wedding were gone—the bride had no friends in America to sing the songs; the groom had friends, but often not a brother or a cousin to answer in kind, nor to descend on the bride's house while the wedding bread was being kneaded to instigate a dough fight with her male relatives.

The rituals were gone. The bride's dowry was not loaded on a mule or a horse to be transported to the groom's house; it came in a hump-backed trunk and was unceremoniously set down in a crowded apartment or a mine-company house. The wedding dinner was held in a Greek restaurant or boardinghouse, where the bride sat among strangers, her husband one of them.

The young mothers continued to follow the old ways, but doctors replaced midwives; folk cures became mixed with prescription drugs; as they grew older the children balked at old-country ways. Another hard blow to

One of the last Death Weddings, the 1935 funeral of a fifteen-year-old Rocks Springs, Wyoming, girl. Her attendants wear the blue and white of the GAPA girls club. Courtesy of Gregory Halles.

Romiosini came with World War II. Wartime upheavals precluded bodies being taken to the dead person's home for the keening of the *mirologhia,* and funeral homes were an improper place for carrying on the ancient rite. Death Weddings were reduced to the occasional wedding gown for an unmarried young woman and a wedding band for her ring finger.

Customs were further lost when the immigrants had achieved some affluence and moved out of the Greek Towns and Greek neighborhoods into larger houses in middle-class neighborhoods. Midwives and other folk healers remained behind; women not only lost the companionship and help of *patriotisses,* but were often isolated among American neighbors. They slowly conformed to new ways. Those who had lived on the outskirts of cities could no longer raise chickens and rabbits, which was prohibited by ordinances, and husbands could no longer slaughter lambs in the back yard or fill the neighborhood with the fumes of fermenting grapes. The mothers especially feared the criticism of their new neighbors and the rebuke of their American-educated children. The mothers, in turn, were highly critical of the neighbors' methods of child rearing and feeding ("They feed their children *samiches*").

With the passing away of Greek Towns, immigrant culture faded. Puerto Ricans, Jamaicans, and many other peoples now live in the once all-Greek town of Astoria, New York; Kitsilano's Greek Town in Vancouver is no more.

The Gregory Halles boardinghouse in Salt Lake City, 1925. Americanization begins in small ways; the decorated Christmas tree was unknown in Greece.

All the while Americanization had been going on without much notice. In Greece, Christmas was a religious celebration only; godparents gave gifts on New Year's, Saint Basil's name day. Yet the Christmas tree became part of the nativity season early; gift-giving began when children heard of it in school and saw Christmas displays in stores. More important changes would come. In 1954, when the first seminary graduates became priests, they encouraged families to sit together. Hardly any challenge was made: men no longer sat exclusively on the right of the nave, women and children on the left.

When the children of pioneer immigrants reached maturity in the World War II years, Greek values began to decline. The many Greek American men and women who served in the armed services traveled far from home; they saw little significance in most old-country rituals, and they began to marry outside Greek culture. Immigrants who arrived after the war retained many of the old customs and were bent on preserving the Greek language, but they too dropped many traditions that appeared unseemly in America.

All generations were affected by the social revolution of the 1960s and 1970s. For the young it went beyond informality in dress to relaxing precepts held nearly sacred by Greeks. Grandmothers, children of immigrants, were taken aback at children calling adults by their first names, even their godparents. Godparenthood lost its great importance in America. Godparents were merely friends of parents, and oaths taken at baptism were devoid of the deep meaning that had once given mothers and fathers assurance that their children would have security throughout their lives. Through such small details as no longer naming children after grandparents, the culture was further diluted.

Most immigrant mothers who became grandmothers and great grand-mothers realized an autonomy in America. Their children and grandchildren saw them assert themselves in old age; they were amused at their possessiveness over their Social Security checks, which were theirs to do with as they wished.

Still, most Greek ethnics feel a warm pride when the Metropolitan Museum displays Greek antiquities, when the white-kilted *evzones* come from Greece to lead the March 25 parade down New York's Fifth Avenue, and when Angelopoulos received the Palm d'Or at Cannes for his poignant *Eternity and a Day*. They listened with enthusiasm to Greek folksingers like Nana Mouskouri and Kokotas, whose death elicited a three-day mourning period in Greece, and listen now to contemporaries like Georgios Dalaras and the showman Yianni at the piano.

Many Greek Americans are involved in campaigns centered on Greece: petitioning England to return the marble statues Lord Elgin took from the Acropolis and other ancient sites; vociferously resenting the use of the word *Macedonia* when Yugoslavia was partitioned and the area adjoining northern Greece became the Former Yugoslav Republic of Macedonia (FY-ROM)—the name *Macedonia* had belonged to the Greeks since the time of Alexander the Great's father; virulently taking sides over Maria Karakasidou's Balkan identity book, *Fields of Wheat, Hills of Blood;* voicing their frustration over the loss of northern Cyprus to Turkey; fearing the continuing isolation and the demeaning of the Greek Patriarchate in Istanbul; and angered over the contentions in the book *Black Athena: the Afro-Asiatic Roots of Classical Civilization.*[22] These Greek Americans subscribe to many publications published in the United States and in Greece.

Greek Americans who are interested in what happens to Greece, the land of their parents and grandparents, but not with overwhelming concern, express a variety of feelings about Greekness in this country once called exile.

I'm a little more comfortable being outside the hard fraternity of Hellenism, then I, like a voyeur, can be less contrived, more benevolently critical and observe idiosyncrasies like those who love Greece, but can't get away from it fast enough. It's being redolent with honor in the past, but having less than impeccable social mores. Its own xenophobia, prejudices and artifices make it stand with most cultures of the world and yet give it its own uniqueness.—Dr. Chris Ghicadas[23]

American Beauty, the carousel horse in A Carousel for Missoula [Montana] that depicts the important aspects of the life of Jim Caras, a Greek immigrant who donated the land for Caras Park. On the saddle are symbols of his Masonic and his wife's Eastern Star lodges, Greek and American flags, a Greek key design, pictures of his children and grandchildren, and the American Beauty rose which he sold in his flower shop. Courtesy of A Carousel for Missoula.

That trip to Greece in '76 made me want to identify myself more as a Greek than as an American. I started listening to the rebetica *and decided to un-Americanize the pronunciation of my family name. . . . My first two years at Georgetown were pretty unpleasant, but that changed dramatically when I met Aki and Spiro, two Greeks who had come to GU to get degrees. The three of us became inseparable. I had never had friends like this before. . . . Up to this point, my Greek identity revolved around the past experiences and lore of my family. Now for the first time I was experiencing Greekness in the present, with Greek-Greeks my own age. They were steeped in Greek culture and it was exhilarating. . . . But the most precious gift of this friendship was the feeling of brotherhood that I felt for the first time in my life. . . . It was through my good friends from Georgetown—Aki and Spiro, and later Pavlo and Yianni, that I understood the meaning of* filotimo *[honor]. It's hard to find* filotimo *even in Greece these days, but I have felt it through my friends and the experience had made me a better person. . . . While I have no regrets about my life here—I have a great education, a wonderful companion, and a fascinating career—I can't help but feel that I'm out of place. I know I'd be miser-*

able were I to move back to Greece, but I feel I must look for ways to sustain my connection to the old country so that I don't disappear into the melting pot.—Taki Telonides[24]

When I was in 3rd or 4th grade in the early forties, the teacher asked that all in the class who were Mormon to stand. When they sat down, she asked that all non-Mormons stand. As I was the only one standing, I recall the stares and whispers which were the first of many such incidents reinforcing how different I felt. . . . At times I felt like a "dirty Greek."

As I look back on many comments and reactions, it saddens me how many of my Greek American women friends experienced similar incidents. As a young adult, I became proud of my heritage. Being Greek American is very much what I am. The family and traditions, Greek school, Greek foods and music, church choir, that Greek simpatico when a person meets someone who is Greek—all have enhanced my life. My heritage has served me well, personally and in my career as a school counselor. There is a touch of hubris among some Greek Americans. Where once we had to be defensive about being Greek, I am now uncomfortable when I hear Greek Americans speaking Greek in front of non-Greeks. This is not because I am embarrassed, but I feel it is insulting to others.—Amy Theodore[25]

There are many facets to being Greek Orthodox and it's not even just carrying on the traditions into your home, the church or community. . . . There's a Greek word that's used called kefi. It's the spirit and excitement of how people act. When you Greek dance there's so much kefi and joy.—Angel Skedros[26]

We Greek-Americans have the best of both worlds, our American life and our Greek heritage. When I visited Greece the first time, I felt I had come home. I love my Greek roots, its soul, heart, spirit, the love of life, and parea [group of friends]. In combination with American life, it is the best of both worlds. What could be better!"—Georgia Hall[27]

Her son writes:

I am one-half Greek and one half English. My mother's parents were born in Greek villages in Asia Minor. I was raised Greek Orthodox in Brooklyn and on Long Island. I can still remember my mother chasing me with the car to go to Greek school. As I've gotten older I have come to appreciate the value of my Greekness. . . . A huge contribution to the humanities was made by the Greeks. I love the fact that I am Greek and that my ancestors contributed so much to western civilization. . . .

I could do with less of the yelling I remember when I was a member of the parish council of our church. Also some of the elitist groups in the church were not very welcoming.

The tough thing about being descended from a culture that was once strong and influential and now is not one of the power-brokers of the world is that we can only enjoy that feeling by looking back. . . . I not only am Greek, I get to teach it as my life's work.—Don Hall[28]

My earliest memories are of the Greek world. Before there were words to put to things, there were the smells of my grandmothers' kitchens, the incense in the church. Later on, when there were words, many of them were Greek. Words for foods, for wants, even words in baby talk were often in Greek. When we moved farther away from my grandparents, and I started school, I also moved farther away from the language, that carried so much a part of me that was Greek.

Much of my Greek identity hinges around the Orthodox church, and, I imagine, that is true for most Greek Americans. This may not have been the center of our lives, and many of us were—and are— "Easter Greeks," but the Church, with its ancient language, its chanting and ethereal music, and those stern icons staring at you, was the farthest point of difference from those other Americans—the Protestant, English speaking, who, when I was growing up, imagined themselves, and were in some sense imagined by others to be the "real" Americans.

At weddings and, sadly these days, more often at funerals, I am still moved by the great beauty of the ancient ritual and the words and music of the ritual. And yet, as a non-believer, I no longer feel at home in the Church into which I was baptized, and whose language and rituals are so familiar to me. I might feel more comfortable as a frank outsider in a Jewish synagogue or Buddhist temple. I don't like to sail under false colors in "my" church. My respect for those who earnestly do believe, as they recite the creed or make the sign of the cross, is too sincere for me to stand next to them as a non-believing connoisseur or tourist.

My Greek heritage has given me much. I know as the generations move farther and farther away from old-country origins, it is inevitable that traditions will fade too, but I try to respect and honor them in my own way, and to pass on what I know of them to my children.—Byron Z. Grivas[29]

The noted Cretan musician Harilaos (Pipirakis) in his old age, seated between two musicians from Crete. Courtesy of Kaliope Sargetakis.

How much do the progeny of the first Greek immigrants know of their people's origins? Have they been told of the prejudices, exploitation by both American and Greek labor agents, the hunger, joblessness, low wages, sacrifices to fulfill family responsibilities, the drive to build churches, and the obsession to retain their Romiosini culture in a foreign land? The generations have come and gone and they know but little. Memoirs abide, but only one immigrant left a diary of those years, and matriarchs and patriarchs are no longer alive. As Kazantzakis said, "No one understands their ancestors less well than the descendants."[30]

Dr. Spyros D. Orphanos, president of a national organization of clinical psychologists, teaches, writes, lectures, and carries on a full-time practice in New York City. Asked how he can do all this, he replied, "I work like an immigrant."

> Nostalgia for the lost years is still alive: We only have ourselves to blame. We Greek-Americans allow little bits and pieces of our rich Hellenic heritage to slowly fade away into lost memories, never pausing to even notice or mourn our losses. Like the current state of live Greek music . . . the old Greek band . . . used to crank out loud, tone deaf cadence while everyone danced a tsamiko or kalamatiano. . . . Lately, I have been attending a series of Greek-American functions where this strange apparition appears on stage. With a single table adorned by a crooked, colorful tablecloth. Surrounded by milk crates

Nick Papadakis, Nick Dugdale, and Greggory Keller in Cretan dress, dancing in the twenty-seventh annual Marin [California] Grecian Festival, 11 June 1998. Courtesy of Cathie Banks.

and boxes filled with CDs. Loudspeakers bigger than my Jeep. Flashing lights on poles or stands. Someone dressed up to look like "disc" John Travolta complete with razor cut hair. You know, "The Greek Deejay." . . . Whatever happened to the cigarette smoking drummer? The old men with the clarinets and mandolins? The bouzoukia and rhythm guitars? It seems they have suddenly faded away.[31]

Individualism has lost its color. George Kourvetaris regrets the passing of Greek immigrant culture, its language and customs, its respect for elders. Most poignant is the loss of the demanding *filotimo,* family and personal honor that the children of immigrants were incessantly taught to uphold. It belongs in the distant past, when houses were never dark at night but glowed faintly with the vigil light of icons.

The children of immigrants—fewer each year—recall that golden icon glow suffusing the dark of night; they remember the scents of oregano, honey, and cinnamon. They often forget the ordeal of learning under unyielding Greek schoolteachers and the restrictions and difficulties of an old culture in a new land, but they remember the cold, clean scent of the spring flowers decorating the bier of Christ on Good Friday. They remember those fathers and mothers who tried valiantly to preserve their culture. The survival and strength of Greek Orthodoxy in America is justification for the great effort they made for that vibrant, unique culture.

ΠOTES

CHAPTER 1

1. Robert Eisner, *Travelers in an Antique Land: The History and Literature of Travel to Greece* (Ann Arbor: University of Michigan Press, 1993), 94.

2. Maria-Fani Tsigakou, *The Rediscovery of Greece: Travelers and Painters of the Romantic Era* (New Rochelle, New York: Caratzas Brothers, 1981), 28.

3. C. Kerényi, *Greece in Colour* (New York: McGraw-Hill, 2d printing, 1959), 5, 10.

4. Nikos Kazantzakis, *Journey to the Morea: Travels in Greece,* trans. F. A. Reed (New York: Simon and Schuster, 1965), 10.

5. Tsigakou, *The Rediscovery of Greece,* 70–71, 83.

6. Hesiod, *Theogony, Works and Days, Shield,* ed. and trans. Apostolos N. Athanassakis (Baltimore: John Hopkins University Press, 1983), 74.

7. G. Athanas, *Traghoudhia ton Vonon* (Songs of the mountains) (Athens: I. M. Shaziki, 1953), 113.

8. Interview with author, Salt Lake City, 1 Dec. 1971, Greek Archives, Special Collections, Marriott Library, University of Utah.

9. The standard work on Greek customs is George A. Megas, *Greek Calender Customs* (Athens: B. and M. Rodis, 1963). See the following publications: Gheorghios K. Spyridakis and Spyros D. Peristeris, *Ellinika Dhimotika Traghoudhia* (Greek Demotic songs) vols. A (1962), B (1965), and C (1968) (Athens: Academy of Athens); N. G. Politis, *Dhimotica Traghoudhia: Eklogai Apo Ta Traghoudhia Tou Ellinikou Laou* (Demotic songs: Selections from the songs of the Greek people) (Athens: Dionysos Press, 1975); Athanasiou H. Graka, *Yperotika Dhimotika Traghoudhia 1000–1958* (Folksongs of Epirus 1000–1958) (Athens: Pyros Press, n.d.); Melpo Merlier, *Traghoudhia Tis Roumelis* (Songs of Roumeli) (Athens: Sidheris Press, 1931); and Ghianni Efthevoulou Tsoudherou, *Kritika Moirologhia* (Cretan laments) (Athens, 1976). Of special interest for those with little or no knowledge of Greek are: Rae Dalven, *Modern Greek Poetry,* 2d ed. (New York: Russell & Russell, 1971); and Ellen Frye, *The Marble Threshing Floor: A Collection of Greek Folksongs* (Austin: American Folklore Society, University of Texas, 1973), in which seven regions are represented with scores and translations: Peloponnesus, Epirus, Macedonia, Crete, and the Sporades, Dodecanese, and Cyclades Islands.

10. "Turk-trodden," in Michael Herzfeld, *Ours Once More: Folklore, Ideology, and the Making of Modern Greece* (New York: Pella, 1986), 69; or "dust-trodden" in Merlier, *Traghoudhia,* p. 19.

11. Politis, *Dhimotica,* 10.

12. Merlier, *Traghoudhia,* 85.

13. *Nea Elliniki Anthologhia* (New Greek anthology) (New York: Atlantis, 1913), 352.

14. Spyridakis and Peristeris, *Ellinika,* vol. C, 152–53.

15. Ibid., vol. A, 460–63.

16. *The Memoirs of General Makriyiannis, 1787–1794,* ed. and trans. H. A. Lidderdale (London: Oxford University Press, 1966). He employed an artist to paint what he described: the pictures appeared in a separate publication.

17. Quoted in Nikos Kazantzakis, *Report to Greco,* trans. P.A. Bien (New York: Simon and Schuster, 1965), 141.

18. Demetrios Fotiadhi, *Karaiskakis* (Athens: Literature Issue, 1959), 378–83; Athan Karras, "Independence Day Combines Religion and Cultural Pride," *The International Greek Folklore Society Laografia* 3, no. 3 (March 1987): 2, 3, 8.

19. Frye, *Marble Threshing Floor,* 23–24.

20. Ibid., 167–68.

21. The words "bared breast" were sung, but were left blank in Soterios M. Kotsopoulos, *Nafpaktias: Geografiki, Istoriki, K.D.P Apopsios* (Nafpaktias: Of geography, history, and other aspects) (Athens: Fokion Stavron, 1924), 134.

22. This song is found in many anthologies; it is especially significant to the people of northern Greece.

23. In *The Marble Threshing Floor: Studies in Modern Greek Poetry* (London: Vallentine, Mitchell, 1956), chap. 6, Philip Sherrard advances the theory that since Greece did not know these forces, the nation did not experience the cultural break with the past that so greatly affected Western Europe.

24. Steven Runciman, *Byzantine Civilization* (New York: St. Martin's Press, 1933; New York: Meridian Press, 1956).

25. Thucydides, *The History of the Peloponnesian War,* trans. Richard Crawley (London: J. M. Dent & Sons, 1910; New York: E. P. Dutton, 1916), 95.

CHAPTER 2

1. John Cuthbert Lawson, *Modern Greek Folklore and Ancient Greek Religion* (New Hyde Park, New York: University Books, 1964), 42, 45, 72, 120.

2. George Florovsky, *Collected Works,* vol. 3: *Creation and Redemption* (Belmont, Massachusetts: Harman Music Group, 1976), 32, 118, 119.

3. Michael Contopoulos, *The Greek Community of New York: Early Years to 1910* (New Rochelle, New York: Aristede D. Caratzas, 1992), 19.

4. Two general books on Eastern Orthodoxy are Timothy Ware, *The Orthodox Church* (Baltimore: Penguin Books, 1963) and Ernst Benz, *The Eastern Orthodox Church: Its Thought and Life* (Garden City, New York: Doubleday & Company, 1963). See pages 48–54 in Benz for a discussion of mysticism and legalism.

5. Bernard Eugene Meland, *Faith and Culture* (Carbondale: Southern Illinois University Press, 1953; Arcturus Books, 1972), 51.

6. Deno John Geanakoplos, *Byzantium: Church, Society, and Civilization Seen through Contemporary Eyes* (Chicago: University of Chicago Press, 1984), 180–81.

7. L. C. Stavrianos, *The Balkans since 1453* (New York: Holt, Rinehart and Winston, 1966), 467–71.

CHAPTER 3

1. J. F. Campbell, *Honour, Family, and Patronage* (London: Oxford University Press, 1964), 145–46.

2. Leviticus 12:13–14.

3. A description of the dowry and its social significance is found in Ernestine Friedl, *Vasilika: A Village in Modern Greece* (New York: Holt, Rinehart and Winston, 1963), 53–60.

4. Kathy Politopoulos, "Weddings of Nysiros," *Laografia* 3, no. 8 (Aug.–Dec. 1986): 13. An article in the March 1989 issue of *Laografia* details the lineup in the wedding dances in Kozani Province, western Macedonia, in which each relative of the bride and groom has a specific place.

5. An Epirus marriage contract is found in *Laografia* 4, no. 2 (July 1987): 6.

6. Dimitri Ntouzou, *Laografika Nafpaktias* (Folklore of Nafpaktias) (Athens: n.p., 1961), 85–93, 90.

7. Ibid., 90.

8. Rennell Rodd, *Customs and Lore of Modern Greece* (Chicago: Argonaut Publishers, 1892), 102.

9. Soterios (Sam) Chianis, "The Folk Music of Skyros," *Laografia* 7, no. 8 (Nov.–Dec. 1990): 6.

10. Irini Stavrakis, "Cretan Marriage customs: Praises to the Bride, *Laografia* 3, no. 8 (Nov. 1986): 3. Bride songs are collected in many books including N. G. Politis, *Dhimotiica Traghoudhia: Eklogai Apo Ta Traghoudhia Tou Ellinikou Laou* (Demotic songs: Selections from the songs of the Greek people) (Athens: Dionysos Press, 1975), 177–82; Ellen Frye, *The Marble Threshing Floor: A Collection of Greek Folksongs* (Austin: American Folklore Society, University of Texas, 1973); Gheorghios K. Spyridakis and Spyros D. Peristeris, *Ellinika Dhimotika Traghoudhia* (Greek Demotic songs), 3 vols. (Athens: Academy of Athens, 1962–68).

11. Richard Blum and Eva Blum, *The Dangerous Hour: The Lore of Crisis and Mystery in Rural Greece* (New York: Charles Scribner's Sons, 1970), 11–12.

12. Politis, *Dhimotica*, 231.

13. D. Loucatos, "E Symasia Tou Iliou Stin Elliniki Zoe Apo Tis Paramies Ke Ta Dhimotika Mas Traghoudhia" (The importance of the sun in Greek life: Indications from proverbs and folk songs), 8. Reprinted from *Solar Energy* 11 (1961): 101–106, 114–16.

CHAPTER 4

1. See Rae Dalven, *Modern Greek Poetry,* 2d ed. (New York: Russell & Russell, 1971), 23–40, for a discussion of the feud between partisans of the *katharevousa* and the demotic.

2. Hellenic Latter-day Saints Life Sketches, s.v. "Theoharis Gheorghios Grivas (Harry Greaves)," 1964, Greek Archives, University of Utah; interview with author, 1971.

3. "Konstandinos Argyres: An Autobiography," trans. George Argyres, photocopy, 1997, collection of the author, 1, 3, 4, 6, 7, 8–12.

4. Quoted in Dalven, *Modern Greek Poetry,* 32.

5. In "The Secret Schools: Chronicles of Myth," *Greek American* (Long Island City, New York), May 16, 1998, 19; *Hellenic Journal* (Brisbane, California), May 28, 1998, 3, Alkis Angelou calls the repression of Greek schools by the Turks a myth. Yet L. C. Stavrianos states that under the Turks, learning lessened with each generation until illiteracy reached into the higher clergy. By the end of the sixteenth century, even archbishops had trouble writing their names correctly (*The Balkans since 1453* [New York: Holt, Rinehart and Winston, 1966], 109–10).

6. Helen Papanikolas, *A Greek Odyssey in the American West* (Lincoln: University of Nebraska Press, Bison Books, 1997), 101. Originally published as *Emily George* (Salt Lake City: University of Utah Press, 1987) in the Utah Centennial series.

7. Greek Archives, University of Utah.

8. "Christmas Customs in Greece," *Laografia* 4, no. 19 (Dec. 1987): 2–5.

CHAPTER 5

1. Patrick Leigh Fermor, *Mani: Travels in the Southern Peloponnese* (New York: Harper & Row, 1958), 57–58.

2. Quoted in Michael Herzfeld, *Ours Once More: Folklore, Ideology, and the Making of Modern Greece* (New York: Pella, 1986), 71.

3. Margaret Alexiou, *The Ritual Lament in Greek Tradition* (London: Cambridge University Press, 1974), 10.

4. John Cuthbert Lawson, *Modern Greek Folklore and Ancient Greek Religion* (New Hyde Park, New York: University Books, 1964), 348. For ancient practices see Donna C. Kurtz and John Boardman, *Greek Burial Customs* (Ithaca, New York: Cornell University, 1971), in the series *Aspects of Greek and Roman Life,* gen. ed. H. H. Scullard.

5. Gheorghios K. Spyridakis and Spyros D. Peristeris, *Ellinika Dhimotika Traghoudhia* (Greek Demotic songs), 3 vols. (Athens: Academy of Athens, 1962–68), vol. C, 349–50.

6. John Addington Symonds, translator.

7. Rae Dalven, *Modern Greek Poetry,* 2d ed. (New York: Russell & Russell, 1971), 45.

8. N. G. Politis, *Dhimotiica Traghoudhia*: *Eklogai Apo Ta Traghoudhia Tou Ellinikou Laou* (Demotic songs: Selections from the songs of the Greek people) (Athens: Dionysos Press, 1975), 209.

9. See the Virgin's lament in Margaret Alexiou, *The Ritual Lament in Greek Tradition* (London: Cambridge University Press, 1974), 63–78. The Orthodox Virgin is active in her suffering, unlike the passive Catholic Virgin.

10. Reminiscence of Nicholas Kotsomichos, Plessa, Province Doridos. Hellenic LDS Life Sketches, 57. In America Kotsomichos changed his name to Philagios (love of the holy).

11. Richard Blum and Eva Blum, *Health and Healing in Greece: A Study of Three Communities* (Stanford: Stanford University Press, 1965), 80; Richard Blum and Eva Blum, *The Dangerous Hour: The Lore of Crisis and Mystery in Rural Greece* (New York: Charles Scribner's Sons, 1970), 313–14; Alexiou, *Ritual Lament,* 5.

12. John Mavrogordato, *Digenis Akrites* (London: Oxford University Press, 1956). Wrestling with Charos (Charon) does not appear in the original Akrites ballad. It is a later accretion. The spelling of was changed to Akritas by folk poets.

13. Lawson, *Modern Greek Folklore,* chap. 4.

CHAPTER 6

1. Richard Blum and Eva Blum, *The Dangerous Hour: The Lore of Crisis and Mystery in Rural Greece* (New York: Charles Scribner's Sons, 1970), 112–18.

2. Gilbert Murray, *The Five Stages of Greek Religion,* 3d ed. (London: Watts & Company, 1935), 132.

3. Told to the author by her husband's mother.

4. Helen Papanikolas, *A Greek Odyssey in the American West* (Lincoln: University of Nebraska Press, Bison Books, 1997), 64, 66.

CHAPTER 7

1. Michael Herzfeld, *Ours Once More: Folklore, Ideology, and the Making of Modern Greece* (New York: Pella, 1986), x.

2. Ibid., 12.

3. John Cuthbert Lawson, *Modern Greek Folklore and Ancient Greek Religion* (New Hyde Park, New York: University Books, 1964), 25–28; Herzfeld, *Ours Once More,* 78, 79.

4. Herzfeld, *Ours Once More,* 7.

5. Ibid., 98.

6. Patrick Leigh Fermor, *Roumeli: Travels in Northern Greece* (New York: Harper & Row, 1962), 144–45. See chap. 3 for the Hellene-Romios comparison. Romiosini is discussed on pp. 96–103, 105–13.

7. Peter Gray, *People of Poros: A Portrait of a Greek Island Village* (New York: McGraw-Hill, 1942), 276.

8. Irwin Sanders, *Rainbow in the Rock: The People of Rural Greece* (Cambridge: Harvard University Press, 1962), 4.

9. Dorothy Demetrakopoulos Lee, "Greece," in *Cultural Patterns and Technical Change,* ed. Margaret Mead, manual prepared for the World Federation for Mental Health (New York: New American Library, 1955), 57, 62.

10. Quoted in Herzfeld, *Ours Once More,* 59.

11. Nikos Kazantzakis, *Journey to the Morea: Travels in Greece,* trans. F. A. Reed (New York: Simon and Schuster, 1965), 167.

12. Robert Georges, "Greek American Folk Beliefs and Narratives: Survivals and Living Traditions" (Ph.D. diss., Indiana University, 1964), 22.

13. Among the Greek orphans of the 1821 Revolution were Alexander George Papatis, doctor of medicine, graduate of Amherst in 1831; Loukas Miltiades, congressman from Wisconsin; John Celivergos Zachos, graduate of Kenyon College in 1836, educator; Captain George Musalas Colvocoresses, graduate of Annapolis, who rose to the rank of rear admiral (See Eva Katafygiotu Topping, "George M. Colvocoresses, USN," in Dan Georgakas and Charles Moskos, eds., *New Directions in Greek American Studies* [New York: Pella, 1991], 17–34). Most important was Michael Anagnostopoulos, later shortened to Anagnos, who worked with Stanley Gridley Howe to help liberate Crete in 1867. He came to America, where he married Howe's daughter and became head of the Perkins Institute of the Blind. There he introduced modern methods for the education of the sightless. In World War II, a Liberty ship was named the S.S. Anagnos.

14. Dean Steve Pastis, "Go West Greek," *Greek Accent,* July–August 1983, 16–19, 45; "The Greek Texans," The University of Texas Institute of Texan Cultures at San Antonio, 1994, 3–4.

15. Michael Contopoulos, *The Greek Community of New York: Early Years to 1910* (New Rochelle, New York: Aristede D. Caratzas, 1992), 37.

CHAPTER 8

1. L. C. Stavrianos, *The Balkans since 1453* (New York: Holt, Rinehart and Winston, 1966), 291.

2. Ibid., 293.

3. Ibid., 144, 478–79.

4. Patrick Leigh Fermor, *Roumeli: Travels in Northern Greece* (New York: Harper & Row, 1962), 190.

5. Soterios M. Kotsopoulos, *Nafpaktias: Geografiki, Istoriki, K.D.P Apopsios* (Nafpaktias: Of geography, history, and other aspects) (Athens: Fokion Stavron, 1924), 34.

6. H. K. Kambouris, "Pages from My Life and Various Poems on My Embarking from Greece for America and My Struggles in America," translation of "Selidhai Ek Tou Viou Mou Ke Dhiafora Poemata Mou Anahorisis ek Elladhos Dhia Ameriki Ke E Dhiamoni Mou En Ameriki" by C. V. Vasilacopoulos, ed. Helen Papanikolas, Greek Archives, University of Utah, 3.

7. Helen Papanikolas, *A Greek Odyssey in the American West* (Lincoln: University of Nebraska Press, Bison Books, 1997), 111.

8. Georgios Drossinis, "Greek Earth," in Rae Dalven, *Modern Greek Poetry,* 2d ed. (New York: Russell & Russell, 1971), 141–42.

9. Gheorghios K. Spyridakis and Spyros D. Peristeris, *Ellinika Dhimotika Traghoudhia* (Greek Demotic songs), 3 vols. (Athens: Academy of Athens, 1962–68), vol. C, 332.

10. Interview with author 2 May 1973.

11. Interview with author 6 July 1974.

12. As told to the author's father. See also an interview with George Cayias, Greek Archives, University of Utah.

13. Conversation with author, summer 1972.

14. Homer P. Balabanis, *The Life and Death of a Greek Village* (Kentfield, California: Western Star Press, 1970), 7, 15, 17, 81.

15. Hellenic LDS Life Sketches, 178–80.

CHAPTER 9

1. James Louis Cononelos, "Greek Immigrant Labor" (Master's thesis, University of Utah, 1979), 60, 64–67.

2. Tom Nicolopulos, "An Ancestor's Journey to America," *Hellenic Journal* (San Francisco, 29 Oct. 1987; 12 Nov. 1987).

3. Dan Georgakas, "Papou" (Grandfather) in "Growing Up Greek and American," *Greek American* (Long Island City, New York), 24 Oct. 1987.

4. Louis Lingos interview, Salt Lake City, 1970, Greek Archives, University of Utah.

5. Takis Telonides, letter to author, typescript, 8 May 2000.

6. N. G. Politis, *Dhimotiica Traghoudhia: Eklogai Apo Ta Traghoudhia Tou Ellinikou Laou* (Demotic songs: Selections from the songs of the Greek people) (Athens: Dionysos Press, 1975), 199.

7. Tetos Demetriadis, "The Banana Is a Sweet Fruit," sung by Demetriadis and his wife Tasia, Columbia Records 56082-F, 1927. Lyrics translated by Andreas Dellis.

8. Hellenic LDS Life Sketches, 128–31.

9. Helen Papanikolas, *A Greek Odyssey in the American West* (Lincoln: University of Nebraska Press, Bison Books, 1997), 143–44.

10. Dan Georgakas, "Greek Immigrants at Work," pamphlet (New York: Greek American Labor Council, 1992).

11. Jack London, "The King of the Greeks" in *Tales of the Fish Patrol* (Oakland: Star Rover House, 1982), 41.

12. Ibid., "Demetrios Contos," 201.

CHAPTER 10

1. George James Patterson, Jr., *The Unassimilated Greeks of Denver* (New York: AMS Press, n.d.), 129–31. No. 14 in Immigrant Communities and Ethnic Minorities in the United States and Canada series, ed. Robert J. Theodoratus.

2. *Reports of the Immigration Commission: Abstracts of Reports of the Immigrant Commission (Dillingham Report)*, vol. 11 (Washington, D.C.: Government Printing Office, 1911), 396. The Greek padrone system is discussed on pages 391–408.

3. Theodore Saloutos, *The Greeks in the United States* (Cambridge, Mass.: Harvard University Press, 1964), 52–53.

4. *Dillingham Report*, 397–98.

CHAPTER 11

1. Nick K. Halkides, "Nickname," *Trapezus* (Boston), March–April 1999.

2. Steve A. Demakopoulos, *Do You Speak Greek?* (New York: Seabream Press, 2000); Steven G. Economou, "Grenglish: An Illustrated Lexicon" (n.p., n.d.).

3. Stanley Feldstein and Lawrence Costello, eds., *The Ordeal of Assimilation: A Documentary History of the White Working Class* (Garden City, New York: Anchor Press, Doubleday, 1974), 4.

4. Linda S. Myrsiades and Kostas Myrsiades, *The Karagiozis Heroic Performances in Greek Shadow Theater* (Hanover, New Hampshire and London: University Press of New England, 1988).

5. Steve Frangos, "The Grecian Gladiators: A Vaudeville Tableau Act," *The Hellenic Journal* (San Francisco), 27 July 1995.

6. Nicholas John Rozakos, *To Neo Elliniko Laiko Theatro stin Ameriki* (The new Greek folk theater in America), *1903–1950* (San Francisco: Falcon Press, 1985).

CHAPTER 12

1. Andrew T. Kopan, "The Greek Press," in Sally M. Miller, ed., *The Ethnic Press in America: Historical Analysis and Handbook* (New York: Greenwood Press, 1987), 161.

2. Ibid., 163.

3. Alexander Karanikas, *Hellenes and Hellions: Modern Greek Characters in American Literature* (Urbana: University of Illinois Press, 1981), 53–60.

4. Yiorgos Kalogeras, "Porfiras," *Kerkyra* (Nov. 1993–March 1994): 17.

CHAPTER 13

1. Theodore Saloutos, *The Greeks in the United States* (Cambridge, Mass.: Harvard University Press, 1964), 121.

2. Helen Papanikolas, *A Greek Odyssey in the American West* (Lincoln: University of Nebraska Press, Bison Books, 1997), 108, 144.

3. The author had seen the book in her father's desk. After she questioned him about it, it disappeared.

4. Told to the author by this long-time friend.

5. Alexander J. Kosta, "Episodes in One Man's Life," typescript, John B.Vlahos collection, 47–51. Saloutos, *Greeks,* chap. 6.

6. Paul G. Manolis, "Raphael (Robert) Morgan, 'The First Black Orthodox Priest in America,'" pamphlet (Athens, 1981), 10.

7. Saloutos, *Greeks,* 121.

8. Ibid., 130.

9. Letter to his grandson Mike Gregory, typescript, collection of the author.

10. Hellenic LDS Life Sketches, 56–64.

11. Ibid., 81–96.

12. Bobby Malfouris, "The Malvis Foundation," in *Ellines Tis Amerikis* (Greeks in America), *1528–1948,* trans. Nenny Panourghia (New York: Isaak Goldman), 451–53; Steve Frangos, "The Malbis [Malvis] Foundation," *Greek American* (Long Island City, New York), 10, 11.

CHAPTER 14

1. James Louis Cononelos, "Greek Immigrant Labor" (Master's thesis, University of Utah, 1979), 141.

2. Governor's Correspondence (April 1909), Governor William Spry, Utah, Box 7, Utah Historical Society.

3. Translation of Maria Sarandopoulou Economidhou's *E Ellines Tis Amerikis Opos Tous Eidha* [The Greeks in America as I saw them] (New York: D. C. Divry, 1916) by Thalia and Katherine Papachristos (n.p., n.d.), 62–63.

CHAPTER 15

1. "Mississippi Melting Pot," *Clarion Ledger,* Jackson, Mississippi, 21 Jan. 1991.

2. Although Euripides Constantine Kehayas did not convert to the Mormon (LDS) church, his brief biography appears in "Record of the Kehayas Family" by Demetri Kehaya in Hellenic LDS Life Sketches, Greek Archives, University of Utah.

3. Elias J. Janetas (Phil Nax), "Ta Loukanika" (The sausages), in *E Aftou Megaliotis: Metanastis* (Their majesties: The immigrants) (New York: Anatolian Press, 1946), 21–26.

4. John Cuthbert Lawson, *Modern Greek Folklore and Ancient Greek Religion* (New Hyde Park, New York: University Books, 1964), 462–84.

5. Patrick Leigh Fermor, *Roumeli: Travels in Northern Greece* (New York: Harper & Row, 1962), 127.

6. Helen Papanikolas, *A Greek Odyssey in the American West* (Lincoln: University of Nebraska Press, Bison Books, 1997), 146.

7. Translation of Maria Sarandopoulou Economidhou's *E Ellines Tis Amerikis Opos Tous Eidha* [The Greeks in America as I saw them] (New York: D. C. Divry, 1916) by Thalia and Katherine Papachristos (n.p., n.d.), 203–4.

8. Helen Papanikolas, "A Sketch of Greek Immigrant Life in the American West," in *Greeks in English-Speaking Countries,* ed. C. P. Ionnides (New York: Melissa Media Associates, 1997), 25–26.

CHAPTER 16

1. James Louis Cononelos, "Greek Immigrant Labor" (Master's thesis, University of Utah, 1979), chap. 4.

2. *Reports of the Immigration Commission: Immigrants in Industries, Part 25: Japanese and Other Immigrant Races in the Pacific Coast and Rocky Mountain States,* vol. III (Washington D.C.: United States Printing Office, 1911), 202.

3. W. M. Leiserson, *Adjusting Immigrants and Industry* (1924; reprint ed., New York: New York Times, 1969), 71–72.

4. Emily G. Balch, *Our Slavic Fellow Citizens* (New York: Arno Press, 1969), 472.

5. *White Pine Daily News* (Ely, Nevada), 28 Oct. 1907.

6. H. K. Kambouris, "Pages from My Life and Various Poems on My Embarking from Greece for America and My Struggles in America," translation of "Selidhai Ek Tou Viou Mou Ke Dhiafora Poemata Mou Anahorisis ek Elladhos Dhia Ameriki Ke E Dhiamoni Mou En Ameriki" by C. V. Vasilacopoulos, ed. Helen Papanikolas, Greek Archives, University of Utah, 64, 65.

7. Ibid., 117, 118, 119.

8. Ibid., 82.

9. Letter to author from James (Demetrios) Galanis of Neohorion, Province Fthiotis, 7 July 1977.

10. Ibid.

11. John G. Bitzes, "The Anti-Greek Riot of 1909—South Omaha," *Nebraska History* 51, no. 2 (1970): 199–224.

12. *Chicago Sunday Tribune,* 1922: 29 April, p. 1; 30 April, p. 21; 1 May, p. 17; *New York Times,* 1922: 29 April, p. 6; 30 April, p. 30. The author thanks Steve Frangos for this information.

13. E. D. Karampetsos, "Nativism in Nevada: Greek Immigrants in White Pine County," *Journal of the Hellenic Diaspora* 24, no. 1 (1998): 61–95.

14. Ibid., 68–69.

15. Ibid., 74–75.

16. Ibid., 84.

17. Margaret Alexiou, *The Ritual Lament in Greek Tradition* (London: Cambridge University Press, 1974), 152–57.

18. Translation of Maria Sarandopoulou Economidhou's *E Ellines Tis Amerikis Opos Tous Eidha* [The Greeks in America as I saw them] (New York: D. C. Divry, 1916) by Thalia and Katherine Papachristos (n.p., n.d.), 133.

19. Helen Papanikolas, *A Greek Odyssey in the American West* (Lincoln: University of Nebraska Press, Bison Books, 1997), 162–63.

20. Louis Lingos interview, Salt Lake City, 9 April 1970, Greek Archives, University of Utah.

21. Notebook in the possession of his nieces Thalia and Katherine Papachristos.

CHAPTER 17

1. Helen Papanikolas, "Magerou: The Greek Midwife," *Utah Historical Quarterly* 38 (winter 1970).

2. L. C. Stavrianos, *The Balkans since 1453* (New York: Holt, Rinehart and Winston, 1966), 472.

CHAPTER 18

1. The Mouyias brothers were fellow villagers of the author's father in Klepa, Nafpaktias. The author and her husband visited them and their wives in their railyard coffee shop, in the early 1950s.

2. Letter to the author from Anastasia Karrant Soteropoulos, 5 July 1970.

3. "To Pimniostasion Ke Tyrokomion Ton Adhelfon Tsiflakou" (The sheepfold and cheese factory of the Tsiflakou brothers) in *Ai Elliniki Parikia Ton Dhitikon Polition Tis Vorion Amerikis* (The Greek colony of the western states of America) (San Francisco: Prometheus Publishing Co., 1918–1919). John B. Vlahos collection.

4. From the back of the Sweet Shop-Copper Kettle Room menu, Raton, New Mexico.

5. Theodore Saloutos, "The Immigrant Contribution to American Agriculture," *Agriculture History* 50, no. 1 (Jan. 1976).

CHAPTER 19

1. Translation of Maria Sarandopoulou Economidhou's *E Ellines Tis Amerikis Opos Tous Eidha* [The Greeks in America as I saw them] (New York: D. C. Divry, 1916) by Thalia and Katherine Papachristos (n.p., n.d.), 37.

2. Ibid., 85.

3. Ibid., 53, 54.

4. Ibid., 124.

5. Ibid.

6. Ibid.

7. Ibid., 223–14.

8. Ibid., 122

9. Ibid., 124.

10. H. K. Kambouris, "Pages from My Life and Various Poems on My Embarking from Greece for America and My Struggles in America," translation of "Selidhai Ek Tou Viou Mou Ke Dhiafora Poemata Mou Anahorisis ek Elladhos Dhia Ameriki Ke E Dhiamoni Mou En Ameriki" by C. V. Vasilacopoulos, ed. Helen Papanikolas, Greek Archives, University of Utah, 45, 52.

11. Economidhou, *E Ellines,* 152.

12. "Biography [autobiography] of George P. Kyranakos," Kastania, Vion Province, Greece. In possession of his niece Mary Ypsilantis Souvall.

13. Elias J. Janetas (Phil Nax), "O Maniolos," in *E Aftou Megaliotis: Metanastis* (Their majesties: The immigrants) (New York: Anatolian Press, 1946), 39–41.

CHAPTER 20

1. Helen Papoulis Koulouris, interview with the author, June 1974.

2. Pearl Kastran Ahnen, *Legends and Legacies* (Glenn, Michigan: Legna Press, 1999), 112.

3. Helen Papanikolas, "Greek Immigrant Women in the Intermountain West," *Journal of the Hellenic Diaspora* 16, nos. 1–4 (1989), 26.

4. "Mama," a biography by a daughter, typescript, collection of the author.

5. Charles C. Moskos, Jr. "Growing up Greek American," *Society* 14, no. 2 (Jan./Feb. 1977): 67.

6. Helen Papanikolas, *A Greek Odyssey in the American West* (Lincoln: University of Nebraska Press, Bison Books, 1997), 200, 201.

7. David M. Schneider, *American Kinship: A Cultural Account* (Englewood Cliffs, New Jersey: Prentice Hall, 1968), 15.

8. Rennell Rodd, *Customs and Lore of Modern Greece* (Chicago: Argonaut Publishers, 1892), 156.

9. Other southern European countries exhibit similar cultural traits. See David M. Schneider and Raymond T. Smith, *Class Differences and Sex Roles in American Kinship and Family Structure* (Englewood Cliffs, New Jersey: Prentice Hall, 1973); Francesco Cordasco and Eugene Bucchioni, eds., *The Italians: Social Backgrounds of an American Group* (Clifton, New Jersey: A.M. Kelly, 1974); Rebecca West, *Black Lamb and Grey Falcon: A Journey through Yugoslavia,* 2 vols. (New York: Viking Press, 1941); and George J. Prpic, *The Croatian Immigrants in America* (New York: Philosophical Library, 1971).

10. Interview with author, Salt Lake City, 20 March 1973, Greek Archives, University of Utah, 23, 24.

11. Told to Theodore Paulos by his grandmother Anna Paulos, Tooele, Utah.

12. Matthew 3:17.

13. See the author's "Wrestling with Death: Greek Immigrant Funeral Customs in Utah," *Utah Historical Quarterly* 52, no. 1, 1955.

14. N. G. Politis, *Dhimotiica Traghoudhia: Eklogai Apo Ta Traghoudhia Tou Ellinikou Laou* (Demotic songs: Selections from the songs of the Greek people) (Athens: Dionysos Press, 1975), 214.

15. Told to the author by Penelope Koulouris, sister of the dead child.

16. John Cuthbert Lawson, *Modern Greek Folklore and Ancient Greek Religion* (New Hyde Park, New York: University Books, 1964), 533–34.

17. Eva Katafygiotu Topping, "Maria Voulgares: Pioneer Model Midwife," *Greek American* (Long Island City, New York), 3 Oct. 1998.

18. Interview with author, 23 Dec. 1980.

19. Gheorghios K. Spyridakis and Spyros D. Peristeris, *Ellinika Dhimotika Traghoudhia* (Greek Demotic songs), 3 vols. (Athens: Academy of Athens, 1962–68), vol. C, 388.

20. Eleni Koulouris interview with the author.

21. Interview with author, 8 Sept. 1974.

22. Artemis Leontis, "Women's Fabric Arts in Greek America," *Laografia* 12, no. 3 (May/June 1995): 5–11.

23. Sophia Elissa Altin, "Growing up Greek American in the South," *Greek Star* (Chicago), 7 May 1998.

CHAPTER 21

1. "Fifth Grader Against Foreigners," *Emery County Progress* (Castle Dale, Utah), 4 May 1912.

2. For labor strife in the fur industry, see Christine Philliou, "Greek Local 70 of the International Fur and Leather Workers Union, 1925–1966: Crossing the Lines" (1994, collection of the author).

3. Arnold Dexter, "Ethnic Diversity and Labor Unity: Reflections on the Lowell Textile Strike of 1912," *Labor's Heritage* 8, no. 2, quarterly of the George Meany Memorial Archives (fall 1996): 59.

4. Ibid., 60.

5. Ibid., 66.

6. Ibid., 70.

7. Philip J. Dreyfus, "The IWW and the Limits of Inter-ethnic Organizing: Reds, Whites, and Greeks in Grays Harbor, Washington, 1912," *Labor History* 38, no. 4 (fall 1997): 450–70.

8. Ibid., 453.

9. Ibid., 454.

10. Ibid., 459.

11. Ibid., 462.

12. Ibid., 466.

13. Helen Zeese Papanikolas, "Life and Labor among the Immigrants of Bingham Canyon," *Utah Historical Quarterly* 33 (fall 1965): 289–315.

14. For accounts of the strike see H. D. Graham and T. R. Gurr, *Violence in America: Historical and Comparative Perspectives* (Washington, D. C.: Bantam Books, 1969), 254–56; *Ludlow: Being the Report of the Special Board of Officers Appointed by the Governor of Colorado*, (Denver, 1914); G. S. McGovern and L. F. Guttridge, *The Great Coal Field War* (Boston: Houghton Mifflin, 1972); B. B. Beshoar, *Out of the Depths: The Story of John R. Lawson, A Labor Leader* (Denver: Golden Bell, 1958); Zeese Papanikolas, *Buried Unsung: Louis Tikas and the Ludlow Massacre* (Lincoln: University of Nebraska Press, Bison Books, 1991; published earlier by University of Utah Press, 1982).

15. *Ludlow, Report of the Special Board*.

16. Zeese Papanikolas, *Buried Unsung*, 241.

17. Helen Papanikolas, "Unionism, Communism, and the Great Depression," *Utah Historical Quarterly* 4, no. 3 (summer 1973): 221–54.

18. Mary Vardoulakis, *Gold in the Streets* (New York: Dodd, Mead and Company, 1945), 235.

CHAPTER 22

1. *News Advocate* (Price, Utah), 3 Jan. 1918.

2. Theodore Saloutos, *The Greeks in the United States* (Cambridge, Mass.: Harvard University Press, 1964), 148.

3. Ibid., 167–68.

4. Told to the author by Theodore Jouflas, spring 1970.

5. Told to the author by Mary Pappas Lines, 22 June 1987.

6. Chicago Hellenic Museum and Cultural Center files.

7. Helen Papanikolas, *A Greek Odyssey in the American West* (Lincoln: University of Nebraska Press, Bison Books, 1997), 269.

8. Helen Papanikolas, *Toil and Rage in a New Land: The Greek Immigrants of Utah*, 2d ed. (revised, reprinted from *Utah Historical Quarterly* 38, no. 2 [1970] in 1983 and 1984), 155–56.

9. W. Augustus Low and Virgil A. Clift, eds., *Encyclopedia of Black Americans* (New York: McGraw-Hill, 1981), 232.

10. *Salt Lake Tribune*, 2 Sept. 1984.

CHAPTER 23

1. Helen Papanikolas, "Greek Folklore of Carbon County," in Thomas E. Cheney, ed., *Lore of Faith and Folly* (Salt Lake City: University of Utah Press, 1971), 61–77.

2. Interview with former Utah Governor Bracken Lee, 16 June 1983.

3. Told by the author's husband.

4. U. S. House of Representatives, Committee on Immigration. *Congressional Record,* vol. 61, Part 9, 4 March; 4 to 23 Nov. 1921. Congressman Knutson, 171; Congressman Box, 174, 20 April 1921.

5. Christopher Xenopoulos Janus, "My Favorite Places, Persons, Quotes," *Greek Star* (Chicago), 2 Sept. 1999, 5.

CHAPTER 25

1. *Standard* (Ogden, Utah), 20, 21, 22 Feb. 1904. The author is indebted to Stella Capitan for research into this explosion, which killed her grandfather.

2. F. Stanley [pseudonym], "The Dawson (New Mexico) Tragedies," pamphlet, Pep, Texas, 1964.

3. *Evening Picketmine* (Trinidad, Colorado), 28 April 1917; H. B. Humphrey, *Summary of Coal Mine Explosions in the United States, 1810–1958,* bulletin 586, Bureau of Mines (Washington, D.C.: United States Printing Office, 1960), 81.

4. Alan Kent Powell, *The Next Time We Strike: Labor in the Utah Coal Fields, 1900–1933* (Ogden: Utah State University Press, 1985); Michael Katsanevas, Jr., "The Emerging Social Worker and the Distribution of the Castle Gate Relief Fund," *Utah Historical Quarterly* 50 (1982); Janeen Arnold Costa, "A Struggle for Survival and Identity: Families in the Aftermath of the Castle Gate Mine Disaster," *Utah Historical Quarterly* 56 (1988).

5. H. L. Mountzoures, *The Bridge* (New York: Charles Scribner's Sons, 1972).

6. "Yes! We Have No Bananas!" Irving Cohn and Frank Silver, Skidmore Music Co., New York, 1923.

7. Charles C. Moskos, Jr. "Growing up Greek American," *Society* 14, no. 2 (Jan./Feb. 1977): 66.

8. "To Alanaki" (The gadabout), Victor Records 7–59034 B, 43934 USA, 30 April 1928. Lyrics translated by Andreas Dellis.

CHAPTER 26

1. Richard Clogg, *A Short History of Modern Greece,* 2d ed. (London: Cambridge University Press, 1986), 118. See Marjorie Housepian, *The Smyrna Affair* (New York: Harcourt Brace Jovanovich, 1971), 121. A novel on the disaster is Richard Reinhart, *The Ashes of Smyrna* (New York: Harper and Row, 1971).

2. Richard Clogg, *A Concise History of Greece* (London: Cambridge University Press, 1992), 98, 99.

3. *Toronto Daily Star,* 20 Oct. 1922. William White, ed., *By-Line: Ernest Hemingway; Selected Articles and Dispatches of Four Decades* (New York: Charles Scribner's Sons, 1967).

4. L. C. Stavrianos, *The Balkans since 1453* (New York: Holt, Rinehart and Winston, 1966), 590.

5. Interview with Louis Cononelos, Salt Lake City, 4 Nov. 1974, Greek Archives, University of Utah.

6. Interview with author, 20 Jan. 1978.

7. Lawrence Durrell, preface to Ilias Venezis, *Beyond the Aegean,* trans. E. D. Scott-Kilvert (New York: Vanguard Press, 1956), v.

8. Stavrianos, *Balkans,* 676, 481.

9. Thomas Doulis, *Disaster and Fiction: Modern Greek Fiction and the Asia Minor Disaster of 1922* (Berkeley: University of California Press, 1977), 42.

10. Richard Clogg, *The Greek Diaspora of the Twentieth Century* (London: MacMillan Press; New York: St. Martin's Press, 1999), 1.

11. *Mikra Assia* (Asia Minor), vocals by Georgos Dalaras and Haris Alexiou, recorded in Greece by Peters International Recording Company, New York, audiocassette

MCDPI–5001. Brought to the author's attention by Georgia Hall. Lyrics translated by Andreas Dellis.

12. "Konstantinoupoli" (Constantinople), Victor 7–59033 B (45667), 1928. Lyrics translated by Andreas Dellis.

13. Takis Telonides to author, typescript, 8 May 2000.

14. Theodore Saloutos, *They Remember America* (Berkeley: University of California Press, 1956), 29.

15. Jim Papadakis telephone conversation with the author, 26 Nov. 1999.

16. Minnie Blackman Theodore to her sister-in-law Josephine Z. Theodore. The difficulties former Greeks had on returning to visit their homeland caused considerable difficulties between the United States and Greece. See Theodore Saloutos, *The Greeks in the United States* (Cambridge, Mass.: Harvard University Press, 1964), chap. 11, on the problems facing Greeks who had not fulfilled their three-year military service before emigrating.

CHAPTER 27

1. Louis Adamic, *A Nation of Nations* (New York: Harper & Brothers, 1944), 274.

2. Rae Dalven, *Modern Greek Poetry,* 2d ed. (New York: Russell & Russell, 1971), 86: "Written in 1823. . . . Liberty is described rising from the bones of all Greek heroes who have died in her defense."

3. Ibid., "The Death of the Klepht," 52.

4. "Kontofarthos and Tzanetos," RCA Victor Comedy Co. 38–3113, sides A and B, trans. Nenny Panourghia.

5. "Patzames" (Pajamas), Columbia 206625; "To Sigareto" (The cigaret), Columbia 205766.

6. Gail Holst, *Road to Rembetika: Music of a Greek Sub-culture: Songs of Love, Sorrow, and Hashish,* 3d ed. (Limni, Evia, Greece: Denise Harvey, 1983), 14, 26.

7. Gail Holst Warhaft, "Rebetika Revisited," *Laografia* 9, no. 4 (Nov./Dec. 1992): 9, 10. The entire issue is devoted to the *rebetika.*

8. See Steve Frangos, "The Last Café-Aman Performer," *Journal of Modern Hellenism* 12/13 (1995–96).

9. Cy Rice, *Nick the Greek: All the Legends Live Again* (New York: Funk and Wagnalls, 1970. Review in *Delaware Today Magazine,* Nov. 1970, 33. See also Harry Mark Petrakis, *Nick the Greek* (Garden City, New York: Doubleday, 1979).

10. The success of Pantages's and the Skouras brothers' theater businesses is discussed in Theodore Saloutos, *The Greeks in the United States* (Cambridge, Mass.: Harvard University Press, 1964), 273–80.

11. Carey Morgan and Arthur M. Swanstrom, Edward B. Marks Music Co. Recorded by Nora Bayes, July 1920. Columbia A–2980.

12. Lucille Richins, "A Social History of Sunnyside," WPA Collection, Utah Historical Society [n.d.].

13. *National Herald* (Washington, D. C.) obituary, 14 Jan. 1921, trans. Efthalia Walsh.

14. *Washington Post,* 11 Jan. 1921.

15. *News Advocate* (Price, Utah), 13 July 1922.

16. Interview, Salt Lake City, 1 March 1969, Greek Archives, University of Utah [part of the tape is missing].

17. Interview, Salt Lake City, 8 Sept. 1972, Greek Archives, University of Utah.

18. Theodore Saloutos, "Growing up Greek in the Greek Community of Milwaukee," *Historical Messenger of the Milwaukee County Historical Society* (summer 1973), 53.

19. Ann Sederocanellis, *Spanning a Century: A Greek-American Odyssey* (New York: Vantage Press, 1995), 67.

20. Helen Papanikolas, *A Greek Odyssey in the American West* (Lincoln: University of Nebraska Press, Bison Books, 1997), 29.

21. *Fort Smith News Examiner* (Arkansas), 25 June 1970. Letter to author from Anastasia Soteropoulos, 3 Dec. 1970; letter to author from Mary Turner, 3 Dec. 1970.

22. Eva Katafygiotu Topping, "From Baptist to Byzantine Hymns," *Greek American* (Long Island City, New York), 22 Nov. 1997.

23. Demetrios Constantelos, "The Greek Orthodox Church and the Future of Greek Identity in America," in *Greeks in English-Speaking Countries,* ed. C. P. Ionnides (New Rochelle, New York: Aristede D. Caratzas, 1997), 55.

24. Mary Veronis Thompson, "The Veronis Story 1889–1992," photocopy, 5.

25. Sederocanellis, *Spanning a Century,* 149.

26. Harry C. Triandis and Pola Triandis, "The Building of Nations," *Psychology Today* 2, no. 10. Pronouncements such as "To the average Greek, neglecting one's wife, children, and family for one's profession is unthinkable. . . . Within the family the child is indulged, protected, and constantly loved and petted" would be puzzling and unbelievable to immigrant Greeks and their children. The author would be interested to know whether rural Greeks were included in their research and what were the economic status and educational backgrounds of the respondents.

27. Pseudonym. Told to the author, 18 Nov. 1999.

28. Mary Pappas Lines, told to the author, 11 April 2000.

29. During a class discussion with the author, University of Utah, autumn 1979.

30. Pseudonym. Told to the author on a lecture tour, New York City, autumn 1990.

31. Pseudonym. Told to the author on a lecture tour, Chicago, spring 1998.

32. Constance Callinicos, *American Aphrodite* (New York: Pella, 1990), 97.

33. Ibid., 288.

34. Pseudonym. Told to the author after a talk at the Greek American Women Network conference, New York City, 7 Oct. 2000.

35. Kallie Souvall Politis, reply to the author, Hellenic Cultural Association meeting, Salt Lake City, Utah, 7 Nov. 1999.

36. P. David Seaman. "Sociological Factors in American Greek Bilingualism" (paper presented to the Modern Greek Studies Association Symposium, University of Chicago, Oct. 1976), 3. Seaman is the author of *Modern Greek and American English in Contact* (The Hague, Paris: Mouton, 1972).

37. Chris Ghicadus, M.D., typescript, autobiographical sketch to author, 20 May 2000.

CHAPTER 28

1. Elias Vlanton, "Greek Immigrants in the Federal Writers Project: A Comprehensive Bibliography of State Holdings," *Journal of the Hellenic Diaspora* 30.1 (1994): 87–96.

2. "Pallios Family Heritage," 19, 20 (author's collection).

3. Thompson, "The Veronis Story 1889–1992," photocopy, 9.

4. Athena K. Pallios, as told to the author many years ago.

5. Deno Pappas, as told to the author, 29 June 1999.

6. Melva Georgelas Kouris, Greek-school classmate of the author.

7. Interview with author.

8. The author's husband.

9. Typescript in the collection of the author.

10. Lela Ioannou Kannes, "The History of the [Salt Lake City] Mothers' Club" (original title is in Greek; n.p., n.d.) trans. Helen Papanikolas.

11. Stephen J. Paitakis, *The Paitakis Family Geneology* (n.p., n.d.), 16.

12. Alice Scourby, "Ethnicity, the Greek Case," *Greek World* (March–April 1977): 18–19. See also Alice Scourby and Harry J. Psomiades, *The Greek American Family in Transition* (New York: Pella, 1982), which includes a bibliographic guide by John G. Zenelis.

13. Greek Archives, University of Utah.

14. Mimis Demetriou (James Demetrius), *Tihi Se Kseni Hora* (Fortune in a foreign land), trans. Nenny Panourghia (New York: n. p., 1934), preface.

15. Mimis Demetriou, *O Brooklis Stin Athina* (The Brooklyner in Athens), trans. Nenny Panourghia (New York: n. p., 1934).

16. The song, a Tsamikos dance, is included in Melpo Merlier, *Traghoudhia Tis Roumelis* (Songs of Roumeli) (Athens: Sidheris Press, 1931), 33 (author's translation).

17. *Ellinikes Horoi* (Greek dances), trans. Th. Stefanidhes (Athens: n.p., 1940), 7.

18. Orthophonic, S–621 B. Recorded in Athens, Greece.

19. Columbia (206624) 56345–F. George Katsaros vocals.

20. An uncle of noted collector Deno Pappas explained this omission to his nephew.

21. Theodore Saloutos, *The Greeks in the United States* (Cambridge, Mass.: Harvard University Press, 1964), 332.

CHAPTER 29

1. Andrew T. Kopan, "Patriarch Athenagoras: A Personal Remembrance," *Greek Star* (Chicago), 19 March 1987.

2. Interview with the author, 22 March 1999.

3. Penelope Koulouris told this anecdote to the author many years ago.

4. Letter to the author, 1 March 1999.

5. L. C. Stavrianos, *The Balkans since 1453* (New York: Holt, Rinehart and Winston, 1966), 681, 683.

6. Dan Georgakas, "Greek Widows," *Greek American* (Long Island City, New York), 7 Nov. 1987.

7. Nick Vidalakis, telephone conversation with the author, 9 Sept. 2000.

8. Evangelos C. Vlahos, *The Assimilation of Greeks in the United States: With Special Reference to the Greek Community of Anderson, Indiana* (Athens: National Centre of Social Researches, 1968), 156, 268.

9. "To Dholario" (The dollar), Orthophonic S–603 A; also RCA Victor 38–3008, recorded in Athens, ca. 1930–31. Trans. Andreas Dellis.

CHAPTER 30

1. "Bleary-eyed Hirohito,"Orthophonic 5–577A; "Bull dog Mussolini," RCA 26–8175A; "Fool Mussolini," RCA Victor 26–8167 A; "Ntouse, Ntoutse" (Duce, duce), RCA Victor 26–8167 B.

2. Steve Frangos, "Vembo: The Voice of Hellenism," *National Herald*, 11–12 Sept. 1999.

3. From the author's cousin, Athens, June 1958.

4. Letter to the author [n.d.]. Andy Katsanevas's father was killed in the Castle Gate, Utah, explosion of 1924. He was plant manager for the EIMCO Steel Company, a worldwide organization.

5. Conversation with the author, 9 April 2001. John Chipian returned from WWII and founded an inventory company.

6. Helen Papanikolas, *The Time of the Little Black Bird* (Athens, Ohio: Swallow Press, 1999), 112–14.

7. *Colorado Springs* (newspaper), 6 March 1943; "The Greek Battalion," *Greek-American Review*, 27 Nov. 1994.

8. Angeline Geo-Karas earned a law degree from De Paul University. She was elected to the Illionis State Senate, 31ˢᵗ District, in 1979.

9. Diamantis Zervos, *Baseball's Golden Greeks: The First Forty Years: 1934–1974* (Canton, Massachusetts: Aegean Books, 1998), 255.

10. Theodore Saloutos, *The Greeks in the United States* (Cambridge, Mass.: Harvard University Press, 1964), 247–50.

11. "Memoirs of Peter Boudoures," typescript, John B. Vlahos collection, 94–95.

12. Andrew T. Kopan, "Defenders of Democracy: Greek Americans in the Military," *Greek-American Review* (Sept. 1998): 11.

13. Nikos Kazantzakis, *Journey to the Morea: Travels in Greece,* trans. F. A. Reed (New York: Simon and Schuster, 1965), 44.

14. See also "Romiossini" in *Yiannis Ritsos: Selected Poems 1938–1988,* ed. and trans. Kimon Friar and Kostas Mysules (Brockport, New York: BOA editions, 1989). The author has used the version found on the back of the pamphlet "Z," where no translator is given. The publication gives a short history of the repressive government of the "Colonels" through a military coup with the help of the United States CIA. The movie *Z* is based on the life of Dr. Gregory Lambrakis, who was murdered under orders of the junta while campaigning against the colonels; the score for the movie was composed by Mikis Theodorakis; and the director was Costas Gavras. The book *Z* was written by Vasili Vassilikos.

15. Elias Vlanton, "Who Killed George Polk?" *Greek American* (Long Island City, New York.), 7 Sept. 1996, 1, the first of three articles. See also Elias Vlanton, *Who Killed George Polk: The Press Covers up a Death in the Family* (Philadelphia: Temple University Press, 1996).

16. Richard Clogg, *A Short History of Modern Greece,* 2d ed. (London: Cambridge University Press, 1986), 179. See John Corry, "Greece: The Death of Liberty," *Harper's* (Oct. 1969): 72–81.

17. George Psychoundakis, *The Cretan Runner* (London: John Murray, 1955).

18. Konstantinos Lardas, "The Burial of Kazantzakis," *Accent* (University of Illinois) 19 no. 2 (spring 1959): 126. See Alexander Karanikas, *Hellenes and Hellions: Modern Greek Characters in American Literature* (Urbana: University of Illinois Press, 1981), 154–59, for a short biography of Lardas.

19. *Introduction to Modern Greek Literature* (Mary P. Gianos, ed. and trans. [New York: Twayne, 1969]) lists the following authors. Fiction: Panayiotis Kanellopoulos, I. M. Panayotopoulos, Emmanuel Roidis, Alexandros Papadiamantis, Konstantinos Theotokis, Andreas Karkavitsas, Konstantinos Hadzopoulos, Startis Myrivilis, Elias Venezis, Kosmas Politis, Petros Haris, Taxis Doxas, Yiannis Manglis, Markos Lazaridis, and Demetrios Yiakos. Drama: Gregorios Xenopoulos, George Theotokas, Pandelis Prevelakis, and Loukis Akritas. Poetry: Constantine Cavafis, Angelos Sikelianos, Nikos Kazantzakis, Kostas Ouranis, Takis Papatzonis, Kostaas Kariotakis, George Seferis, George Themelis, Zoe Kareli, Andreas Embiticos, George Thomas Vafopoulos, Alexander Baras, George Sarandaris, Melissanthi, Yiannis Ritsos, Nikos Engonopoulos, Alexander Matsas, Odysseus Elytis, Nikiphoros Vrettakos, Nikos Gatsos, and Takis Varvitsiotis.

20. Vasiliki Tsitsopoulou, "Greekness, Gender Stereotypes, and the Hollywood Musical," *Journal of Modern Greek Studies* 18, no. 1 (May 2000): 79.

21. Andrew Horton, *Angelopoulos: A Cinema of Contemplation,* 2d ed. with afterword (Princeton: Princeton University Press, 1999).

22. Eleni Karras, "Living in My Grandmother's Name," winner of the 2000 Merit award from the Arts Recognition and Talent Search (ARTS), a program of the National Foundation for Advancement in the Arts, 7.

23. Letter to the author, 20 Nov. 2001. Margaret Matson Katsanevas is a retired registered nurse and a convert to the Greek Orthodox church.

24. Interview with the author, autumn 1975.

25. Pearl Kastran Ahnen, *Legends and Legacies* (Glenn, Michigan: Legna Press, 1999), 129.

26. Ibid., 140–41.

27. Conversation with author, Stockton, California, 16 June 2001.

CHAPTER 31

1. Dorothy Demetrakopoulos Lee, "Greece," in *Cultural Patterns and Technical Change,* ed. Margaret Mead, manual prepared for the World Federation for Mental Health (New York: New American Library, 1955), 62.

2. John L. Kallas, "Agapi: The Greek Word for Love," one-act play in *Growing up As a Greek-American* (New York: KAV Books, 1992), 119–22.

3. Told to the author by her cousins Thalia and Katherine Papachristos, who heard this story from the young man involved.

4. Roxanne Cotsakis, *The Wing and the Thorn* (Atlanta: Tupper & Love, 1952), 352.

5. Nicholas Gage, *Eleni: A Savage War, A Mother's Love, and a Son's Revenge: A Personal Story* (New York: Random House, 1983).

6. Greek American Women's Network (GAWN), annual meeting, New York City, 7 Oct. 2000.

7. Ibid.

8. Ibid.

9. Ibid.

10. Dan Georgakas, "The Changing Face of Astoria," *Greek American* (Long Island City, New York), 29 March 1997, 12.

11. James G. Patterson, "The Greeks of Vancouver," National Museum of Man Mercury Series, Canadian Centre for Folk Culture, Studies Paper no. 18 (Ottowa, 1976), 17. The epilogue describes how the ethnic scene has changed.

12. Alexander Karanikas, *Hellenes and Hellions: Modern Greek Characters in American Literature* (Urbana: University of Illinois Press, 1981), chaps. 3, 7, 9, 16.

CHAPTER 32

1. Telephone interview with the author, 22 March 2001. Georgia Hall earned a Ph.D. in anthropology with a specialty in gerontology. She lives in Phoenix and works with the Indian tribes of Arizona.

2. Letter to the author [n.d.]. Amy Theodore is retired from the Denver public school system, where she was a counselor.

3. Constance Callinicos, *American Aphrodite* (New York: Pella, 1990), 153–54.

4. Ibid.

5. Theano Papazoglou-Margaris, "Amen," in *A Tear for Uncle Jimmy* (Athens: Diphros, 1958). Alexander Karanikas, *Hellenes and Hellions: Modern Greek Characters in American Literature* (Urbana: University of Illinois Press, 1981), 97.

6. Roxanne Cotsakis, *The Wing and the Thorn* (Atlanta: Tupper & Love, 1952).

7. Dorothy Demetrakopoulos, "Greek Tales of Priest and Priestwife," *Journal of American Folklore* 60 (April 1947): 163–67; "Greek Accounts of the Vrykolakas," *Journal of American Folklore* 55 (July 1942): 121–32; "Greek Personal Anecdotes of the Supernatural," *Journal of American Folklore* 64 (July 1951): 307–12.

8. James A. Notopoulos, *Modern Greek Heroic Oral Poetry,* Ethnic Folkways Library Album F E 4468, with notes (New York: Folkways Records and Service Corp., 1959).

9. Robert Georges, "Greek-American Folk Beliefs and Narratives: Survivals and Living Traditions" (Ph.D. diss., Indiana University, 1964).

10. Elias Kulukundis, *The Feasts of Memory* (New York: Holt, Rineheart & Winston, 1967); Daphne Athas, *Entering Ephesus* (New York: Viking Press, 1971); Thomas Doulis, *Disaster and Fiction: Modern Greek Fiction and the Asia Minor Disaster of 1922* (Berkeley: University of California Press, 1977).

11. Karanikas, *Hellenes,* 53, 49.

12. Ibid., 312–15. Her biography by her daughter, Vivian Margaris Kallen, appears in *Greek American Pioneer Women of Illinois,* ed. Elaine Thomopoulos (Chicago: Arcadia

Publishing, 2000). Yiorgos D. Kalogeras, "Suspended Souls, Ensnaring Discourses: Theano Papazoglou-Margaris's Immigration Stories," *Journal of Modern Greek Studies* 8 (1990): 85–96.

13. Thalia Selz, "The Education of a Queen," *Partisan Review* 28 (1961): 151; *Best American Short Stories of 1962* (Boston, New York: Houghton Mifflin). See also Karanikas, *Hellenes,* 149–51.

14. Karanikas, *Hellenes,* chap. 11.

CHAPTER 33

1. Dimitri Mitropoulos, Great Conductors Online.

2. John Dizekes, *Opera in America: A Cultural History* (New Haven: Yale University Press, 1993), 498.

3. Ibid., 555–61.

4. Ibid., 519.

5. Ibid., 555.

6. Ibid., 558.

7. Nicholas Gage, *Greek Fire: The Story of Maria Callas and Aristotle Onassis* (New York: Alfred A. Knopf, 2000).

CHAPTER 34

1. Letter to the author, 23 Dec. 2000. Marcus G. Theodore is a patent attorney practicing in Salt Lake City. His mother is American-born, his father Greek-born.

2. James Becket, *Barbarism in Greece* (New York: Walker and Company, 1970); Richard Clogg, *A Short History of Modern Greece,* 2d ed. (London: Cambridge University Press, 1986), 186–202; John Corry, "Greece: The Death of Liberty," *Harper's,* Oct. 1969, 72–81.

3. Jessica Suchy-Pilalis did her doctoral work in the history, theory, and practice of Byzantine music. She also studied under leading Byzantine musicologists in Greece. In 1984, she became the first officially titled female *psalti* (chanter) of the Greek Orthodox Church of North and South America by assuming the lead position of *protopsalti* in the Holy Trinity Church in Indianapolis, Indiana.

4. Ricky Holden and Mary Vouras, *Greek Folk Dances* (Newark, New Jersey: Folkcraft, 1965); Constantine Manos, photographs, and Mary Vouras, music, *Greek Villages: A Portfolio of Photography and Sound,* vol. 2 (no city: James Metzner, 1975). See also Constantine Manos, *A Greek Portfolio* (New York: Viking Press, 1972).

5. Anna Caraveli, *Scattered in Foreign Lands: A Greek Village in Baltimore,* an exhibition and catalog at the Baltimore Museum of Art, 30 June–18 August 1985.

6. Soterios (Sam) Chianis, *Folksongs of Mantinea, Greece* (Berkeley: University of California Press, 1965).

7. Ted Alevezos and Susan Alevezos, *Folk Songs of Greece* (New York: Oak Publications, 1968); Ted Alevezos, *Songs of Greece,* Tradition Records, Everest Records Production. TLP 1037.

8. Ellen Frye, *The Marble Threshing Floor: A Collection of Greek Folksongs* (Austin: American Folklore Society, University of Texas, 1973); Gail Holst, *Road to Rembetika: Music of a Greek Sub-culture: Songs of Love, Sorrow, and Hashish,* 3d ed. (Limni, Evia, Greece: Denise Harvey, 1983).

9. "Modern Essays: Greek American Artists of the Twentieth Century," catalog of the exhibition at the Queens Museum of Art, 6 Oct. 1999–30 Jan. 2000. Biographical curators: Peter Selz and William Valerio; notes by Thalia Cheronis Selz include Stephen Antonakos, William Baziotes, Lynda Benglis, Chryssa, George Constant, Nassos Daphnis, Electrus, Cristos Gianakos, Stee Gianakos, Morfy Giakas, Mary Grigoriadis, Mark Hadjipateras, Dimitri Hadzi, Theo Hios, Aristodimos Kaldis, Zoe Keramea, Carole Ann Klonar-

ides, Michael Lekakis, Constantine Manos, Jenny Marketou, Jim Morphesis, Eleni Mylonas, George Negroponte, Lucas Samaras, Theodora Skipitares, Andrea Spiros, Theodoros Stamos, Athena Tacha, Philip Tsiaras, Polygnotos Vagis, John Vassos, Costa Vavagiakis, Peter Voulkos, and Jean Xceron.

EPILOGUE

1. Susan Kiesel Keleides, "You Can Fight City Hall," an interview with Helen Boosalis, *Greek American* (Long Island City, New York), 13 August 1988.

2. Donald J. Albers, "An Interview with Tom Apostol," *The College Mathematics Journal* 28, no. 4 (Sept. 1997). *M! Project Mathematics: Program Guide and Workbook to Accompany the Videotape on the Tunnel of Samos,* California Institute of Technology, 1995.

3. Letter to author, 12 Nov. 2000. Theodore Theodoratos teaches mathematics in Oakland, California.

4. Diamantis Zervos, *Baseball's Golden Greeks: The First Forty Years: 1934–1974* (Canton, Massachusetts: Aegean Books, 1998).

5. A good regional history is George P. Daskarolis, *San Francisco's Greek Colony: The Evolution of an Ethnic Community* (Minneapolis: Light & Life Publishing, 1995).

6. Marilyn Rouvelas, *A Guide to Greek Traditions and Customs in America* (Bethesda, Maryland: Attica Press, 1993).

7. The Reverend James Dokos, "Ask Father Jim," *Greek Star* (Chicago), 21 Sept. 2000.

8. Sam J. Tsemberis, Harry J. Psomiades, and Anna Karpathakis, eds., *Greek American Families: Traditions and Transformations* (New York: Pella, 1999), 11.

9. Mavis Manus, "At the Olympics of Greek Folk Dance," *Greek American* (Long Island City, New York), 26 Feb. 1999, 1; *"Glendi"* (Joyful amusement) *Odyssey Magazine* (Feb. 1999).

10. Report to author, 20 Sept. 2000. John Chipian has devised many labor-saving machines to reduce the time for food preparation in the yearly Salt Lake City festivals. He has been in charge of *loukoumadhes* for more than twenty-five years.

11. Eva Katafygiotu Topping, "Greek Orthodox Women USA: Do We Stand a Prayer?" *Greek American* (Long Island City, New York), 21 April 1990.

12. Conversation with author, 15 March 2000. Niki Georgeson is a university graduate and a director of business technology at American Express in Salt Lake City.

13. Letter to author, 20 May 2000. Dean Athens is an education major with a Master's degree in theology from Holy Cross Greek Orthodox School of Theology. He is prominent in Orthodox adult education in Salt Lake City.

14. Constance Callinicos, *American Aphrodite* (New York: Pella, 1990), 129–30.

15. "Schools Running on Willpower," *Greek American* (Long Island City, New York), 14 Nov. 1998.

16. "A New Path to Greek Education," *Greek American* (Long Island City, New York), 2 April 1999.

17. Andrew T. Kopan, "Preservation of Greek Language Seen Hopeless," *Hellenic Chronicle* (Boston), 26 August 1971.

18. Byron G. Massialas, "The Education of Hellenes in America: From Melting Pot to Cultural Pluralism," *Ahepan* (fall 1984): 24.

19. George A. Kourvetaris, "The Future of the Greek Ethnic Identity and Culture in the 21st Century," *Greek-American Review* (May 1999): 10.

20. James Steve Counelis, "A New Church: The Americanization of the Greek Orthodox Church" (paper presented to the Modern Greek Studies Association Symposium, University of Chicago, Oct. 1976).

21. *Washington Post,* 17 Nov. 1997.

22. Mary Lefkowitz, who is not Greek, has refuted Martin Bernal's thesis in essays, on television, and in a book (*Not out of Africa: How Afrocentricism Became an Excuse to Teach Myth as History* [New York: Basic Books, 1996]).

23. Autobiographical sketch, 20 May 2000, collection of the author.

24. Letter to author, 8 May 2000. Taki Telonides is a folklorist.

25. Letter to author, 19 May 2000. Amy Theodore is now retired; she was a counselor in the Denver public schools.

26. Angel Skedros is the granddaughter of immigrants and a university graduate.

27. Telephone interwiew, 15 Sept. 2000. Georgia Hall's parents were immigrants from Asia Minor. In addition to her work with Indian tribes, she is actively involved in researching the Greek American history of Arizona.

28. Letter to author, 22 Sept. 2000. Don Hall teaches humanities in a Phoenix, Arizona, community college.

29. Pseudonym. Letter to author, 22 Oct. 2000.

30. Nikos Kazantzakis, *Journey to the Morea: Travels in Greece,* trans. F. A. Reed (New York: Simon and Schuster, 1965), 170.

31. Louis Geo. Atsaves, "At Random," *Greek Star* (Chicago), 17 August 2000.

SELECTED GLOSSARY OF GREEK WORDS

While all Greek words are explained in the text, some are defined only when they first appear. This glossary is provided for those readers who are not reading from cover to cover.

filotimo: honor, self respect

foustanella: a pleated, knee-length skirt similar to a kilt; see page 55

kafejis: coffeehouse owner

kalimafkion: tall hats worn by priests; see page 85

katharevousa: a formal, pure form of the Greek language

kilimi: goat-hair blankets in which travelers wrapped their belongings

klefts: guerrilla freedom fighters who battled the Turks in the revolution of 1821−29

ksenitia: foreign lands

ksenoi: strangers; foreigners

mami: midwife

mirologhia: words of fate, sung as laments for the dead

patridha: Greece; homeland

patriotes: countrymen

Romaioi: a name for Greeks coined in the Byzantine era, prior to which Greeks were subjects of Rome

Romiosini: the culture of Romaioi; Greek culture; Greek identity

topos: the region of one's birth; ancestral place

vrakes: baggy pants worn by Cretans; see page 56

vrykolakes: vampires

yiayia: grandmother

Index

Note: Italicized page numbers refer to illustrations and their captions.